ACHIEVING RACIAL BALANCE

Case Studies of Contemporary School Desegregation

SONDRA ASTOR STAVE

Contributions to the Study of Education, Number 65

GREENWOOD PRESS
Westport, Connecticut • London

Library of Congress Cataloging-in-Publication Data

Stave, Sondra Astor.
   Achieving racial balance : case studies of contemporary school
desegregation / Sondra Astor Stave.
     p.   cm.—(Contributions to the study of education, ISSN
0196–707X ; no. 65)
   Includes bibliographical references (p.   ) and index.
   ISBN 0–313–29523–9 (alk. paper)
   1. School integration—United States—Case studies. I. Title.
II. Series.
LC214.2.S73 1995
370.19'342—dc20   95–16146

British Library Cataloguing in Publication Data is available.

Library of Congress Catalog Card Number: 95–16146
ISBN: 0–313–29523–9
ISSN: 0196–707X

First published in 1995

Greenwood Press, 88 Post Road West, Westport, CT 06881
An imprint of Greenwood Publishing Group, Inc.

Printed in the United States of America

The paper used in this book complies with the
Permanent Paper Standard issued by the National
Information Standards Organization (Z39.48–1984).

10 9 8 7 6 5 4 3

This book is lovingly dedicated

to three men who share the surname Stave:

my father-in-law, Bernard R.,

whose zest for life and accomplishment

serves as a model for us all;

my husband, Bruce M.,

who inspires and sets in motion

almost every significant event in my life; and

my son, Channing M-L,

whose expectations of me keep me constantly challenged

and who provides my window into the future.

Contents

Illustrations

MAPS

TABLES

Preface

This study owes much to Dean Charles W. Case of The University of Connecticut. From our first meeting, he provided the highest level of encouragement and enthusiasm. Our discussions were always stimulating, and I felt continually both challenged and supported as we proceeded through the various phases of the project. I cannot imagine a better working relationship than the one that we shared. Helpful criticism also was offered by two other members of the Administration Department of the School of Education: Barry Goff and Timothy Reagan.

I am tremendously indebted to the more than one hundred interviewees who took time from their busy schedules to share their experiences and insights. I offer my thanks to these educators, administrators, and public officials in Connecticut, Delaware, New Jersey, New York, and Ohio whom I had the pleasure to meet and engage in conversation. I was tremendously impressed with their dedication and expertise; our schools are in very good hands.

The computer has made a work of this type much easier to do; however, it can occasionally be a daunting piece of equipment for someone who prepared her first papers on a manual typewriter. I appreciate the aid afforded me in keeping my Macintosh friendly from my son, Channing, and from Tasha Bouchard, R. Craig Branning, Jack Polidoro, and my soon-to-be daughter-in-law Sara Schloss. My secretary, Amy Bassett, was extremely helpful in the preparation of the tables in this volume while Bill and Chris Keegan introduced me to the world of computer cartography when they prepared the maps. I am grateful for the assistance rendered by James T. Sabin, Executive Vice President of the Greenwood Publishing Group, and Bridget M. Austiguy, my production editor.

A project of this kind spills over into all facets of one's life. I am most appreciative of the interest and support shown by my colleagues at the Mansfield Board of Education Central Office. My

dear friend, Ann Kouatly, shared weekly in the triumphs of a
finished chapter or the frustration of tracking down an elusive piece
of data. Toni Robinson, offered appropriate words of encouragement
on this project as she has throughout our long and very special
friendship. My fellow doctoral student and subsequent good friend,
Jean Egan, provided support and the wonderful sharing of
information available only from someone who has very successfully
trod the same path. My father-in-law, Bernard R. Stave, has, for
many years, served as both supporter and inspiration. My husband,
Bruce M. Stave, has been an integral part of this effort, as he has
been in every other part of my adult life. It was in discussion with
him, seven years ago, that I determined to pursue this topic.
Subsequently, he shared his ideas, accompanied me on my out-of-
state interviews, critiqued almost-completed chapters, and performed
myriad lesser tasks as well.

Chapter 1

Introduction

Since the United States Supreme Court decision in the landmark *Brown v. Board of Education* case on May 17, 1954, cities throughout the nation have been engaged in the process of school desegregation. Generally by court order, occasionally initiated by civic-minded citizens, cities and metropolitan areas have wrestled with the issue of how to enable their schools to appropriately reflect their changing racial demography.

This study seeks to describe and analyze how five communities in the northeastern quadrant of the United States have addressed the subject of desegregation. Dayton, Ohio; Hartford, Connecticut; Rochester, New York; Trenton, New Jersey; and Wilmington, Delaware share the experience of having increasingly large, poor, minority populations surrounded by mostly white, generally affluent suburbs. All five are mid-sized urban communities with standard metropolitan statistical areas (SMSAs) of less than one million inhabitants. Since the 1960s, each has been consistently or intermittently involved with school desegregation.

The following questions were addressed for each of the five communities:

1. What factors related to historic and demographic issues are most likely to advance or inhibit successful desegregation and the achievement of racial balance?
2. What factors related to legal issues are most likely to advance or inhibit successful desegregation and the achievement of racial balance?
3. What factors related to political responsibility are most likely to advance or inhibit successful desegregation and the achievement of racial balance?
4. What factors related to administrative responsibility are most likely to advance or inhibit successful desegregation and the achievement of racial balance?

5. What factors related to community responsibility are most likely
to advance or inhibit successful desegregation and the achievement of racial balance?

Chapters 2, 3, 4, 5, and 6 contain the case studies of the five
communities selected for analytical and comparative purposes. The
case studies for Dayton, Hartford, Rochester, Trenton, and Wilmington define the sequence of desegregation events; key issues and
periods of time have been determined. The existence of critical
incidents, such as court challenges and citizen action or reaction, has
been established.

In each case study, the investigation of legal issues includes a
review of court cases and decisions. To ascertain political actions,
newspaper coverage has been augmented by interviews with active
participants in each of the areas under study. Administrative efforts
have been revealed through interviews and the study of planning
documents, implementation reports, and evaluations. Reports and
interviews with leaders of citizen groups elicited community response.
All interviews were open ended. The interview schedule for Dayton,
Rochester, Trenton, and Wilmington appears in Appendix A; because
Hartford is at an earlier phase of desegregation activity, a separate
interview schedule was prepared and appears in Appendix B.

Chapter 7 selects and discusses the most important factors in the
desegregation efforts in the five case study cities and determines why
those factors are the most significant. Dayton is instructive in
demonstrating the advantages of strong, charismatic leadership; its
highest level school administrators have worked in the system for
long periods of time and have fostered a level of trust that is crucial
when changes frightening to much of the population are to be
implemented. The study of Rochester establishes the importance of
community participation and the benefits of strong educational
components, such as the World of Inquiry School, in the desegregation plan; there is a strong history of community involvement in
this metropolis and a sense of civic pride that has resulted in its
being one of the very few cities in the nation to initiate desegregation
efforts without the prodding of a court action. Trenton serves as a
warning of the difficulty of achieving progress when communication
between state and city is strained; although representatives of both
the city and the state sought and continue to seek desegregation and
improvement to the educational experience of Trenton schoolchildren,
lack of trust has totally frustrated that effort. Wilmington
demonstrates that when a mandatory, regional desegregation plan is
implemented, it is more likely to succeed if the district is made too
large for "white flight" to be easily accomplished. Once even initially
unenthusiastic parents gave the new districts a chance, the
overwhelming majority realized that their children's education was
not negatively affected and the population remained relatively stable.

The chapter also highlights those issues raised by the Hartford interviewees, particularly concerns for safety and educational quality. Safety has proven to be an understandable concern of parents both in the city and in its surrounding suburbs when the issue of desegregation and possible busing has been raised. Suburban parents are reluctant to have their children sent into the perceived-to-be dangerous city; urban parents fear both the perils of the city and the possible hostility their children might experience in the culturally different areas outside. Yet, there is little opposition to school transportation when it is voluntary--the overwhelming multitude of Connecticut children are transported by bus to schools in their town since, in the gross majority of cases, they are deemed too far away for children to walk. Conversely, busing is the term applied to involuntary transportation, and resistance to busing has become synonymous with resistance to integration.

Achieving the highest possible quality of education has also been shown to be of general concern. When a school, such as a magnet or private one, is perceived to offer a better educational experience, transportation is rarely an issue. Buses are happily boarded and/or parents drive their children distances far greater than would be necessary to reach the neighborhood school.

The bibliographic essay that appears at the end of this study reviews the literature relevant to school desegregation. This appendix begins with a compendium of the legal cases related to school desegregation, starting with *Plessy v. Ferguson* in 1896 and continuing through to the present decade. Cases which bear particular relevance to the case study areas are discussed in greater detail. The remainder of the essay is devoted to description and analysis of the writings on school desegregation, including the diverse methods in favor at various times; these include voluntary and mandatory busing, schools of choice and controlled choice, magnet schools, and metropolitan regionalization.

Social action is generally predicated on advancing the perceived self-interest of those encouraging it. However, what may seem to be enlightened, desirable action in the short run may be much less desirable overall. The United States is rapidly becoming a more multicultural society than ever before in the history of the nation, and the education of its children must address this reality. Among its many effects, integration tends to diminish the political power of minorities within city schools and requires a broader vision from many suburban residents than they have so far exhibited. However, the value to society of quality, integrated education cannot be minimized.

Yet, at least two other factors must be considered. The demography of the decade just after World War II, when major population shifts were increasing the size of cities, differs significantly from the last decade of this century, when citizens, both white and of color, are fleeing these same central areas for perceived better and safer lives in the suburbs. As the inner suburbs become more integrated, options for the increasingly segregated central cities are diminished.

Further, as all levels of government feel growing financial pressures, the cost of integration is likewise increasingly challenged. Educators as well as parents and lay citizens question whether moving students for the purpose of desegregation is the best use of the education dollar. In early 1995, 40 years after *Brown v. Board of Education,* this concern has been demonstrated in *Missouri v. Jenkins* where the State of Missouri contested a court order that had required the expenditure of 1.3 billion dollars during the previous decade to integrate its overwhelmingly black inner-city schools. Although 56 magnet schools were created in the system and 1500 suburban students voluntarily transferred to the Kansas City schools, test scores, especially at the high school level, did not show the progress expected. In the 1990s, the quality of education and the results achieved are as much discussed as the racial composition of the student body (*The Christian Science Monitor,* January 10, 1995, p. 10).

In the 1950s, once *Brown* was accepted as the law of the land, it was generally assumed that desegregating those schools that were racially unbalanced, whether by *de jure* or *de facto* circumstances, would sufficiently address the issue. Viewed from the perspective of the 1990s, the situation seems far more complex. School districts that voluntarily or under court order, desegregated their schools may become resegregated as students and their parents choose to move into or out of the district.

Desegregation was assumed to have educational as well as social benefits. This hypothesis is now being called into question. While the circumstances of the next century will differ significantly from what already has transpired, we still benefit from an awareness of past successes and failures.

Chapter 2

Dayton

When the Dayton schools, under court order, desegregated in the fall of 1976, then Superintendent of Schools John B. Maxwell, contended it was "without violence and with minimal disruption to the students' learning process." He credited Dayton's relatively positive experience to community leaders championing what was an equitable plan, parents being encouraging, and a court-appointed monitoring committee that was concerned and supportive rather than antagonistic to school administration (*Dayton Cares for Kids: From Court Order to Implementation*, 1977, unpaged).

Attempts to desegregate the Dayton Public Schools reached the United States District Court for the Southern District of Ohio, Eastern Division on April 17, 1972 when plaintiff-appellants Mark Brinkman et al., black and white parents, represented themselves, their minor children, and all others similarly situated. The National Association for the Advancement of Colored People (NAACP) joined as a party plaintiff. The complaint named the Governor and Attorney General of Ohio, the Ohio State Board of Education, the Superintendent of Public Instruction of the Ohio Department of Education, the Dayton Board of Education, its six individual members, and the Superintendent of the Dayton School District as parties defendants. The Dayton Board of Education cross appealed (503 F.2d 684, 1974).

Geography has played an important role in the development of Dayton. Due to its location at the confluence of Wolf Creek and the Mad, Stillwater, and Great Miami Rivers, boundaries are naturally formed, historically dividing the city both ethnically and economically. At the time of the suit, the Dayton School District population was approximately 48 percent black and 52 percent white. The southwest quadrant of the city, located between Wolf Creek and the Great Miami River, was predominantly black in the early 1970s, while the eastern part of the city remained mostly white. The northwestern

2.1 Dayton SMSA (Ohio), 1970

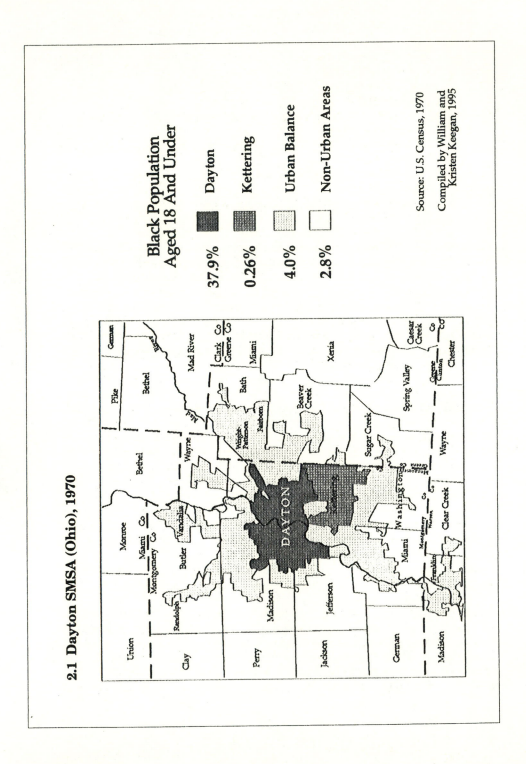

Black Population
Aged 18 And Under

37.9%   Dayton

0.26%   Kettering

4.0%   Urban Balance

2.8%   Non-Urban Areas

Source: U.S. Census, 1970

Compiled by William and
Kristen Keegan, 1995

area was racially mixed (*Dayton Cares for Kids: From Court Order to Implementation*, 1977; *Brinkman v. Gilligan*, Civil No. C-3-75-304, p. 5).

The City of Dayton was first settled by four Revolutionary War soldiers who traveled up the Miami River from Cincinnati in 1796. In 1803, the year in which Ohio was granted statehood, Montgomery County was created and Dayton was selected as the county seat. In 1805, with an area of one square mile and an annual budget of one hundred dollars, Dayton was incorporated as a town by special act of the Ohio legislature. It grew with the opening in 1829 of the first section of the Miami and Erie Canal, which allowed barges to travel along the waterways in the area. The arrival of the railroad in the 1850s, as well as the first steam engine and the first steam bakery in 1851, encouraged further development. During the Civil War, Dayton's industres boomed. In 1889, when natural gas supplemented steam, the city gained an even cheaper and more efficient source of fuel. The city's riverfront became crowded with factories specializing in farm machinery and wood products. Dayton's population of 30,473 in 1870 doubled to 61,220 in 1890 and increased significantly again to 85,333 at the turn of the century (Magnet School Assistance Program Application, 1989, p. 2; *Metropolitan Challenge*, pp. 52-53; Sealander, 1988, p. 1; *American Academic Encyclopedia*, 1980, 6:57).

Dayton became known as the "birthplace of aviation" when Orville and Wilbur Wright conducted experiments in that city, which then led to the first successful flight at Kitty Hawk, North Carolina in 1903. Dayton was also closely associated with the automobile industry. It was here that Charles F. Kettering invented the ignition system, self-starter, and leaded gasoline for cars. Through the mid-twentieth century, Dayton remained a primarily blue collar town dependent upon heavy manufacturing jobs in the automotive industry. Currently, approximately 1500 manufacturing firms remain in the metropolitan area where they have been joined by high technology production as well as research and development companies. In 1989, there were more than 300 advanced technology and aerospace companies employing approximately 18,000 workers creating, in the Miami Valley, one of the highest concentrations of aerospace scientists, engineers, and technical experts in the world. These businesses increased jobs in Dayton from 374,000 to 444,000 between 1982 and 1987 (Magnet School Assistance Program Application, 1989, pp. 2-3).

In 1913, Dayton became the first city of significant size to adopt the city manager form of government. With the exception of New England, where town meetings were the rule, in the early twentieth century, most municipalities had a mayor and some form of city council. The commission form of government was being tried in some locations, but while it diminished corruption, some felt that it was inefficient. The structure in Dayton, created by a committee chaired by John Henry Patterson, the founder of the National Cash Register Company (NCR), featured a commission of five members elected on a non-partisan, at-large basis to make policy. They served part-time for a nominal salary, and the implementation of policy was undertaken by a full-time chief administrator. The idea of running the city in a way analogous to the organization of a business had great appeal to this committee of commercial leaders charged with reviewing governmental options. Fortunately for Dayton, its first city manager, Henry Waite, was both vigorous and effective and showed that the new system could be a sound way to run city government (Sealander, 1988, pp. 96-97; Ronald & Ronald, 1981, pp. 108-9).

While some, such as Sealander, view the efforts of the reformers as totally benign or even as "a disinterested crusade to improve the lot of the downtrodden," others such as historian Samuel P. Hays are a bit more questioning. While conceding that benefits accrued to those served, it is Hays's position that these reformers, in their "search for order," also desired to centralize authority and to achieve and maintain control over newer residents whose style of life might not totally accord with their own (Hays in Brownell and Stickle, 1973, pp. 137-59).

The same John Henry Patterson, sometimes called the father of welfare capitalism, who was responsible for changing Dayton's governmental structure and one of the most constructive participants in dealing with Dayton's severe flood of March, 1913, was also influential in changing its school system. As a progressive in both business and government, he was concerned with the educational system that prepared the citizens of Dayton to subsequently work in his company. In concert with Arthur Morgan, an engineer closely involved with the highly regarded Miami Conservancy District for flood control, Patterson helped to introduce progressive education to Dayton. Morgan saw the schools as substitute parents for those children, rich or poor, whose mothers and/or fathers did not have the time to supervise their education personally (Ronald & Ronald, 1981, pp. 96, 102; Sealander, 1988, pp. 13, 129-34).

According to Frank Slutz, the first principal of the private Moraine Park School, where progressive ideas ruled from 1917 to 1927 in a most hospitable environment in a southern suburb of Dayton, the key to this type of education was the integration of schooling and life. The Moraine Park School was funded and supported by the business elite for their own children and was lavishly equipped. A huge success for its affluent pupils, who ultimately went on to enjoy successful and socially responsible lives, it closed when the participating families' children reached adulthood and no longer required such a facility (Sealander, 1988, pp. 135-41) .

Progressive education had come even earlier to the public school system, at the turn of the century, under the superintendency of

Edwin Brown. During the latter part of the nineteenth century, while there were more than 12,000 young people between the ages of 15 and 19 living in the city, attendance at Dayton's only high school varied between 250 and 300 students. The traditional curriculum, emphasizing "Latin, German, Greek, philosophy, history, algebra, and rhetoric," was irrelevant for all but those young women who were preparing to become schoolteachers and some few fortunate young men. By 1927, the school system offered seven alternative tracks, including "General, Commercial, College Preparatory, College Preparatory in Engineering, Cooperative Industrial, Cooperative Retail, and Cooperative Commercial." A huge new vocational high school as well as six new junior and senior high schools had been added to the Dayton school structure to enable the offering of this far more varied curricula to a greatly expanded high school student population that numbered 3680 in 1927 (Sealander, 1988, pp. 140-42).

Progressive education began as part of the humanitarian effort to apply the promise of American life to the urban-industrial civilization coming into being during the second half of the nineteenth century. It included numerous functions: broadening the schools' responsibilities to encompass concerns for health, vocation, and quality of family and community life; applying new pedagogical principles to classroom teaching; designing instruction to meet the needs of the different kinds and classes of children coming into the public schools; and proving viable "the radical faith that culture could be democratized without being vulgarized" and "that everyone could share not only in the benefits of the new sciences but in the pursuit of the arts as well" (Cremin, 1964, pp. viii-ix).

Progressive goals went beyond those espoused in the mid-nineteenth century by early school reformers such as Horace Mann. Mann assured businessmen that "public schools would preserve order, extend wealth and secure property"; his common school was to "contribute substantially to fashioning an emerging social order governed by a new public philosophy." On the other hand, William Torrey Harris, the United States Commissioner of Education between 1889 and 1906, the beginning of the Progressive era, spoke in another tone. For him, the school was the "greatest instrumentality to lift all classes of people into a participation in civilized life." He defined this as "a life of order, self-discipline, civic loyalty, and respect for private property." Therefore, "the purpose of education must be tied to time-honored principles deeply imbedded in the wisdom of the race" (Cremin, 1964, pp. 14-17).

For at least some of those who accepted the theories expounded by progressive educators, vocational education and tracking were generally of benefit to everyone involved. Under the modern factory system, in place by the late nineteenth century, "apprenticeships had deteriorated into a haphazard arrangement in which masters no longer cared to teach, in which boys were no longer prepared to accept prolonged periods of indenture, and in which child labor had therefore become exploitive rather than educative" (Cremin, 1964, pp. 34-35).

This was one justification for those advocating vocational education. Others were even more vehement regarding its desirability. According to William Maxwell, the superintendent of the New York schools, who in 1900 advocated placing trade training in elementary schools in tenement districts, traditional education might give the tenement child tastes and desires "higher and better than those which he finds in his sordid surroundings," but it would not afford him "any art by which he may earn a living" (Violas, 1978, p. 140).

Vocational education and tracking, purported by the Progressives as occupationally desirable and helpful to lower class immigrants in the early twentieth century, or seen by others as a way to keep them as a permanent underclass, was viewed as having similar effects on black students 50 years later. In *Hobson v. Hansen*, J. Skelly Wright, a Circuit Judge in the District of Columbia, was required to determine whether ability grouping or tracking systems, "by which students at the elementary and secondary level are placed in tracks or curriculum levels according to the school's assessment of each student's ability to learn" benefits or retards the educational process for these students. While Superintendent of the Washington, D.C. Schools Hansen argued that "the comprehensive high school (and the school system generally) must be systematically organized and structured to provide differing levels of education for students with widely differing levels of academic ability," Judge Wright decided otherwise (*Hobson v. Hansen*, 269 F. Supp 401 (DDC 1967), *aff'd sub nom, Smuck v. Hobson* 408 F.2d 175 (DC Cir. 1969) (en banc)) (Kirp & Yudof, 1974, p. 674).

In declaring that the District of Columbia's tracking procedures must be abolished, Judge Wright criticized its then current implementation by noting that the system failed "to translate into practice one of the most critical tenets of the tracking system: 'Pupil placement in a curriculum must never be static or unchangeable. Otherwise the four-track system will degenerate into a four-rut system.'" The judge's opinion continued that tracking encouraged self-fulfilling prophesy in that those placed in the lowest track "will act out that judgment and confirm it by achieving only at the expected level . . . [T]here is strong evidence that the performance in fact *declines*" (Kirp & Yudof, 1974, pp. 677, 680).

Judge Wright saw none of the benefits of tracking, as advocated by the Progressives, for the students of mid-twentieth century Washington. He noted that "in practice, if not in concept, [tracking] discriminates against the disadvantaged child . . . Designed in 1955, as a means of protecting the school system against the ill-effects of integrating with white children the Negro victims of *de jure* separate but equal education, it has survived to stigmatize the disadvantaged child of whatever race relegated to its lower tracks--from which tracks the possibility of switching upward . . . is remote." (Kirp & Yudof, 1974, p. 682).

The two-year tenure of Superintendent J. J. Burns, beginning in 1885, brought to public attention the rote and drill methods used by most teachers in the Dayton system at that time. However, during the next twenty years, four superintendents followed each other in rapid succession, two lasting only two years each, enabling few really significant changes to take place. In that interval, the greatest force for reform was Patterson himself, and this was best exemplified in his support of the Patterson School. Between 1891 and 1908, it sought to remove the walls between school and society and enable children to study mechanical drawing, machining, carpentry, applied chemistry, and millinery in addition to the more traditional subjects. While the addition of more practical areas of study ultimately benefited employers such as Patterson, only the most cynical observers of the time have suggested that his motives were totally selfish. For at least some of those young people not going on for further education, the expanded offerings were appropriate and relevant (Sealander, 1988, pp. 142-44).

Edwin Brown's eight-year tenure as superintendent, begun in 1908 when he was 37 and lasting until his death, solidified the progressive vision begun by Patterson. Brown introduced an elaborate program of night schools attended yearly by an average of 3000 students. Most were young men who worked during the day and recent immigrants seeking occupational skills and an opportunity to study English. Brown also introduced an extensive physical education curriculum, summer classes and programs for the deaf and crippled, as well as those diagnosed as "backward." "About the only identifiable group left to languish was a tiny population of black children . . . composing only four or five percent of children in most age groups in the city. . . . Their race and not their numbers explained the slighting of black children. Their segregated school received little attention from Edwin Brown or any other administrator" (Sealander, 1988, pp. 144-46).

Brown's implementation of progressive educational ideas included medical and dental inspections and treatment for pupils whose parents could not afford such services, as well as intelligence and "efficiency" testing to determine how much teachers might properly expect from individual students. School buildings truly became city "social centers" available to the general public during and after school hours as the site for films, lectures, and debates (Sealander, 1988, pp. 146-47).

The superintendents who followed Brown, after his death in 1916, continued to combine educational innovation with progressive, business-minded concerns for efficiency. School administration was reorganized, placing department heads between the superintendent and the building principals. Janitorial and cafeteria services were centralized, as were purchasing, transportation and building construction, maintenance, and repair. In 1923, to maximize the use of school space, students were divided into platoons to alternately work on academic and non-academic subjects. This proved particularly desirable during this decade when Dayton's population doubled and its school population more than tripled. Even with this efficiency, classes still had to be held in hallways and, when the weather permitted, on the schools' front steps (Sealander, 1988, pp. 147-49).

Night school enrollments peaked in the school year 1927-28, when approximately "five thousand teenagers and adults studied everything from Shakespeare to automobile repair." Hundreds of other young people were enrolled in the cooperative high school, working at an outside job one week and attending school full-time the next. Businesses not only provided jobs but scholarships as well. Without question, the programs profited the employers, who gained a better trained and more appreciative work force, but in many cases, the students who subsequently became those workers benefited as well (Sealander, 1988, pp. 149-50, 152-53).

The Depression hit Dayton's schools especially hard. The system, which in 1927-28 had a total of 165 schools and 1188 teachers, had to cut 90 teachers a year. The pride of the business interests and the community at large could not compete with the economic realities. Teachers, who had little input regarding what they considered progressive intrusions into their traditional teaching responsibilities, now had larger classes to contend with as well. Minimum class sizes were mandated between 30 and 40 depending upon grade level. Retrenchment became school policy for the next several years (Sealander, 1988, pp. 150-52, 154-55).

The Dayton black community which, in the first three decades of the twentieth century, appeared to be the only group to be denied the benefits of the progressive educational movement, by the 1970s was no longer willing to be neglected. On April 17, 1972, appellants in *Brinkman v. Gilligan* "sought, *inter alia*, an injunction enjoining the Dayton defendants from continuing their allegedly unconstitutional policy of operating the public schools in Dayton in a manner that perpetrated racial segregation." The plaintiffs charged that the Dayton Board of Education ignored the law of the State of Ohio, in effect since February 22, 1887, that mandated an integrated public school system. Ohio Revised Code, 3313.48 declared that:

The board of education of each city, exempted village, local, and joint vocational school district shall provide for the free education of the youth of school age within the district under its jurisdiction, at such places as will be most convenient for the attendance of the largest number thereof. (503 F.2d 684, 1974)

This statute had been upheld by the Supreme Court of Ohio in 1888 in *Board of Education v. State*, 45 Ohio St. 555, 556, 16 N.E. 373, 373 in which the court declared that "separate schools for colored children have been abolished and no regulation can be made . . . that does not apply to all children irrespective of race or color." In continuing the historical review of the racial policies of the Dayton Board of Education, the District Court noted that:

The evidence presented has established isolated but repeated instances of failure by the Dayton School Board to meet the standards of the Ohio law mandating an integrated school system. Such instances include a physical segregation into separate buildings of pupils and teachers by race at the Garfield School in the early 1920's, a denial of blacks to access to swimming pools in high schools in the 1930's and 1940's and the exclusion, between 1938 and 1948, of black high school teams from the city athletic conference" (503 F.2d 684, 1974). The physical segregation into separate buildings of pupils and teachers by race was ruled illegal in *Board of Education of School District of City of Dayton v. State ex rel. Reese*. (114 Ohio St. 188, 189, 151 N.E. 39, 1926)

The Court's historical review continued by noting that in 1956, following the *Brown* decision "the Ohio Attorney General had ruled that the Ohio State Board of Education had the primary responsibility for administering the laws relating to the distribution of state and federal funds to local school districts" and that such funds should not be distributed to local districts which "segregated pupils on the basis of race in violation of *Brown*." For twenty years, the Dayton branch of the NAACP and other groups had protested that, in fact, the Dayton school population was racially imbalanced, yet the funding continued (*Brinkman v. Gilligan*, 689).

The Acting Director of the Office of Civil Rights notified Dayton school authorities, on March 17, 1969, that the district was not in compliance with Title VI of the Civil Rights Act of 1964, particularly regarding "the assignment of teachers and other professional staff. Thus, all Negro principals are assigned to predominantly Negro schools as are 11 of the 14 Negro assistant principals. "Similar charges were made regarding teachers and coaches (*Brinkman v. Gilligan*, 689).

The distribution of pupils also was criticized. It was noted that 85 percent of Negro pupils were concentrated in three high schools, where the percentage of Negro attendance ranged from 92.3 to 100 percent. Similarly, approximately 85 percent of Negro elementary school students attended 20 of the 53 elementary schools in the district. In 17 of those 20 schools, Negroes comprised 90 to 100 percent of total enrollment (*Brinkman v. Gilligan*, 689-90).

The Ohio State Department of Education made recommendations to the Dayton Board with regard to how to achieve constitutionally required desegregation. The State Board, noting that the Dayton Board serves "as an agency of state government," indicated a strong feeling of obligation. The State Department emphasized that rather than improving, racial imbalance in particular schools was getting worse. Although Dayton's efforts to address the state's recommendations did not lead to full compliance, state financing was continued (*Brinkman v. Gilligan,* 690).

The Dayton Board recognized that it was "guilty of procedures that led to the racial isolation of school children," when, on April 29, 1971, it appointed "a broadly representative committee to evaluate and advise it on plans to reduce racial isolation and improve educational opportunities." The group was referred to as the Committee of 75, although eleven students were later added. In its charge to the committee, the Board admitted that "unequal educational opportunities for the poor and black students now exist in the Dayton School District." The Board set "quality integrated education" as its goal and asked the committee "to establish evaluation elements to be applied to a developed plan . . . and to set up guidelines and/or methods by which the community will become meaningfully involved" (*Brinkman v. Gilligan*, 690-91).

In late fall, 1971, the committee issued its report, which "recognized the Dayton Board's causal responsibility for the condition of segregation and the imperative need to end one race schooling." The committee concluded the summary of its report by noting that "quality integrated education can help stop the flight to the suburbs, break the cycle of poor education, and the lack of job skills which handicap the minorities. The cost of this type of education will be small in relation to the total benefits society will reap" (*Brinkman v. Gilligan*, 691-92).

At its meeting on December 8, 1971, the Board passed three resolutions admitting that the Board was responsible for racial and economic segregation in the Dayton schools, suggesting that the problem was a metropolitan one that demanded a metropolitan solution, requesting assistance from state and federal governments in desegregating the schools, and declaring that the Board policy would henceforth be that each school's enrollment would substantially reflect the racial and economic characteristics of the district as a whole. The superintendent of schools was directed to implement the desegregation plan, which rescinded the existing attendance districts as of September 1, 1972. Pupil assignments would be made to appropriately mix the student body of each school in proportion to the city as a whole, and transportation would be used when necessary. Magnet and demonstration schools that met desegregation criteria were to be encouraged (*Brinkman v. Gilligan*, 692-93).

Table 2.1
Dayton Population by Race: SMSA and City, 1970 and 1980;
County and City, 1990

	1970		1980		1990	
	N	%	N	%	N	%
TOTAL CITY	243,601		203,371		182,044	
WHITE	168,407	69%	126,188	62%	106,258	58%
BLACK	74,284	30%	75,016	37%	73,595	40%
HISPANIC	N/A		1,744	1%	1,356	1%
SMSA OR COUNTY	850,266		830,070		573,809	
WHITE	752,933	89%	716,453	86%	463,551	81%
BLACK	93,676	11%	105,261	13%	101,817	18%
HISPANIC	N/A		5,653	1%	4,539	1%

Note: Categories may not total to 100% because of other groups and because Hispanics may also be listed as White or Black.

Source: U.S. Census, 1970, 1980, 1990

The resolutions were short lived. The Board that passed them in December had been voted out of office the month before, and when the new Board was seated in January, 1972, it rescinded the three resolutions of its predecessor Board. The three resolutions, which had all originally passed on 5 to 2 votes, were now negated by votes of 4 to 3, 4 to 2, and 4 to 2. The racially isolating attendance zones were reinstated, including the system's Freedom of Enrollment program. *Brinkman v. Gilligan* was filed on April 17, 1972 (*Brinkman v. Gilligan*, 693).

On July 24, 1972, the Dayton defendants and the State defendants filed their answers, denying the material allegations of the plaintiffs' complaint. An expedited hearing before District Judge Carl B. Rubin took place between November 13 and December 1, 1972. The single issue to be determined was whether the Dayton school system was segregated due to acts of the Dayton Board of Education. On February 7, 1973, the District Court found that "(1) racially imbalanced schools, (2) optional attendance zones, and (3) rescission by the Dayton Board of Education of the three resolutions calling for racial and economic balance in each school in the Dayton system were 'cumulatively in violation of the Equal Protection Clause' of the Constitution" (*Brinkman v. Gilligan*, 693).

The District Court ordered the Dayton Board to submit a plan that would

(1) abolish all optional zones, (2) restate the priorities of the Board's Freedom of Enrollment program so that racial transfers would take precedence over curriculum transfers, (3) maintain faculty assignment practices so that each school would continue to reflect the approximate ratio of the total black-to-white faculty in the Dayton system, and (4) establish hiring practices that would enable the clerical and maintenance personnel employed by the Board to approximate the proportion of black-to-white population existing in the Dayton system. (*Brinkman v. Gilligan*)

The Court further stated that the four elements noted above "shall be considered as a minimum" and that the plan to be submit-ted by the Board was to conform to all requirements of the law. *Swann v. Charlotte-Mecklenburg Board of Education* and *Davis v. School Commissioners of Mobile County* were cited as examples (*Brinkman v. Gilligan*).

On March 19, the Dayton Board complied with the District Court order and submitted a desegregation plan containing eleven points:

1. Elimination of Optional Zones-for both elementary and high school students;
2. Freedom of Enrollment Priorities-revised criteria;
3. Faculty Assignment Practices-faculty assignments for each school should reflect the white-to-black ratio of the entire system;
4. Hiring Policies for Classified Personnel-blacks would be hired for clerical, custodial, and food service positions in proportion to the black-to-white population residing within the Dayton School District;
5. Science Environmental Program-all children would be bused to this mandatory program which would be held in four centers. The groupings would be racially mixed to reflect the black-to-white student ratio;
6 Patterson-Stivers Vocational High School-combined two vocational schools into a unified cooperative school with districtwide enrollment;
7. Musical Stereopticon-created districtwide elementary and high school band, orchestra, and chorus;
8. Integrated Athletics-required that schools without minority athletes play those with such players; high school schedules to be centrally administered to eliminate racial isolation;
9. Minority Language Program-instituted mandatory in-service workshops on linguistic differences in American English for teachers and administrators;

10. Living Arts Center-departments of art, creative writing, dance, and drama were organized;
11. Control Center-created rumor control centers, school guidance centers, and area learning centers to encourage a more secure climate for quality education. (*Brinkman v. Gilligan*)

Alternate plans were submitted by the Dayton Board minority members as well as the Dayton Classroom Teachers' Association, the former group feeling that the Board plan did not go far enough. The Court, however, essentially accepted the plan of the Board majority despite protest from the plaintiff-appellants that the plan "froze in" the then current segregated system. The Court, however, did express its "disappointment at the limited nature" of points five through eleven and stated that "the desired goal was not attained completely by the majority plan" (*Brinkman v. Gilligan*).

The District Court continued: "There remains for consideration two further questions which the Court has reserved: The matter of the so-called Metropolitan School District and the status of defendants State of Ohio through its Governor and the Ohio Department of Education." The Court then declared the metropolitan question moot and dismissed the non-Dayton defendants. It declared its support of the neighborhood school concept as long as no "improper racial intent" could be demonstrated. Paraphrasing *Swann v. Charlotte-Mecklenburg Board of Education*, the Court declared: "It is the functions of the federal courts only to eliminate a deprivation of constitutional rights; it is the duty of local school boards to operate and maintain integrated school systems" (*Brinkman v. Gilligan*).

The United States Court of Appeals, Sixth Circuit reviewed the case in April, 1974 and issued its decision the following August. It concluded that the remedy prescribed by the District Court was inadequate and that the State of Ohio was also culpable. It directed that court to revise and supplement its order in accord with remedy guidelines as outlined in *Keyes, Swann,* and *Milliken v. Bradley* (*Brinkman v. Gilligan,* 704-5).

The *Brinkman* plaintiffs were not satisfied with the Board of Education plan and appealed the court ruling. The petition was heard by the United States Court of Appeals, Sixth Circuit on June 24, 1975. The Appeals Court agreed to the findings of fact by the District Court that the Dayton school system was "guilty of *de jure* segregation practices." The Appeals Court also agreed with the plaintiff-appellants that "the remedy ordered by that court [was] inadequate, considering the scope of the constitutional violations . . . [U]nder the plan approved by the District Court the basic pattern of one-race schools will continue largely unabated." The Appeals Court concluded that "the District Court's plan fail[ed] to eliminate the continuing effects of past segregation," rendering it "inadequate" (*Brinkman v. Gilligan,* 518 F.2d 853, 1975, 853-56).

The Appeals Court stated that if time were not a factor, it would have granted the relief requested by the plaintiffs, which was to overturn the original judgment. Instead of summary reversal, the case was remanded to the District Court with directions to modify the plan "so as to improve the racial balance before September 1, 1975 in as many of the remaining racially identifiable schools in the Dayton system as feasible." The Appeals Court also directed that there be "a system-wide plan for the 1976-77 school year" to "conform to the previous mandate" no later than December 31, 1975 so that it would be in place for the new school year to begin in September, 1976. This plan was to include the mandate that each school reflect the total district's black/white racial balance of 48 percent/52 percent, plus or minus 15 percent (*Brinkman v. Gilligan* 1975, 857; *Dayton Cares For Kids: From Court Order to Implementation*, 1977).

When the Dayton Board of Education challenged the appeals ruling in 1977, the Supreme Court sided with the Board. While agreeing with the original plaintiffs that there had been violations by the school board, the Supreme Court determined that the remedy prescribed had been excessive. In the opinion as delivered by Justice Rehnquist: "If such violations are found, the District Court . . . must determine how much incremental segregative effect these violations had on the racial distribution of the Dayton school population as presently constituted, when that distribution is compared to what it would have been in the absence of such constitutional violations. The remedy must be designed to redress that difference, and only if there has been a systemwide impact may there be a systemwide remedy" (*Dayton Board v. Brinkman* No. 76-539, 420).

The case was returned to the Court of Appeals in 1978 and to the Supreme Court in 1979 where the systemwide remedy was finally affirmed. It was concluded that the radiating effects of segregative acts ultimately do become systemwide in scope even if they are not so initially. The 1977 decision was unanimous with Justice Marshall not participating; in 1979, the Court supported the Sixth Circuit by a vote of 5-4. In explaining the reversal, Justice White described a series of segregative practices going back more than two decades that were not limited to isolated violations, thus justifying a systemwide remedy (Frank Goodman in Yarmolinsky, Liebman, & Schelling, 1981, p. 53; Metcalf, 1983, pp. 261-62).

Even though the Supreme Court, in the first instance, attempted to limit the accountability of the school board to intentional discrimination, by the late 1970s, the Dayton schools were in the throes of creating a systemwide plan for desegregation. Dayton was very conscious of its public image and had no desire to repeat the experiences of Boston and Louisville. The brochure, prepared by Superintendent John B. Maxwell's office to explain the desegregation process to the community, refers to the difficulties in those two cities

(Mark F. Yudof in Stephan & Feagin, 1980, p. 113; *Dayton Cares for Kids: From Court Order to Implementation*, 1977).

Because of the numerous appeals with regard to the court action, Dayton's desegregation efforts proceeded in an incremental fashion. In February, 1973, part-time magnet centers were introduced at both the elementary and secondary level. The former offered programs in career motivation (grades 4-5), business skills (grades 6-8), foreign languages (grades 6-8), and extended outdoor education (grade 5), while the latter provided experiences in communications, computer technology, advanced math, and science and museum studies. At the same time, full-time magnet schools offered a structured alternative school for grades K-8 and a co-op program for grades 9-12. In addition, the freedom of enrollment policy was modified to allow elementary students to enroll in any school in the city "provided such enrollment improved the racial balance in the receiving school and did not diminish it in the sending school." High school students could enroll in any school in the district (*Dayton Cares for Kids: From Court Order to Implementation*, 1977).

In early 1976, the pairing of predominantly black and predominantly white elementary schools was added to the plan; middle schools were abolished and students and teachers in the paired schools were to change buildings at mid-year. Subsequently, the paired schools alternated the students and teachers annually, and still later it was determined to keep all kindergarten children in their neighborhood school and make half of the schools K-3 and the other half K, 4-6. Ultimately, the schools were returned to a K-6 pattern (*Dayton Cares for Kids: From Court Order to Implementation*, 1977; interview with James Williams, June 23-24, 1991).

Those high schools that had appropriate black/white ratios remained neighborhood schools with attendance zones designed to encourage the maintenance of an integrated student body. The other four schools, two predominantly black and two predominantly white, were paired much like the elementary schools (*Dayton Cares for Kids: From Court Order to Implementation*, 1977).

Providing opportunities for community involvement in the implementation of the various desegregation plans received at least as much attention as the creation of the plans themselves. The literature prepared by the Superintendent's office emphasized the importance of community input. Advisory boards, which met every Saturday, were created that included business and religious leaders, social agencies and the police, parents and other grass roots groups. The murder of court monitor Charles Glatt, by an irate white citizen opposed to desegregation, shocked the community and served as a compelling impetus for people to work together. John B. Maxwell's successor after Richard Hunter, the city's first black school superintendent, was Dr. Franklin Smith, who during the summer of 1991 became the superintendent of schools in Washington, D.C. Dr.

Smith was universally described as a master of public relations
(*Dayton Cares for Kids: From Court Order to Implementation*, 1977;
interviews with James Williams and Dale Frederick, June 23-24,
1991; interview with C. Benjamin Kirby, June 24, 1991).

Miley O. Williamson, Executive Secretary of the Dayton NAACP,
concurs that the community groups and community participation in
general was extremely important in implementing the desegregation
efforts. Although some people, both white and minority, were and
still are opposed to transporting children, students are nonetheless
bused to enable desegregation efforts to take place. Prior to
desegregation, according to Ms. Williamson, black schools were
clearly inferior to those for whites and only with integration have they
achieved a reasonable level of equality. She noted that the high
school had two pools, supposedly one each for boys and girls, but
used instead to separate blacks and whites. There were even two
senior proms, one for each race. "Anything separate will never be
equal," she contended emphatically (Interview with Miley O.
Williamson, June 29, 1992).

Ms. Williamson identified the churches, the business community,
the NAACP, and the Urban League as the groups within the area
working with municipal and school officials that were most
responsible for Dayton being one of the few cities not to "have
problems" implementing integration in its schools. She also stressed
"strong leadership at the top" being a requirement for ensuring that
people work together (Williamson interview).

School desegregation, aided undoubtedly by the proportionate
increase of the minority population, has resulted in housing becoming
less segregated as well. Previous to 1978, blacks lived almost
exclusively on the west side. Now housing opportunities are more
equal, with African-Americans gaining access to previously all-white
areas such as Trotwood and Oakwood. White lending institutions
have made more money available to blacks as well (Williamson
interview).

While there was general agreement among those interviewed that
Dayton's business community continued its legacy of cooperation with
and in support of the schools, opinions were more varied regarding
the role that teachers have played and continue to play in
desegregation efforts. These differing opinions probably reflect the
variety of responses from the faculty in the same way that some feel
that the in-service provided for the teachers met their needs, while
others reported great dissatisfaction with administrative efforts in
this regard (Williams, Kirby, and Frederick interviews, interviews
with Mary Moore and Mary Robinson, June 24, 1991).

In 1991, seventy percent of Dayton's teachers were white;
aggressive efforts were being instituted to recruit more minority
faculty and to assist teaching aides in continuing their education to
earn teaching credentials. It was hoped and expected that the ratio

would soon more closely approximate that of the students. A dozen schools were moving toward site-based management and decentralized administration; merit pay was being discussed. While at the end of the nineteenth century, reformers blamed the failure of the schools on decentralized and unprofessional administration, at the end of the twentieth century, the effective schools movement views decentralization and the empowerment of individual principals, groups of teachers, and neighborhoods of parents as the means to enable the schools to solve all of society's problems. The primary mission of the schools was to address the needs of pupils, even, if necessary, in preference to adult needs. According to Dr. Williams: "If the system is good enough, integration is no longer the paramount issue" (Williams interview, Katz, 1987, pp. 124-28).

The actions of the media likewise had supporters and detractors. While the superintendent's office praised the role played by the media, the current magnet school director, Benjamin Kirby, felt that the media exaggerated the difficulties involved in the implementation of the desegregation programs and inaccurately attributed declining school enrollments to white flight as a result of the desegregation efforts, despite the fact that suburban school districts were experiencing a similar loss of school population. A *Dayton Daily News* special series on race relations, published between December 13-19, 1987, overwhelmingly emphasized the separation, rather than the integration, of the races in Dayton and its suburbs (*Dayton Cares*, Kirby interview, *Dayton Daily News*).

There was absolutely no disagreement among those interviewed that parents' feeling they had some control over the destiny of their children was the most important factor in enabling desegregation to take place in Dayton. Recollections of riots in West Dayton in 1967 and of racial violence in local high schools the following year made most Dayton residents desirous of not repeating the frightening experiences of Boston and Louisville. The magnet school concept allowed for an element of choice within a context of an imposed court-ordered action. Rossell argues in *The Carrot or the Stick*, comparing Dayton with Buffalo, that voluntary plans result in less white flight. It seems likely that white parents would have been less accepting of desegregation if they felt that they had no choice in the school their children attended (*Dayton Daily News* supplement, p. 5; Rossell, 1990, pp. 87-91).

By 1989-90, magnet school choices had increased to include classical/traditional academies and structured/traditional academies, both with uniforms, as well as Montessori programs and schools that emphasized professional studies, computer technology, environmental science, and the visual and performing arts. Five-year and ten-year plans were conceived in 1990 designed to emphasize individual achievement and the widest variety of choices of both how and what to learn (*Dayton Public Schools Annual Report*, 1989-90, pp. 6-13).

In addition to the extensive opportunities offered, one of the most positive forces promoting desegregation is the new school superintendent, James Williams. As Miley O. Williamson of the NAACP noted, no idea can succeed without someone who fully embraces it and can share that enthusiasm with others. Staff describe Dr. Williams as inspirational; there is little doubt of his commitment to the programs he helped construct as assistant superintendent (Williams interview; Williamson interview).

It is harder to determine whether those less enthusiastic are opposed to desegregation per se or merely to the busing. While few children travel more than 20 minutes to school, the majority of parents still prefer the concept of neighborhood schools. Even with the wide variety of choices available, many parents select a school for their children more on the basis of proximity than program. Additionally, Benjamin Kirby suggests that integration works best in integrated neighborhoods, among those with higher incomes, and in areas with more stable families. "Segregation may be just a habit." With the Dayton school population approaching two-thirds minority in 1989, and Dr. Williams convinced that the suburban towns in Montgomery County would strongly resist moving to a countywide school district, it becomes all the more important to maintain a commitment to the city's schools by all segments of the city's population (Williams interview, Williamson interview, Kirby interview, *Just the Facts, 1988-89*, p. 15).

By late 1994, Dayton's minority population had reached 70 percent, 98 percent of that group being African-American. There were modest increases in minority populations in the northern and western suburbs contiguous to the areas where Dayton's minority population concentrated. Most of those migrating outward were middle class. Fewer minorities moved to the southern and eastern suburbs, which abut areas within the cities that were primarily white. A levee passed in 1991 guaranteed more generous funding for the city's schools and enabled the expansion of the magnet school program. Academic offerings were increased and student achievement rose. Administrators did not foresee any significant changes in school organization in the near future (Interview with Jane Rafal, Executive Assistant to the Superintendent, November 17 and 22, 1994).

Chapter 3

Rochester

When Rochester, New York initiated a serious attempt to desegregate its schools in 1969, it was not in response to outside pressure or judicial decree. The city had a population of 296,000 and a school enrollment of 46,000 students, 68 percent of whom were white. As an aggregate, the number of minority students in the city would have allowed for integrated education; however, the distribution of those students was racially very uneven. "In 1963, schools were predominantly either black or white," but, by 1968, all but two schools had significantly increased in minority population. Whereas in 1963, only 8 of the 43 city schools had minority populations greater than 50 percent, six years later 11 schools of 45 had a preponderance of minority students and of those 11, 6 were more than 90 percent minority (*U.S. Census; Grade Reorganization and Desegregation of the Rochester Public Schools,* 1969, p. 18).

Rochester's first experience in race relations took place at the end of the eighteenth century when white settlers discovered the charms of the Genessee River area. In 1788, during the westward movement in the early years of the Republic, Oliver Phelps realized the potential of the Genessee Falls as a source of power when he negotiated with the Indians at nearby Buffalo Creek. While attempting to purchase most of the Seneca lands in western New York, he noted the reluctance of the Indians to part with any territory west of the Genessee River. These earliest residents took as much pride in the area as those who were to follow. Phelps offered to construct mills for their use at the small upper falls in exchange for the grant of a mill lot west of the river. The tract that was agreed upon comprised what is now the western half of Monroe County, of which Rochester is the major city (McKelvey, 1973, pp. 1-3).

Ebenezer Allan was hired a year later to build the grist mill just north of the Upper Falls of the Genessee River on the two and a half million acres purchased from the Indians. By 1811, swamps and

3.1 Rochester SMSA (New York), 1970

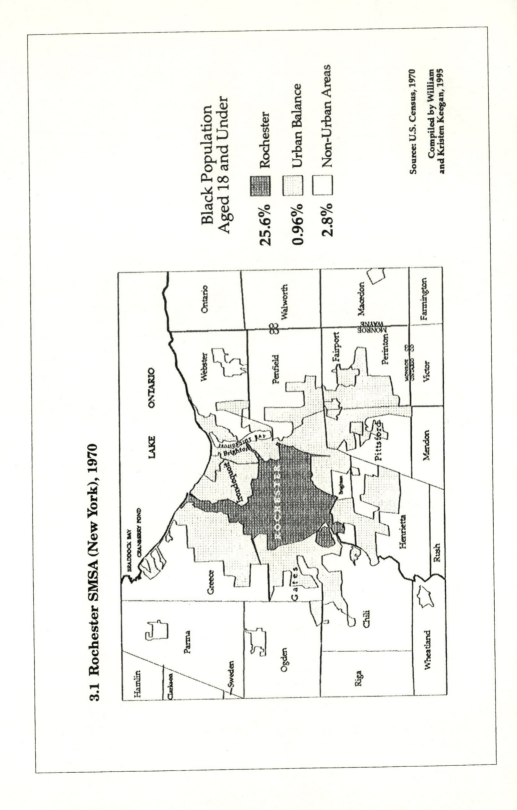

Black Population
Aged 18 and Under

- 25.6% Rochester
- 0.96% Urban Balance
- 2.8% Non-Urban Areas

Source: U.S. Census, 1970

Compiled by William
and Kristen Keegan, 1995

rattlesnakes were being replaced by additional flour mills when
Colonel Nathaniel Rochester and his partners bought Allan's site.
Rochester became America's first boomtown and, as the village of
Rochesterville, it was known as the "Flour Capital of the Nation."
Long lines of barges loaded with flour, potash, and lumber moved
along the Erie Canal, built in 1822, which was routed over the
Genessee River by means of a stone aqueduct (McKelvey, 1973, pp.
3-4; *A Visitor's Guide to Rochester,* 1991, p. 1).

The Civil War's requirement for uniforms fueled Rochester's
rapidly growing garment industry and, after the war, work continued
in supplying ready-made suits to the West. By the end of the
nineteenth century, the men's clothing industry was second only to
the flour mills in importance. Rochester's fame as the "Flour City"
became homonymic when two leading nurserymen, George Ellwanger
and Patrick Barry, enhanced the city's impressive park system and
lovely gardens to international standards, resulting in Rochester
being known as the "Flower City" as well (McKelvey, 1973, pp. 48,
87, 89).

The second half of the nineteenth century witnessed the
beginnings of two of Rochester's most important and longest
sustained industries. In 1853, John Jacob Bausch and Henry Lomb
opened the small optical shop that was to become today's Fortune
500 optical and health care company. In 1888, George Eastman,
then a young bank clerk, began experimenting with dry plates and
film in his mother's kitchen in the evenings. Eastman's first camera
launched the industry that, as Eastman Kodak, currently employs
approximately 45,000 Rochesterians (McKelvey, 1973, pp. 106-08).

The Xerox Corporation began as the Haloid Company in 1906.
When it developed the world's first plain paper copier in 1950, it
totally changed the way information could be transmitted. At
present, almost 12,000 residents of Monroe County are employed by
the company manufacturing copiers, terminals, and laser printers
(McKelvey, 1961, pp. 17, 196-97, 213-14).

Schooling for Rochester's children was first provided by the nearby
Gates and Brighton School Districts. But, when the 480 children
enrolled in 1821 increased to 2000 by 1827, "only the brief terms
attended by most pupils saved the system from collapse." Colonel
Rochester was unsuccessful in his attempt to form a Lancastrian
Society to operate the Gates and Brighton schools as a union district,
Albany turning down the proposal in 1821. Private academies for
boys and seminaries for girls were established, and their modest fees
enabled those able to pay an alternative to the crowded public
system. A union high school was created in Brighton in 1828, but its
high cost resulted in its becoming a private seminary in 1831
(McKelvey, 1973, pp. 30-31).

During the 1830s and '40s, education was among the most
significant civic advances. In 1835, the old Gates District No. 2,

renamed Rochester District No. 1, constructed a four-room stone schoolhouse at a cost of $3000. When it was soon outgrown and an annex request denied by the aldermen, a movement to create an independent school board developed. In May, 1841, Rochester's first elective board of education was established "to control a system of free, tax-supported common schools." By 1844, 4200 pupils were being taught by 44 teachers in 15 district schools. A high school was recommended by the new school board superintendent, Isaac Mack, "but mounting demands for economy" delayed it for a decade. The free schools diminished the activities and enrollment of both the charity and select schools but the arrival of increasing numbers of Irish and German immigrants prompted the establishment of religious schools to meet their needs (McKelvey, 1973, pp. 52-55).

By 1851, state law required that all children be enrolled in school for at least part of the year. The city expended $30,000 on new buildings, bringing the total number of schools to 16. However, it was not until 1857 that Rochester remodeled old School No. 1 to serve as its first public high school. Meanwhile, Catholic and Lutheran parochial schools continued to serve immigrant wards, particularly those that were predominantly German (McKelvey, 1973, pp. 66, 76).

The 1890s depression hit the schools especially hard. The city could not meet its payroll, and teachers did not get their 50 dollars a month salary in January of 1894. The city's budgetary difficulties prompted examination of the school system, and educational preparation in general was found to be wanting. The Citizen's Political Reform Association was created with businessman Joseph T. Alling, Alderman James Johnson, and the Reverend Dr. Algernon Crapsey at its helm. They soon determined that the schools had been used for political patronage by George Aldridge, who served first as mayor and then as Republican party leader. The large school board had been easy for the mayor to pack (McKelvey, 1973, pp. 130-31).

By 1899, the critical shortage of public school facilities had attracted state censure. A bill directing Rochester to borrow $100,000 for school expansion was proposed, but Mayor George E. Warner vetoed it. By the end of the year, 1000 youngsters were still without school facilities, the mayor had been discredited, and, in an attempt at reform, a small, elected, politically independent school board was made responsible for the education of Rochester's children. As the new board took over, it was discovered that the outgoing superintendent had pocketed funds that were supposed to be used for non-resident tuition payments. The construction of East High was among the first acts of the new school board (McKelvey, 1973, pp. 132-35; McKelvey, 1961, p. 21).

Reform groups worked with the Board of Education and the city's churches to support a Social Center program that included evening schools, which were begun in 1907, and a "Labor Lyceum," which was initiated in 1910. The city's social and economic leaders, reacting to the influx of new immigrants from southern and eastern Europe, were determined to be positively responsive to the needs of Rochester's most recently arrived citizens (McKelvey, 1973, pp. 136-40).

Rochester renewed its civic pride when, in 1910, the Federation of Social Centers joined the Board of Education in staging the city's first public art exhibit in East High School. The city's musical opportunities had been similarly enhanced when George Eastman launched a program of Sunday musicales earlier in the decade (McKelvey, 1973, pp. 142-43).

Eastman's interest in the cultural life of Rochester extended far beyond music. In concert with other business leaders, he encouraged movement toward professional standards and administration in the schools. During the 1920s, School Superintendent Herbert S. Weet improved educational methods and standards, among which was the introduction of the junior high school. This new concept in school organization enabled students continuing their education beyond primary school to do so in a setting more congenial than the mammoth high schools. The success of this approach was greeted with great enthusiasm by national educators (McKelvey, 1973, pp. 182-83).

During this same period, alternatives to the traditional school program were augmented. Carl F. Lomb, vice-president of Bausch & Lomb, aided by a generous pledge from George Eastman and "pegged as was his custom to the success of a public drive for funds," was the spearhead for the expansion of the Mechanics Institute, one of several special business and trade schools within the system. Meanwhile, the parochial schools reorganized their programs in light of increasing numbers of students as a result of the new immigration and took advantage of the public schools' willingness to provide released time for religious education. In 1929, 36 parochial and special schools provided education for 18,000 Rochester youngsters (McKelvey, 1961, p. 47).

Concomitantly, the public schools were feeling similar enrollment pressures. While the number of new students was no longer increasing dramatically, pupils were staying in school longer. The 6-3-3 organizational system implemented by Superintendent Weet allowed the scheduling of students to be more flexible, but it did not fully relieve the need for new facilities. Despite the peaking of elementary school students at 35,486 in 1927, a request for three elementary schools had to be tabled to allow for the building of an addition to the Washington Junior High School and to hasten the construction of the new Benjamin Franklin High School. Concomitantly, the Monroe Junior High was converted to a senior high school with the provision of new laboratories and other facilities (McKelvey, 1961, pp. 47-48).

The movement of many families to the suburbs and the creation of free-school tracts in Brighton, Greece, and Irondequoit, just beyond the city limits, brought an additional burden. Ten years earlier, when the city annexed a part of these districts, including their district schools, they were promised free admission into the Rochester schools. In 1929, the 684 students were ten times the original number, and the Rochester system wanted them incorporated into the city system as taxpayers as well. However, the towns successfully blocked the measure and the city tabled it (McKelvey, 1961, p. 48).

The schools were even harder hit a year later when severe budget cutting deprived them of approximately two million dollars that had previously been allotted to them. Only the possibility of federal or state relief work projects offered any hope of additional support. During the early 1930s, the business community joined with the schools in launching the New Era Collegiate program and several similar projects to employ some of the city's idle talent (McKelvey, 1961, pp. 63, 66, 70, 79).

As the Depression deepened, the schools cut back portions of their extra-curricular activities but intensified their efforts to serve teenage youths. In 1931, teachers volunteered to accept a ten-percent cut in salary, while the average class size was allowed to increase to 36 as the school population began a decline from its all-time high of 71,871 in 1930. Summer programming, speech correction, and instrumental music instruction were among the casualties of reluctant budget slashing. The effect on the music program, however, was diminished by a gift by George Eastman of 29 radios that enabled the system to reproduce the Civic Orchestra programs to all schools and to feature additional Sunday radio concerts (McKelvey, 1961, pp. 104-5).

Rochester schools weathered the Depression with the assistance of federal programs and strong local support. PWA funds aided in the building of the John Marshall High School, and WPA monies allowed for maintenance work. While some kindergarten programs were cut, support for evening schools was so strong that they were maintained at East High School. James M. Spinning succeeded Herbert S. Weet as superintendent in December, 1933 and continued the school reorganization process. Working cooperatively with the new Democratic Board of Education, he avoided further cuts in the kindergarten and guidance programs while expanding the Rochester School of the Air and visual education work (McKelvey, 1961, pp. 104-6).

Rochester's private and parochial schools were also affected by the faltering economy. While the private schools stabilized and the three that survived constructed new facilities, the enrollments at the parochial schools began to fall. The more recent immigrants sent their children to the public schools, taking advantage of catechetical classes offered on a part-time basis (McKelvey, 1961, pp. 106-7).

The black migration to Rochester resulted in a population of approximately 400 by the year 1900. While to that date none had enrolled in the city's colleges, several had been graduated from the old Free Academy or the new East High School. The city, in an attempt to reach out to new citizen groups, had honored Frederick Douglass at his death with a solemn march and erected a monument to his memory in June, 1899 (McKelvey, 1973, pp. 146-47).

By 1930, the black population had increased to 2679. While almost half of that number lived in the third and fifth wards, comprising a tenth of the residents, the remainder were scattered throughout the city in every ward except the twenty-third. The increase in the black population encouraged civic-minded Rochesterians to augment social services. During the 1920s, branches of the YWCA, the YMCA, the Presbyterian old folks home, and the Rochester Association for the Blind were opened in areas where blacks could be conveniently served (McKelvey, 1961, pp. 8, 40).

The advent of the Second World War brought both economic and social benefits to the black community in Rochester, as it did in many other cities. A labor shortage forced five large firms to relax their resistance to Negro job applicants, and the United Service Organizations, Inc. (USO), with generous support from the Community Chest, founded a club house for Negroes known as Carver House (McKelvey, 1961, pp. 140, 148).

The city's problem with juvenile delinquency emphasized the need for programs in social integration and accentuated the trend toward segregation. School Superintendent Spinning was facing similar problems in the public schools. The combination of war-time funding economies, declining enrollments concomitant with the closing of three school buildings, and the movement of many Negroes into the old immigrant district in the northeastern part of the city created overcrowding and stress on the antiquated schools located there. Working mothers needed kindergarten care for their children, pre-induction youth required summer classes while awaiting the draft, and evening classes were needed for both industrial and civilian defense workers (McKelvey, 1961, pp. 163-64).

The post-war period saw the greatest number of Negro Rochester residents to that time and the greatest amount of hostility to their presence. While "most community leaders were outspoken in their respect for Negroes in the abstract," this respect did not translate automatically to individual men and women of color. The traditional Negro areas of Clarissa and Baden-Ormond, rapidly deteriorating and becoming slum-like, could not support their growing proportion of the 16,000 Negroes in Rochester in 1957. Those with good jobs made easier to acquire as a result of the Ives-Quinn fair employment bill were frustrated by the strong hostilities they encountered when they attempted to find housing in more desirable neighborhoods. The

NAACP membership drives profited from this discrimination as 2600 Negroes and sympathetic whites joined together in an attempt to advance the cause of those qualified to live and work in areas previously denied. The white community divided between those such as Dr. Wilbour E. Saunders, the newly appointed head of the Colgate-Rochester Divinity School, who cautioned Negro graduates not to press their demands for equality too rapidly, and those like Mrs. Harper Sibley, who protested vigorously against discrimination in housing, employment, and social relationships and won commendation from many Negroes for her forthright stand (McKelvey, 1961, pp. 237, 241-42).

In 1950, a new component was added to ethnic relations with the arrival of a few families from Puerto Rico. Five years later, the city had 3000 primarily Spanish-speaking residents sharing most of the same handicaps as the Negroes, with the additional burden of language. While their labor was desired at the canneries and for other unskilled jobs, "those with special talents or higher aspirations faced discouraging obstacles." By the mid-fifties, the Puerto Ricans had organized a council to address their problems as a united group. In the course of the decade, Rochester's non-white population increased from 7845 to 24,214 (McKelvey, 1961, pp. 242-43; 1973, p. 232).

A baby boom reached kindergarten classes in 1947 and exacerbated the school enrollment pressures brought about by the black and Puerto Rican migrations. Teachers added increased class size and student-teacher ratios to their feelings of neglect with regard to salaries. Despite support from Governor Thomas Dewey, recommending a subsidy to allow for a statewide minimum salary of $2000, wages remained an issue for several years. Dr. Howard C. Seymour wrestled with the issue as head of the Rochester Teachers Association during the late 1940s and still had to contend with it, from another perspective, when he became superintendent of the city's schools in 1954 (McKelvey, 1973, pp. 226-27; 1961, p. 285).

Teacher-pupil ratios, which had dropped to 1:20 during the war, increased to 1:25 or in some cases 1:30, as was the standard in New York City. Fiscal pressures on the public schools were eased somewhat by a rapid expansion of the parochial school system, whose enrollments increased from 14,000 to 24,000 within a decade. Suburban communities, such as Irondequoit, hugely affected by suburban migrations, were also required to expand their facilities to deal with rapidly growing enrollments (McKelvey, 1961, pp. 286-87; 1973, pp. 226-27).

In 1952, the Board of Education secured approval for the construction of a new East High School, but repeated delays resulted in the building not being completed for eight years. Early in the fifties, the city, with its traditional generosity and desire to be innovative, spearheaded by a half dozen junior executives at

Eastman, founded Teen-Age Diplomats, Inc., a pioneer student exchange program. However, by the end of the decade, the Rochester Area Council of Parent Teachers Associations was calling for more direct and significant reforms, such as more homework, longer hours, and an enriched curriculum to respond to the launching of the Russian Sputnik (McKelvey, 1961, pp. 231-32, 244-45, 330-31).

The beginning of the 1960s found Rochester schools suffering from a shortage of both classroom space and teachers. More attractive salaries lured many teachers-turned-housewives back into the classroom; however, the problems persisted. When the Board of Education majority shifted to the Democrats, there was the expectation of radical changes, but rifts between school board members and the superintendent over salaries resulted in the termination of the previously popular Dr. Seymour. The *Times-Union* declared the firing shameful and foolish, and two top aides refused the opportunity to serve as interim superintendent. An attempt was made to change the school board to an appointed non-partisan body, but that endeavor failed. Meanwhile, the uninvolved citizens could take pride in the quality of the schools, both public and parochial (at 36 percent, Rochester's Catholic schools served the greatest proportion of those students in the state), as members of both student bodies consistently won national prizes in impressive numbers (McKelvey, 1961, pp. 330-33).

Although Rochester won the first World Brotherhood Award in June, 1958, it manifested shameful shortcomings in significant areas. A state survey determined that, in its "better neighborhoods," it exhibited greater reluctance to sell to Negroes than any other city in the state. In January, 1959, the City Council created an independent Housing Authority and took more responsibility for the rehousing of residents in the dilapidated, and primarily black, Baden-Ormond district. Negroes were also provided increased opportunities for promotion in the police department and for slots in ward elections (McKelvey, 1961, pp. 336-37).

The *Times-Union* chose this time to prepare a series on the Negro in Rochester. Desmond Stone and Jack Germond uncovered "a sorry record of discrimination," which was leavened only slightly by the activities of some church groups and other bodies. While some blacks were being welcomed into the better neighborhoods of city and suburb, the general situation was found to be embarrassing. The city named Loftus C. Carson as full-time director of its Human Relations Committee and vowed, in the words of committee member Elmer Lewis, to "make the city's name a symbol not only of quality but of equality as well" (McKelvey, 1961, pp. 337-38).

The 1960s witnessed the most dramatic transformations in Rochester's history. The combination of declining immigration from abroad with swelling in-migration of blacks from the South accompanied by a movement of city residents to the suburbs, significantly altered the racial and socio-economic proportions of those who remained. Rochester's population peaked at 332,488 in 1950; those residing in surrounding Monroe County numbered 155,144. During the decade of the 1950s, the central city population dropped by 16,000; during the following decade the decrease was 25,000. The non-white population meanwhile tripled through the 1950s and increased by 110 percent in the subsequent ten years. Rochester's ratio of one black to five whites in 1970 was not comparatively high for an urban area; however, the rate of increase was the most rapid of any northern city. While some Negroes and a few Puerto Ricans were moving to the suburbs as well, as in Henrietta, the fastest growing suburb in Monroe County, a black increase of 192 percent still resulted in a total black population of only 72 (McKelvey, 1973, pp. 240-42).

Owing primarily to the launching of the Xerox Copier 914 in 1961, which resulted in thousands of new jobs, Rochester's economy was among the healthiest in the Northeast; however, its rapidly changing demographic variables were creating social unrest. Beginning in August, 1962, with the unsubstantiated arrest of Rufus Fairwell, a series of loosely related incidents put the community on edge. The NAACP, the Human Relations Commission, and the Federation of Churches appealed the treatment accorded blacks by policemen at religious meetings and when they might be charged with drunken driving. A newly formed Integrated Non-Violence Committee staged a day-long sit-in vigil at police headquarters; the appointment of a Police Advisory Board dimished tensions somewhat (McKelvey, 1973, pp. 243-45, 249-50).

Unrest in the city was accompanied by a different type of disagreement in the educational community. While the Rochester Advisory Planning Council and City School District prepared their report relevant to grade reorganization and desegregation, the Division of Research of the New York State Education Department compiled a major document entitled *Racial and Social Class Isolation in the Schools*. The principal findings of this study cited research indicating that

schools isolated on the basis of race may be decidedly harmful to the academic achievement of their students. . . . The problem of racial isolation is a part of the broader problem of social class isolation. Negroes and certain other minority group members are proportionately more disadvantaged because of the close correlation between race and economic status and the continuing and exacerbating influence of residential and school segregation. However, any student--whether he be Negro, Puerto Rican, white or a member of any other identifiable group-- is likely to suffer some degree of underachievement as a result of attendance in schools and classrooms with predominantly lower social and economic status children. (*Grade Reorganization*, 1969, p. 4)

The state report, citing the research of the time, added that "a wide variety of integration efforts involving transfer programs within the urban setting or busing from urban to suburban areas generally facilitated the educational development of Negro students while white students continued to make the usual achievement gains. . . . [I]ntegration is more effective in promoting educational development among Negroes than is compensatory educational development in segregated school settings" (*Grade Reorganization*, 1969, pp. 4-5).

The state report continued by advising that transfers begin at the earliest possible grade, that the proportion of lower-status students be kept below 30 percent, and that the classrooms as well as the schools be integrated. Continued residence in the lower-status neighborhood should not interfere with the achievement gain expected to occur. Interracial understanding and interracial friendships were cited as important conditions of facilitating the educational and psychological development of the disadvantaged minority group students (*Grade Reorganization*, 1969, p. 5).

In committing itself to the elimination of racial segregation in its schools, the New York State Board of Regents aligned itself with the then recent Supreme Court decision in the case of *Alexander v. Holmes County Board of Education*. While this decision related to *de jure* segregation in Mississippi, New York State Commissioner of Education Ewald B. Nyquist saw this as an opportunity to support the developing national policy (*Grade Reorganization*, 1969, p.6).

The first steps toward desegregation had actually been taken in 1963, when the Rochester Board of Education responded affirmatively and unanimously to a directive from the New York State Commissioner of Education to reduce significantly the racial imbalance in the Rochester Public Schools. During the next six years, efforts included an open enrollment plan, which was implemented to allow students from six inner-city schools to attend classes in any of eighteen receiving schools elsewhere in the system. Also implemented were summer programs, which invited inner-city Rochester students to Brighton and other suburbs, and regular school-year transfer programs, which enrolled 25 first grade pupils each year from an inner-city school to suburban West Irondequoit, where it was intended that they would complete their school career. Unfortunately, some of the parents in the receiving schools unleashed an outburst of protest, and two districts in particular actually instituted legal suits in an attempt to safeguard their schools from "a black invasion" (*Grade Reorganization*, 1969, pp. 9, 11; McKelvey, 1973, pp. 250-51).

This affront so offended the black community that integrated efforts previously in place were shaken. Whites were discouraged from membership in groups such as the NAACP, and blacks lost status among their own if they achieved recognition by predominantly white groups. Only in the arts, sports, and politics, where distinctions had to be won competitively, was it still possible for the groups to interact naturally. Most white Rochesterians, who took pride in their city's reputation for tolerance and humanity, were bewildered and unprepared for this rebuff. They were even more astonished by the rioting that began in July, 1964 (McKelvey, 1973, pp. 251-52).

Earlier that year, newspapers had reported incidents of gangs of Italian and Puerto Rican youths engaged in skirmishes; rumors of rumbles involving hundreds of teenagers circulated throughout the city. The YMCA's Operation Outreach formed a corps of street workers in an attempt to diffuse the rising gang threat (*Democrat and Chronicle*, March 14, 1964, p. 1; April 8, 1964).

For three days beginning on a hot Friday evening in July, 1964, Rochester reeled in a riot that resulted in the ultimate arrests of 792 blacks, 153 whites, and 31 Puerto Ricans; 85 of that total were women. The precipitating incident was the attempted arrest of a drunken man from a street dance. When a number of young blacks tried to prevent the incarceration, additional police were called. Their presence heightened tempers, and before long the crowd had become a mob of looters and rioters (McKelvey, 1973, pp. 252-55).

Once order had been restored, the citizens of Rochester reviewed with horror events that most believed could not have taken place in their city. A curfew had been put into effect, the militia had been called out, four accidental deaths had occurred, 35 police had been injured, and 300 civilians required hospital care. Emotional damage was as significant as that to property. White residents of the low-income, integrated Chatham Gardens renewal project debated joining the white exodus to the suburbs. Civic groups renewed social efforts; business groups, always active in Rochester, redoubled their energies regarding those who were unemployed; and the Board of Education endeavored to upgrade its inner-city schools by installing closed-circuit television in 12 elementary and two high schools and launching the Beacon Project, under which "the ethnic and racial experiences and traditions of local children were drawn into classroom programs." Eastman joined the Board of Education in securing federal grants for school and neighborhood programs, which included the Lighted Schoolhouses and the Neighborhood Youth Corps summer supplement (McKelvey, 1973, pp. 252-56).

As various groups responded to the needs of the community, rivalries erupted. The Board of Urban Ministry invited Saul Alinsky, who had achieved particular success with The Woodlawn Organization of Chicago, to organize Rochester's Negroes for their own protection and improvement. Although Alinsky's presence was backed by funds from the Office of Economic Opportunity and Minister Franklin D. R. Florence of the Church of Christ and his organization, Freedom, Integration, God, Honor, and Today (FIGHT), many of the supposedly represented churches, the Gannett newspapers, a local radio station, and numerous other community

Table 3.1
**Rochester Population by Race: SMSA and City, 1970 and
1980; County and City, 1990**

	1970		1980		1990	
	N	%	N	%	N	%
TOTAL CITY	296,233		241,741		231,636	
WHITE	244,118	82%	168,102	70%	141,503	61%
BLACK	49,647	17%	62,332	26%	73,024	32%
HISPANIC	N/A		13,153	8%	20,055	9%
SMSA OR COUNTY	882,667		971,230		713,968	
WHITE	820,520	93%	873,099	90%	600,328	84%
BLACK	57,688	7%	77,881	8%	85,041	12%
HISPANIC	N/A		19,328	2%	26,450	4%

Note: Categories may not total to 100% because of other groups and
because Hispanics may also be listed as White or Black.

Source: U.S. Census, 1970, 1980, 1990.

leaders opposed his appointment, fearing that his abrasive methods
might alienate more than unify (McKelvey, 1973, pp. 257-58).

Alinsky and FIGHT sought to become the sole representatives of
the black community in its negotiations with the corporate structure.
Eastman Kodak, never enthusiastic about dealing with a union, was
no more desirous of being coerced by FIGHT; other local pressure
groups such as Action for a Better Community (ABC) resented being
pushed aside. The internecine squabbling served to delay more than
expedite, and it was not until June, 1967 that Rochester Jobs,
Incorporated, with Edward S. Croft as director, was able to bring the
divergent groups together to develop an effective program to train and
hire the hard-core unemployed. The city weathered the national
unrest during the summer of 1967 with only a few contained
outbreaks and considered itself fortunate in having achieved a
greater maturity (McKelvey, 1973, pp. 258-62).

Rochester's educators, like its industrialists, were committed to
the idea of integration, but implementation was another matter. In
1967, at the request of the Rochester City School District Board,

Superintendent Herman R. Goldberg prepared a report that included four possible plans to desegregate the Rochester elementary schools. The most ambitious, The Natural Educational Park Plan, required the scrapping of all of the existing elementary school buildings and the construction of a new educational park complex; 80 percent of the city's schoolchildren would have required busing (*Desegregation of the Elementary Schools*, 1967, p. 11).

The Rochester Plan, the second alternative, featured primary (K-3) and intermediate (4-6) schools allowing many of the existing schools to continue in service and reducing the proportion of students needing transportation to 37 percent. While the primary schools remained in the neighborhoods and stayed small, the intermediate schools were to be larger and closer to the center of the city, encouraging a more integrated student body (*Desegregation of the Elementary Schools*, 1967, p. 22).

The Combination Plan, as the name of the third proposal suggests, incorporated elements of the two previously described plans. The intermediate schools were to be built in an educational park, and the possibility existed that primary schools would be added at a later time. While the primary schools were to remain on the periphery of the city, they would also be racially balanced (*Desegregation of the Elementary Schools*, 1967, pp. 38-39).

The fourth plan, the Home-Base Plan, was contributed by the Center for Urban Education of New York City. The plan proposed by the Center was to concentrate first on racial balance and subsequently "initiate a gradual movement toward a more long-range program for achieving quality integrated education for all children." The plan was built on the premise that "desegregation (or racial balance) is not an end in itself, but a means to an end--the maximization of the individual child's potential through quality education." Further, it was assumed, "based on the findings of social research, that, where the poor are segregated together, achievement levels cannot be raised significantly unless more money and more professional talent and resources than could possibly be found in any one city are made available" (*Desegregation of the Elementary Schools*, 1967, p. 56).

The proposal was intended to be sufficiently appealing to minimize white flight and to enable increased urban-suburban cooperation. All of the children were to be transported at some time, but the trips were designed to be short. The major costs would be for buses. Students would be based in a school close to home but spend part of two days each week at another school where a program specifically designed to meet their needs, abilities, and interests would be arranged. Racial balance would also be a factor in determining the make-up of these groupings (*Desegregation of the Elementary Schools*, 1967, pp. 57-63).

The report, in addition to providing four possible ways to reorganize the Rochester schools, also clearly delineated a distinction between desegregation and integration. "Desegregation" was defined as "an administrative act which can be immediate in implementation. It is primarily concerned with logistics and its direct result will tend to be reported statistically." The report continued that "integration . . . is instructional in nature and is primarily concerned with changing attitudes and behavior. It may, for these reasons, be slow to achieve. The most significant measure of the success of Rochester's program will be the extent to which schools are able to move from the logistics of desegregation to the attitudinal changes of integration" (*Desegregation of the Elementary Schools*, 1967, p. 44).

Concomitant with the presentation of the superintendent's report including the four desegregation plan options in February, 1967, a group called the Student Union for Integrated Education (SUIE) was formed. This association, which included blacks and whites, city and suburban dwellers, public and non-public students, pressed for a reduction in racial isolation in Monroe County, in which Rochester is the major city   (*Grade Reorganization and Desegregation of the Rochester Public Schools,* 1969, p. 13).

In March, 1967, the Board of Education adopted a 15-point plan. Among those points, and most important, was the determination to use selected features of the Combination Plan. Other parts of the program included voluntary open enrollment plans and reverse open enrollment plans, accompanied by a similar program in the Catholic schools, to bring suburban children into city schools. A World of Inquiry School, with 130 places, was implemented at the elementary level under Title III. The Demonstration Cities Program was to be tapped to help with the funding of new educational facilities and services (*Grade Reorganization and Desegregation of the Rochester Public Schools*, 1969, pp. 13-14).

The appointment of school advisors to parents, community teachers, and other innovations that comprised Project Unique won a grant from the United States Office of Education in 1967 and attracted nationwide praise. The World of Inquiry school appeared so promising that Bernard Gifford, who succeeded the Minister Florence as president of FIGHT, enrolled his daughter, Antoinette, in it (McKelvey, 1973, pp. 264-65).

Between 1967 and 1969 several dozen additional voluntary transfer programs were begun and continued both within the city of Rochester and between the city and its suburban neighbors in Monroe County. However, despite these efforts (by June, 1969, more than 3000 pupils were involved in transfer programs), in June, 1969, ten elementary schools were still *de facto* segregated and there was evidence of increasing imbalance in the high schools (*Grade*

Reorganization and Desegregation in the Rochester Public Schools,
1969, p. 17).

In 1968, Laplois Ashford won a seat on the Board of Education
and became the first Negro to win a citywide election. He soon
became president of the board and encouraged Goldberg's programs
and the attempt to hire more qualified black teachers throughout the
system. However, the addition to the board shortly after of two new
members, elected on an anti-busing platform, diminished the
momentum of the Advisory Planning Council on Quality Integrated
Education and created dissention among the Rochester Teachers
Association, FIGHT, and numerous other advocates of integration. In
what appeared to be an acceptable compromise, a modified
reorganization plan was adopted, and instruction in Spanish was
institiuted in those schools attended by Puerto Rican students
(McKelvey, 1973, pp. 265-66).

During the last quarter of 1969, the Advisory Planning Council on
Quality Integrated Education met with school officials to discuss a
proposed reorganization. The Council comprised a wide
representation of the citizenry of Rochester and had as its goal both
desegregation and quality education. The report, *Grade Reorganization and Desegregation of the Rochester Public Schools,* was
presented to the Board of Education in December, 1969 (p.17).

The plan divided the 43 elementary schools into primary schools
(grades K-3) and intermediate schools (grades 4-6). There were 11
Enlarged Home Zones, each of which contained two or more primary
schools and one intermediate school. When necessary, non-contiguous
schools were grouped together to achieve proper racial balance. While
many students still could walk to school in their own home zone, the
districts were designed to also balance socio-economic differences as
well as those of race (*Grade Reorganization and Desegregation of the
Rochester Public Schools,* 1969, p. 28).

Because quality of education was noted to be as important as
desegregation, the report devoted considerable effort and space to
describing instructional advantages of separating the primary and
intermediate schools. Among the advantages noted were: increased
opportunities to group according to social, physical, emotional, and
academic needs; the ability to provide a stronger focus on reading,
especially in the lower grades; and an environment more hospitable
to attempting team teaching, pupil teaming, and non-graded
instructional programs (*Grade Reorganization and Desegregation of
the Rochester Public Schools,* 1969, p. 30).

The five junior high schools (grades 7-8) and the four high schools
(grades 9-12) had a feeder pattern of almost contiguous elementary
school districts. Separating the junior and senior high schools
achieved good racial balance with a minimal amount of
transportation necessary. The instructional advantages of separating
the junior from senior high schools were felt to be upgraded

instruction, optimum use of available facilities, and greater distance between younger and older high school pupils (*Grade Reorganization and Desegregation of the Rochester Public Schools*, 1969, p. 24).

Between 1969 and 1971, the plan was approved, rescinded, modified, and approved once more. Some members of the originally approving board were voted out of office during the intervening election, and block schools were set up by those parents most opposed to the school reorganization plan. The area's Catholic schools contended that they did not wish to be used as an escape for parents opposing desegregation but, in a time of dropping enrollments, did accept students where places existed (Reid, 1984; Curry interview, June 4, 1991).

However, pressures from the teachers for increased salaries and busing opponents achieving control of the board made the integration victory a brief one. John Franco, who succeeded Herman Goldberg as Superintendent in June, 1971, while convinced of the merits of integration, was unsure as to the proper course of action. Adding to the confusion, Minister Raymond Scott, who became the fourth president of FIGHT, changed the thrust of its activities by demanding that the school system improve inner city schools rather than bus blacks into white neighborhoods where they were not welcome (McKelvey, 1973, p. 271).

The 1972 federal Emergency School Assistance Act (ESAA), created to provide technical and financial assistance to public schools that voluntarily or involuntarily developed remedies to desegregate their schools, served as an additional incentive to the Rochester school system to develop a plan that would be acceptable to the majority of its citizenry. Monies from this source did indeed fund a significant portion of the ultimate plan, until 1980 when the program was cut (Reid, p. 1).

The mid-1970s saw a re-activation of parent and neighborhood groups, especially the Nineteenth Ward Community Association and the Citizens for Quality Integrated Education. Desegregation efforts began to focus on unique instructional programs, such as foreign languages, performing arts, and enrichment classrooms at target schools (Reid, p.2; *CQIE Newsletter*, April, 1972).

By 1979, the magnet program as currently operating was basically in place. The two broad objectives of racial balance through voluntary desegregation and educational reform to improve instruction were being accomplished. Racial balance was gradually implemented. The concept employed a dissimilarity index as its method of measuring integration and is defined as being within plus or minus ten percentage points of the percent of non-whites within the total school population. By 1989-90, minority population at the elementary schools averaged 71 percent, at the middle schools 74 percent, and at the high schools 72 percent. Every middle school, most of the high schools, and more than half of the elementary schools were racially balanced. Virtually all of those schools not yet in compliance were making strides in the appropriate direction (*Rochester City School District Magnet Schools*, 1989-90, pp. 1-5).

Elementary magnet schools (grades K-5) are divided into three general themes: math/science, humanities, and early childhood schools. Within these broad areas are schools that provide special opportunities in bilingual and bicultural education; foreign language immersion; science, computers and technology; performing arts; as well as programs for academically talented students, and schools that emphasize developmental learning styles (*Magnet Schools*, 1989-90, p. 8; *Magnet Schools: Elementary Programs*, 1991).

The Rochester City School District is divided into four quadrants, and schools in each sector offer a variety of educational programs and opportunities. Depending upon current enrollments, some schools will accept only minority transfers, some only non-minority transfers, and some either. Parents complete an application form in the spring for the school year beginning the following autumn (*Magnet Schools: Elementary Programs*, 1991, p. 3).

Enrollment in a magnet school is voluntary but may not negatively affect the racial balance of the student's neighborhood school. While in the abstract, this principle appears sound, according to one white interviewee, it resulted in his son being denied admission to a magnet middle school while his African-American best friend was accepted. In the interest of maintaining racial balance, true interracial exposure and a real friendship was sacrificed (*Magnet Schools: Elementary Programs*, 1991, p. 3; Sette interview, June 3, 1991).

Five middle schools, encompassing sixth through eighth grades, were established during the 1988-89 school year. Four are combinations of magnet and comprehensive middle schools; the fifth, the Nathaniel Rochester Community School, is a total magnet. All middle schools are schools of choice. Special programs include natural science, liberal arts, performing arts, and technology. Natural and cultural resources are used wherever possible to augment and enrich both the special and comprehensive programs (*Magnet Schools*, 1989-90, p. 12).

Middle school open houses are held in the fall, and students must apply for placement by mid-December of the year preceding their entry. Students are notified of their placement in March. Those applying for special programs may do so at any of the middle schools in the city. Those choosing the comprehensive option are assigned to the school in their district (*Selections*, 1990, pp. 2-3).

The four city high schools offer a combination of comprehensive and special programs similar to those in the middle schools. Magnet programs include bioscience and health, business, communication arts, law and government, technology and computer science. A special high school for the performing arts continues a similar program available in the sixth to eighth grade School of the Arts (*Selections*, 1990, pp. 3-14).

At all grade levels, children who live more than a mile and a half from the school they attend and children with handicapping conditions are provided with free transportation. This may be a chartered school bus or a pass for the Regional Transit System (*Selections*, 1990, p. 1).

Of the four cities included in this study, Rochester is the only community to voluntarily implement its desegregation program. School officials, parents, and community representatives were uniform in their pride that Rochester had chosen to desegregate on its own rather than being pressured to do so by outside agencies.

It is generally agreed that a fortuitous combination of dedicated and capable administrators and strong community support was responsible for the ultimate success of the desegregation efforts in the Rochester school system. While the period from 1969 to 1971 was frustrating and counterproductive, once the magnet concept was made the cornerstone of the desegregation efforts, parents felt they had choice and control over the destinies of their children and support for the desegregation concept grew (All interviews, especially Curry, Sette).

The magnet school concept also emphasized the goal of quality as well as integrated education. There were no "sticks," and the choice of "carrots" included programs in foreign languages, technology, computer sciences, and the performing arts (*Magnet School: Elementary Programs*, 1991; *Selections*, 1990).

The political parties were not active in the desegregation debate, except during the 1969-71 period. It was a Democratic board that accepted the first desegregation plan, and it was Republicans who ousted them and gained a majority to rescind that action. But even some of those who supported the plan in principle felt that its original inception was not well conceived and that it required children to spend too long a time being transported. The decade of the '70s saw the Board of Education become for a time non-partisan, but by the 1980s it was once again a part of the two-party system (Curry interview).

Community groups played a far more central role in the desegregation debate and its ultimate implementation than the political parties. The Nineteenth Ward Community Association, in particular, was supportive of desegregation efforts from the early 1960s. Located in the southwestern quadrant of the city, on the west bank of the Genesee River, which bisects the city, the nineteenth ward has for many years been an integrated, middle-class neighborhood with a population approximately two-thirds white and one-third African-American. According to Alfred Sette, currently Budget Director for the City of Rochester and longterm resident of the nineteenth ward and member and former president of its community association, desegregation efforts began in 1963 with the formation of the United Federation of Inner City Parents. This black citizens' group was created to advocate better schools for its children during a time of inner city tension and rioting. Concern for the quality of education was particularly great in the heavily minority fifth and seventh wards in the northern part of the city. While a metropolitan solution to enable desegregation was deemed impossible, according to Mr. Sette, "supporters would be euthanized," attempts to achieve racial balance within the city would be tolerated. The Spanish Action Coalition and the Apartment Owners Association were also cited as being very much involved in the positive dialogue toward desegregation (Sette interview; Corryn interview, June 3, 1991).

Archie Curry, an African-American 13-year veteran of the school board, concurs with the view that community groups and community pride were the overwhelming positive forces in enabling desegregation to be effected. The riots in 1964-65 upset many community members who felt that they placed the city in a poor light. Positive action needed to be taken to remove the blot on the city's image. Wide opportunities for public discussion allowed parents and other members of the community to feel they could influence the decisions being made. Curry also praised the parochial schools for not creating additional places when some parents resisted the original desegregation efforts (Interview).

Teachers and administrators were also credited with serving as a positive force toward desegregation. However, two interviewees were careful to distinguish between those teachers who were truly dedicated to their profession and those who were merely marking time until retirement. One interviewee, the summer lunch coordinator, suggested that recent salary increases, to an average of $45,000 per year, encourage some teachers to remain on the job solely for the money. He also reported being told by some teachers that they cannot discipline their students because school administrators do not back them up. This is because the system is pressured to keep young people in school even if their behavior is lax and students are undisciplined. Economic factors that force good programs to be discontinued or curtailed were also looked upon as having a negative influence (Kiner interview, June 2, 1991; Corryn interview; Curry interview).

Parents who removed their children from the public schools when desegregation programs were first implemented were singled out as negative forces during the reorganization efforts. However, other parents participated in the school district's Neighborhood Diplomatic Corps, a parent-to-parent support system created to develop a link between the school and the home. A "Home Visiting Registry," designed to resemble a passport and delineating how the program operated and listing those in the program, was provided to each parent-diplomat (Corryn interview; *Neighborhood Diplomatic Corps Home Visiting Registry*, 1989).

When asked to advise a community embarking upon a desegregation effort, respondents were unanimous in advocating the greatest amount of public involvement. "People resent being overlooked." Even if there seems to be too much and contradictory input, it is imperative that people feel that they are being heard. Those who will follow through are especially vital to the process. Find that "magic something" that makes the community get involved (Corryn interview; all interviews).

Choice was also cited as one of the most appealing and important elements of the Rochester program. People very much appreciated the voluntary nature of the process and took pride in the fact that no court action or outside pressure was responsible for the city's desegregation efforts. The process was an open one with the community, teachers, and parents all able to influence the ultimate outcome (Andia interview; Reichardt interview; Schloss interview).

However, as the minority population of the city increases by approximately one percent per year, Rochester's successful voluntary efforts are rapidly being eroded. Again, there is agreement among those interviewed, but here the prognosis is extremely discouraging. While the surrounding suburbs have been amenable to token and voluntary mixing with the central city, those Rochester residents interviewed are certain that there would be little acceptance of a true metropolitan solution to the problem of a diminishing base of whites, which now number only 26 percent of the inner city population. Whenever the question was raised, the subject was changed. In the 1970s and 1980s, "a commitment of individuals" was what was deemed to work, and it was thought to be somewhat easier "at a time and in a political climate when liberal was not a dirty word." A similar commitment, based on the values of the 1990s, is what is necessary now for Rochester (Andia interview; Reichardt interview; Schloss interview).

No substantial changes had been undertaken by late 1994. Limited voluntary transfers continued between city and suburbs, but at a rate far too small to be statistically significant. The minority population has continued to increase; at that time, it was 57 percent African-American, 17 percent Hispanic, 3 percent Asian and Native American, and 23 percent white. This growth of minority population was due far less to whites leaving and more the result of the minority birthrate being higher; concomitantly, the number of those living in poverty has increased proportionately as well. The suburbs continue to lack enthusiasm for interdistrict exchanges despite the federal monies that would be available for such enterprises. Only the suburb of Henrietta has seen an appreciable increase in non-white population; that increase is primarily Chinese, although it also has the greatest proportion of African-Americans and Hispanics of

Rochester's suburbs. Board of Education statistics record white populations of 58.3 percent in the city of Rochester, 94.3 percent in Rochester's suburbs, and 82.6 percent in Monroe County as a whole. Conventional wisdom promotes the view that urban problems are more severe than those in the suburbs; those who have moved out seek to protect their children from these perceived dangers (Nella Corryn interviews, November 15 and 22, 1994).

Chapter 4

Trenton

The City of Trenton, which in the twentieth century is a prototype of a city in decline, in earlier times had its moments of glory. The capital of New Jersey since 1790, and the seat of Mercer County, it began as the site of a log mill and residence in 1679. The settlement, built by an English Quaker, Mahlon Stacy, was first known as The Falls, then as Stacy's Mills and ultimately, in 1721, it was named Trenton in honor of a Philadelphia merchant, William Trent, who laid out the town (*Academic American Encyclopedia*, 1980, 19:291).

Hessian mercenaries and George Washington's soldiers engaged in a famous Revolutionary War battle in the city during December, 1776, and Trenton served as the capital of the newly established United States briefly in 1784 and again in 1799. The arrival of the railroad and the construction of the Delaware and Raritan Canal in the 1830s stimulated the growth of this city located on the Delaware River about 30 miles north of Philadelphia. The coalfields of northeastern Pennsylvania and the iron mines of northwestern New Jersey enabled Trenton to become a major manufacturing center. By the middle of the nineteenth century, spurred by the efforts of locomotive pioneer Peter Cooper and iron-rope producer John A. Roebling, Trenton was the nation's leading iron manufacturer producing wrought-iron beams and rods, railroad ties, and iron cables (*AAE*, 1980, 19:291; Cumbler, 1989, p. 2).

Trenton's golden age came in the 1880s. With a population of more than 57,000, it was the nation's fiftieth largest city. Ready-made clothing, cigars, and rubber joined pottery and machine tools as the city's leading industries. Trenton suffered with the rest of the country through the depression of the 1890s and then enjoyed a rejuvenation until the 1920s. The city was proud of its motto "Trenton Makes and the World Takes" (Cumbler, 1989, pp. 1-3).

4.1 Trenton SMSA (New Jersey), 1970

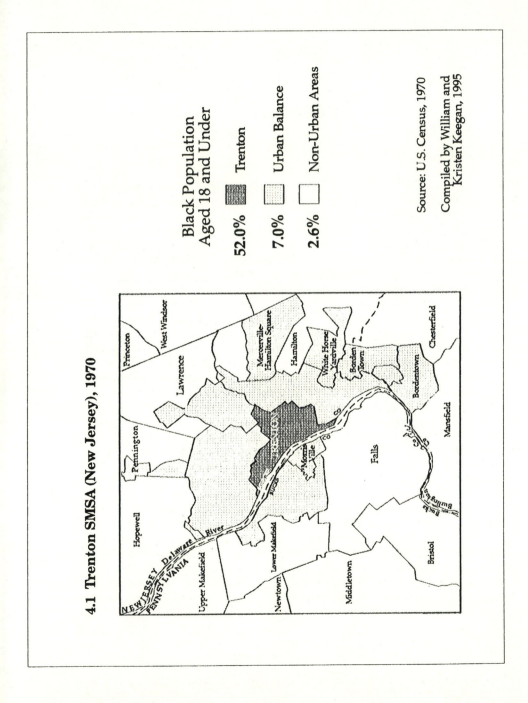

Black Population
Aged 18 and Under

52.0% ■ Trenton

7.0% ☐ Urban Balance

2.6% ☐ Non-Urban Areas

Source: U.S. Census, 1970

Compiled by William and
      Kristen Keegan, 1995

Trenton's period of prosperity coincided with the age of industry and civic capitalism, "an age of individual entrepreneurs who mastered new methods of production and marketing and who mobilized the labor needed to make their machines productive." The entrepreneurs had a self-conscious class outlook and were linked to each other by family connections and a common world view that extended through the economy and government from the city hall to the statehouse and then to Washington. The era of civic capitalism was the era of the owner and employer (Cumbler, 1989, p. 3).

Trenton's decline paralleled the decline of civic capitalism, which was being superseded by national capitalism. In Trenton, this first occurred in 1904 when U.S. Steel bought the Trenton Iron Works. It continued into the 1920s as local pottery and rubber companies were bought by and absorbed into nationally integrated corporations. The process was complete when Colorado Fuel and Iron purchased the gigantic John A. Roebling's Sons Company in 1952. The transition altered the entire infrastructure of the city: its social setting, class relations, political organization, and economic base (Cumbler, 1989, pp. 5-6).

Trenton's industrialization required an extensive labor force, and waves of immigrants arrived in the city eager to fill manufacturing jobs. German and Irish workers supplanted the English in the nineteenth century and, in the twentieth century, Italians and Jews comprised the largest groups of foreign born. Hungarians and Poles were also well represented in the rubber and iron trades. (Cumbler, 1989, p. 105).

The city realized that the children of these new immigrants would be the next generation of workers and, in 1922, Trenton embarked upon an extensive school building program. During the next four years, $3.2 million was spent for new schools and, in 1928, a $2.5 million high school was constructed. During the 1923 election campaign for city commission, all of the candidates agreed on the need for more schools. However, the lone labor candidate pointed out that, to that time, the schools on the more privileged West Side were being significantly better supported than those in poorer neighborhoods (Cumbler, 1989, pp. 105-6).

The schools were viewed as serving numerous purposes. Certainly, it was necessary that they teach English to a student body that was less than 50 percent native born children of native born parents and for 40 percent of whom English was a second language. But, for the industrialists who would ultimately hire these students, the teaching of obedience and patriotism was seen as equally important. Through the 1920s, attendance dropped as the building program progressed. For the industrialists who benefited most, the schools were a bargain, as it was the homeowners who shouldered the majority of the financial burden (Cumbler, 1989, p. 106).

Many of the first blacks to live in Trenton were slaves, since that institution was not outlawed in New Jersey until 1846. By 1860, 700 blacks resided in the city. Most earned their living as domestics; few owned property. All had been born in northern states and whether "classified as being black, mulatto or colored" they were relegated to living in the old northern section of Trenton, which offered few municipal services. A "rigid color line" divided the races; segregation was a way of life. Even the city directories listed the races separately (Washington, 1990, pp. 2-4).

Although there had been white-run and white-staffed schools for African-American children as early as 1801 and the Society of Friends established a Sabbath School in 1809, it was not until the implementation of the 1824 Common School Law that formal public schools existed for either white or African-American children. In 1844, the Common Council set up the present Trenton public schools; Dr. Charles Skelton served as the system's first superintendent (Washington, 1990, pp. 41-42).

At the beginning, African-American children were required to pay tuition: one dollar for spelling and reading, slightly more if writing, arithmetic, and geography were included. By 1848, the tuition requirements were dropped and at least one colored teacher was employed. New Jersey state law, in an 1850 ruling related to Morris County, sanctioned separate school districts for colored children. In 1855, Jackson Hall, the African-American schoolhouse since 1809, was demolished. It had been poorly maintained and by mid-century its condition was beyond repair. Sixty-three black children were left without a school building (Washington, 1990, pp. 43-44; Daniel, 1959, p. 38).

After two years of makeshift arrangements, a two-story brick building was constructed on Higbee Street (later renamed Bellevue Avenue) "to provide general and basic education for the African-American community." Schooling was offered only through fifth grade; however, even white students in Trenton did not have access to a high school until 1874 (Washington, 1990, pp. 46-47).

Poor maintenance and an increased population caused the Higbee School to fall into disrepair by 1872, and for that year its students were transferred to a rented structure on Belvidere Street. The new and larger two-story, two-room brick school built on Ringold Street was deemed appropriate for the African-American pupils, and the former Higbee Street School was renovated for use by whites. It was renamed the Bellevue Avenue School to reflect the change in the street name as well. In dedicating the Ringold Street School, then Superintendent of Schools Dr. C. Shepherd declared that the building satisfied his desires to see equal educational opportunities for the two races (Washington, 1990, pp. 47-48).

Dr. Shepherd's assessment of adequacy was not universally accepted. Public education in the 1870s in Trenton was "not a right, but a privilege." Before enrolling in school, applications had to be made to the school board. By Dr. Shepherd's own admission, of the 6000 children in Trenton in 1872, only 2500 were entered on the school rolls, and of that number, less than 1800 actually attended school. The Ringold School alone had a waiting list of 200 permits for admission (Washington, 1990, p. 49).

By 1879, it was evident to the committee on school conditions that the new Ringold School was totally unable to meet the needs of the African-American community. Constructed of inferior materials, it was also severely overcrowded and poorly equipped. The community demanded that the building be repaired, renovated, or demolished. Some members of the African-American community even suggested that their children be permitted to attend one of the white schools that, if not much better, were at least closer to their home (Washington, 1990, pp. 49-50).

The Board of Education's Rule Number 17, in fact, required that children attend the school nearest to their home. However, when the matter was brought to Dr. Shepherd, he stated that the Ringold School had been built specifically for African-American children and that if "one person should be allowed to send his children to the white school nearest to where he resided, all the African-Americans would claim the right to a like privilege." The permit was denied and the Trenton schools remained effectively segregated until 1944 (Washington, 1990, pp. 50-51).

As frustrations intensifed, African-Americans began to organize and marshall their political strength. R. Henri Herbert, a leading figure in the black community and the editor of the *Sentinel*, an African-American newspaper published between 1880 and 1883, led the drive to abolish the dual system. Two Republican state senators, Francis of Essex County, which includes Newark, and Charles Youngblood of Morris County introduced the bill designed to desegregate the public schools of New Jersey. Senate Bill 209 declared that "no child between the ages of five and eighteen years of age [should] be excluded from any public school in [the] state on account of his or her religion, nationality or color." A monetary fine and imprisonment were to await to those who disregarded the act. The primary goal of the legislation was for African-Americans to gain access to the all-white Trenton High School (Washington, 1990, pp. 51-54).

The bill was passed in 1881 on a vote of 37 to 18. But, despite the impression given by the Trenton School Board that it would comply with the law, it admitted only two African-American children to a previously all white elementary school. The daughters of John Walser were "light complexioned, well behaved and in every way unobjectionable." While African-American children were now legally allowed to attend Trenton High School, erected in 1874, they were placed in special classes and allowed to use the swimming pool only during specific time periods (Washington, 1990, pp. 54-57).

Senate Bill 209 was a mixed blessing with regard to elementary education as well. Prior to its passage, there was little enthusiasm for building a second primary school for African-Americans. After the bill was passed, white opposition to the new school vanished. However, the location selected was on Bellevue Avenue, far from the residences of most African-American children. This also resulted in two schools on the same street with the same name, one for blacks and one for whites. African-American leaders resented having their school referred to as the "Colored School" and asked that the school be renamed the Frederick Douglass School after the African-American abolitionist. The board rejected the name and Lincoln School was selected as a compromise. At the same time, additional rooms and staff were added. Three teachers, two janitors, and a principal served the school population. The New Lincoln School (Junior 5) replaced the building on Bellevue in 1923, and black students in grades seven through nine were placed in the Livingston School (Washington, 1990, pp. 57-59; Daniels, 1959, p. 34).

In the 1880s, with a population of 29,910, of which five percent were black, Trenton had begun its century-long confrontation with the illegality of its segregated schools. During the 1940-41 school year, a black mother sought to have her children remain in the mostly white Calwalader School when she moved, contending that the all-black New Lincoln School was overcrowded. Although, as she noted, the class size at New Lincoln was twice that of Calwalader and therefore could not offer the same level of instruction and individual care, her request was denied. In 1943, the Trenton School Superintendent, in taking no action on a request to allow black children to attend a white junior high school in their neighborhood instead of the Lincoln School, argued that the segregated school gave them the desirable opportunity to be in the majority for the three years between sixth grade and high school (Washington, 1990, p. 48; Daniels, 1959, pp. 40-41, 58-63).

In 1970, the city, whose population had reached 128,009 in 1950 and was now down to 104,638, of which 37.9 percent were African-American, was still trying to solve its problems of balancing the races in its schools. On November 5, 1969, the State Board of Education passed a resolution that directed the Commissioner of Education to "undertake to determine in which school districts in the State of New Jersey racially imbalanced schools [were] maintained" and to "undertake such steps as he [should] deem necessary to correct such conditions of racial imbalance as may be found" (Washington, 1990, p. 48; *Questions and Answers on Commissioner Marburger's Trenton Decision on Desegregation*, 1970, p. 6; *Demographic and Geographic Considerations*, 1986; Daniels, 1959, p. 21).

The assassination of Martin Luther King, Jr., in April, 1968, had brought to a head the frustrations of both blacks and whites in Trenton. Whites were angered by a loss of job security and falling property values as the city's industry continued to decline. Blacks, "having endured years of discrimination and humiliation," saw the whites remaining in the city as the cause of their distress. The two groups transmitted their hostility to their children. Students who, because of both residential segregation and racially drawn school districts, were not integrated until high school, enjoyed little social interaction once they finally occupied the same building (Cumbler, 1989, pp. 174-75).

The primarily white school board disregarded the increasing number of black students. It encouraged the proprietary view of the school held by the whites, who saw it as an instrument for "ensuring that the few jobs still available went to whites." Few of the blacks were enrolled in the college preparatory courses or the enrichment programs, which Trenton was among the first systems to offer despite a general insuffiency of funds that deprived both constituencies of desirable educational opportunities. The social conflict, which raged for a year in the form of "shoving in the halls, racial fights and spontaneous walkouts of black students," finally exploded with the murder of King (Cumbler, 1989, pp. 174-76).

The student population, responding to national movements for civil rights and racist resistance, erupted in bitterness and militancy. White parents demanded the expulsion of black students; black parents argued for more racial understanding. King, the spokesperson for peaceful change, became the excuse in his death for the burning of automobiles and abandoned buildings, the smashing of windows, the looting of stores, and the stoning of police cars. The predominantly white police force exacerbated the situation by exerting a massive show of force resulting in the death of one youth, the wounding of several others, and the scarring of the lives of even more with police records. The already weakened city now also had to contend with $2.5 million in damages and increased white flight (Cumbler, 1989, pp. 175-76).

In reaction to the King riots and in response to a directive by the State Board of Education's newly created Office of Equal Opportunity, an attempt was made to begin to correct racial balance in the city's schools. The district decided to bus approximately 100 elementary school students from predominantly minority schools to non-minority schools. At the same time, 55 white students would be transported from the white populated Mott School to the mostly black Parker School. This effort resulted in major unrest in every ward in the city. Responses to the tentative effort at desegregation included rioting, overturned buses, and a suit brought against the Trenton Board of Education by "Clyde E. Christner and Maryann N. Christner, individually and as the parents and natural guardians of

R. Kenneth Christner, an infant, on behalf of the 55 children involuntarily reassigned from the Mott School to the Parker School." Commissioner of Education Marburger, in a decision delivered on November 14, 1970, found in favor of the plaintiffs and declared the Trenton plan unacceptable. The Commissioner rejected the plan "because of its counterproductivity, its lack of educational goals, and the absence of community involvement in the planning and development stages of the 'Plan' " (*Trenton Plan for Educational Excellence*, 1984, p. 1; interview with Marcellus Smith, March 5, 1992; *Questions and Answers on Commissioner Marburger's Trenton Decision on Desegregation*, 1970, pp. 1-2).

New Jersey is one of a minority of states where the Commissioner of Education is an officer of the court. Therefore, an order of the Commissioner carries the force of law. A district that disregards a directive by the Commissioner is also challenging the first level of the New Jersey court system. Trenton was therefore being ordered to provide a plan for desegregation and then having that plan judged by two branches of the same office. Thus, although it implemented its initial desegregation effort at the behest of the State Board of Education, when the plan proved to be ill-advised, it was the head of that agency, the Commissioner of Education, who ordered the plan to be discontinued (Interview, Smith; *Questions and Answers on Commissioner Marburger's Trenton Decision on Desegregation*, 1970, p. 1).

Trenton's inability to satisfy the State Board and the Commissioner in the late 1960s and early 1970s set the pattern for relations between the city and the state that have continued to at least some extent up to this writing. By administering the school system for the state capital, the Trenton Board of Education is particularly vulnerable; everything that occurs, or what does not when it should, is immediately visible to the state agencies. During the past twenty years a variety of plans have been proposed, modified, implemented, modified, found insufficient or ineffective, and ultimately superseded by a new proposal. During that time, making the issue infinitely more complicated, the proportion of black and Hispanic students had risen while those who are white diminished. Between 1970 and 1990, the total Trenton Public School enrollment declined from 17,081 to 12,222. Of those numbers, in 1970, 67.9 percent were black, 24.8 percent were white, 7.1 percent were Hispanic, and 0.2 percent were other. In 1990, the district was just over 90 percent minority: 69.7 percent African-American, 19.8 percent Hispanic, 9.9 percent white, and 0.6 other minorities (Interview with Mark Raivetz, June 17, 1991; *Trenton Demographic and Geographic Considerations*, 1986, p. 6; *Trenton Public Schools, Districtwide Enrollment, 1990-91*, p. i).

As part of the Christener decision of 1970, Commissioner Marburger advised that any district "developing plans for desegregation should make certain of the following":

1. There is involvement of all groups of people representative of the community in drawing up the plan.
2. There is adequate preparation of parents, teachers, and children who would be affected by the plan.
3. Deadlines must be set for the implementation of the plan which realistically allow for sufficient community involvement and preparation of parents, teachers and children to be affected.
4. Consideration must be given to the pulse of the community, so that the plan may be carried out in such a way as to minimize reaction.
5. The plan should create a genuine racial balance in the district. It should not be the mere shifting of small numbers of students.
6. Means for desegregation other than involuntary busing should be found in any districts which are:
   a. Urban
   b. Where the majority of public school students are from minority groups. (*Questions and Answers on Commissioner Marburger's Trenton Decision on Desegregation*, 1970, pp. 4-5)

The decision also noted that when the Commissioner rejected a plan, he might either require the local district to develop another plan that would be acceptable or construct such a plan himself. Commissioner Marburger had maintained a policy of preserving local control by allowing districts to propose their own plans rather than drawing them up himself. "As long as a district genuinely desegregates, it can do so whatever way it chooses consistent with the statutes" (*Questions and Answers on Commissioner Marburger's Trenton Decision on Desegregation*, 1970, p. 13).

Since 1970, the Trenton Board of Education has recognized that "equality *in* education and the quality *of* education [could] better be achieved in a desegregated school system." It also acknowledged that "meaningful desegregation [could] scarcely be achieved in a district that has [a] great majority of 'minority' pupils." In January of 1970, the Superintendent of Schools noted that "short of regionalization in the Mercer Community real integration of students would be impossible." The Superintendent chided the State Board of Education for its "reticence" in "the matter of addressing itself to the real issue which underlies [its] mandate. . . . [T]he matter of *regionalization . . . is essential* to effect meaningful and productive integration" (*Trenton Public Schools Plan for Educational Excellence*, 1984, p. 3).

The Superintendent continued that it was incumbent upon the State Board to take "a definitive stand on this problem." If this was not done, he warned, "the public schools, particularly those in the old, impacted cities, [would be] faced with the problem of designing

Table 4.1
Trenton Population by Race: SMSA and City, 1970 and 1980;
County and City, 1990

	1970		1980		1990	
	N	%	N	%	N	%
TOTAL CITY	104,638		92,124		88,675	
WHITE	64,305	61%	45,087	49%	37,392	42%
BLACK	39,671	38%	41,860	45%	43,689	49%
HISPANIC	N/A		7,360	8%	12,530	14%
SMSA OR COUNTY	303,968		307,863		325,824	
WHITE	252,202	83%	242,097	79%	244,880	75%
BLACK	49,802	16%	55,545	18%	61,253	19%
HISPANIC	N/A		10,580	3%	18,723	6%

Note: Categories may not total to 100% because of other groups and
  because Hispanics may also be listed as White or Black.

Source: U.S. Census, 1970, 1980, 1990.

plans of integration which could be exercises in futility." He advised
that these cities "were already impacted and segregated '*de facto*'"
and plagued with related problems. "[E]ven though costly and
complex measures are undertaken to 'solve' the problem of
desegregation, it may be at best a most *temporary* solution. *Unless
the matter of regionalization is given careful consideration and
implementation, the cities' efforts will be but a shallow attempt at
providing education opportunity through integration*" (*Trenton Public
School Plan for Educational Excellence*, 1984, p. 3).

According to Mark Raivetz, who since 1985 has been Director of
Planning, Research, and Evaluation for the Trenton Board of
Education and in charge of the desegregation program, only a few
New Jersey cities were selected for desegregation efforts. Trenton, as
the state capital, as the only city of size in Mercer County (the others
being small, suburban or rural, and wealthy), was a logical choice
(Interview with Mark Raivetz, June 17, 1991).

Fred Burke had become State Commissioner of Education prior to
Trenton's second effort toward desegregation. He remembers that the
city's population was primarily Italian and black and racial

animosity was fierce. In September, 1975, an educational support team was established. Its membership, 36 representatives of the Trenton community, was entrusted with two goals:

1. to develop a desegregation plan and a plea to the State for regionalization of county schools to achieve that end; and
2. to provide community-based support for the implementation of the plan. (Interview with Fred Burke, March 4, 1992; *Trenton Public Schools Plan for Educational Excellence*, 1984, p. 1)

Since the district was, at that time, under the direction of an interim superintendent, the plan was set aside until 1977. When a new superintendent was appointed, he, along with directors, principals, teachers, and board members "reviewed the data and convened a task force of more than one hundred persons from the educational field and the community." The task force developed six "ideas" as Board options to desegregate the city's schools. Components of the ideas included:

- the pairing of three elementary schools in the South Ward with three others with redistribution of students to achieve racial balance,
- the closing of one elementary school in the South Ward with the building of an addition to another South Ward school,
- grade reassignments of K-3 students, combining students in grades 4-6 from two schools, and
- centralizing special education students into one building. (*Trenton Public Schools Plan for Educational Excellence*, 1984, pp. 1-2)

Other ideas included "the creation of an educational/community center to house resources that the community could use twelve months a year, including a pre-school and senior citizen planned activities," and "pairing" by assigning "all K-3 students from six South ward schools to three schools and students from grades 4-6 in the remaining three schools." None of the six ideas, either in whole or in part, was deemed viable as a district desegregation plan and nothing from this exercise came to fruition (*Trenton Public Schools Plan for Educational Excellence*, 1984, p. 2).

The State monitored the district between 1979 and 1981 while another plan was developed and submitted to the Office of Equal Educational Opportunity and the County Superintendent. A team from the two offices rated this plan unsatisfactory as well, claiming that it lacked direction (*Trenton Public Schools Plan for Educational Excellence*, 1984, p. 2).

In May, 1983, a committee of teachers and administrators convened to seek possible directions and strategies that could develop into an acceptable plan. In June and July of that year, a committee comprised of teachers first recommended a "magnet projects" plan for the new Mott School. The *Plan for Educational Excellence*, ultimately created in 1984, significantly modified and approved but never satisfactorily implemented, was offered as providing both short- and long-range strategies. Its intent was to enable the district to expand upon already existing opportunities for children, parents, teachers, and the community-at-large. The plan was expected to "enable persons to work, plan, exchange ideas, and to interact in multiethnic educational environments." Further, there were to be "opportunities to implement new strategies . . . to enable the district to concentrate resources more effectively, to seek out new resources and to institute sound educational processes . . . to reduce racial isolation in Trenton Public Schools" (*Trenton Public Schools Plan for Educational Excellence*, 1984, pp. 2, 4).

The committee appointed by the Trenton Public Schools selected, by consensus, three of the six guidelines outlined by the State Board of Education, Office of Equal Educational Opportunity (OEEO), in the development of its 1984 desegregation plan. It determined that effective strategies would include:

1. The identification and consideration of "alternative courses leading to solutions"; seventy factors were identified as being relevant to successful educational programs, "particularly in urban districts."
2. The projection of "the racial composition of each elementary and secondary school attendance area and the racial composition of its staff"; school-pairing was to be determined by the characteristics of the schools. Test scores, attendance patterns, student/teacher ratios, and per pupil expenditures in each school were among the characteristics to be examined.
3. The selection of the "location of proposed school building sites and the utiliz[ation of] existing buildings so that each school [would] represent as nearly as possible a cross section of the population of the entire district"; ethnic balance would be a primary goal. Magnet schools would be method of achieving this goal. (*Trenton Public Schools Plan for Educational Excellence*, 1984, pp. 20-21)

The Master Plan attempted to implement all five of the guidelines suggested by the State Board's OEEO. These guidelines recommended:

1. Involving school staff.
2. Providing opportunities for in-service training of administrators, school board members, teachers, and other school officials to mitigate "problems arising from the implementation of desegregation plans."

3. Furnishing "opportunities for students and parents to work with staff in pooling creative ideas for the instructional program and student activities."
4. Organizing "a curriculum review committee to select relevant textbooks and other teaching materials."
5. Encouraging "opportunities for interracial and intercultural experiences" in racially isolated schools by integrating staff and/or resource people. (*Trenton Public Schools Plan for Educational Excellence*, 1984, pp. 21-23)

The State Department of Education suggested eight options for implementation of the plan. The Trenton Master Plan incorporated four of these strategies:

1. Pairing of schools. Children would continue to attend their own schools; staff members would participate in workshops and school-specific projects; students would work on the common projects and meet periodically to share results. Research has shown that these activities stimulate both the learner and the teacher.
2. Transferring students from racially imbalanced schools to others that have available space. This strategy was both to relieve overcrowding and to provide a more balanced ethnic mix in the receiving schools.
3. Volunteer exchange of students between schools. Trenton already practiced open enrollment for special reasons. Attendance in pilot/magnet programs was added to the reasons to petition an alternate assignment. Requests to attend a magnet school would be honored in such order as to promote ethnic balance.
4. Attendance of students at a school other than their own for limited portions of time for special courses or activities. The then new Mott School was to offer programs that would provide opportunities for students and staff to interact in multicultural and multiethnic settings. (*Trenton Public Schools Plan for Educational Excellence*, 1984, pp. 24-25; 40-41)

One of the major components of the 1984 plan was a magnet schools program. In support of that effort, the district, on June 25, 1985, submitted "an application to the Federal Government in an attempt to obtain funding from the Magnet Schools Assistance Program." The sum of $1,085,541 was requested for magnet programs at two elementary schools and an academic magnet junior high, for school pairings, for science and mathematics, music and art, gifted and talented program expansion, basic skills realignment, and a drop-out/drop-in program for at-risk secondary students. In an irony that seems to capture the history of desegregation efforts in Trenton, the application was rejected and the system received no funding because "monies were distributed only to those districts who had been previous recipients of Emergency School Aid Act (ESAA) funding before it was discontinued in 1981. [Then,] when the District made application for this funding [again] for 1986-87, it was told it would not be allowed to do so. The reason . . . it did not receive any magnet funds for 1985-86" (*Desegregation Plan for Educational Excellence*, Revised August 1, 1986, Trenton Public Schools, pp. 15-16).

Apparently abandoned, for the most part, by the federal government, Trenton was unable to implement most of what had been planned. In the first year of what was to be a five-year plan for the period 1985-90, limited Chapter Two funding enabled only a full-day kindergarten program and a Computer Education Program at the Gregory School and a Mott-Kilmer-Hill Computer Language Arts Program for gifted and talented students (*Desegregation Plan for Educational Excellence*, Revised, 1986, p. 16).

During the next four years, magnet activities were to continue; a review of 7-9 grade organization was to take place; methods were to be determined to more effectively meet desegregation requirements; teachers were to receive in-service training to increase their understandings of diverse backgrounds and to develop school-pairing activities that would be introduced in approximately half a dozen additional schools each year; auxiliary staff were to receive in-service training to improve interpersonal relations as plans continued to maintain staff racial and ethnic balance; and community support for the desegregation effort was to be developed through community meetings, the distribution of information through the media, direct mailings to parents, and the development of School Councils for Desegregation. The 1986 plan also reemphasized the 1982 Board policy that called for textbook review relevant to appropriate representation of minorities. By the end of the fifth year, the Board was to develop a plan that would detail how all remaining schools would be integrated (*Desegregation Plan for Educational Excellence*, Revised, 1986, pp. 17-20; appendix, pp. 10, 14-16).

Community support was deemed to be among the most important elements necessary to ensure the success of the desegregation efforts. The 1986 plan emphasized that racially isolated schools tend to be located in racially identifiable neighborhoods. "The pervasiveness of racially identifiable neighborhoods demands that racially isolated schools not be viewed in a vacuum." Racial isolation must be reduced to help "prepare children to live in a diverse, pluralistic, democratic society," and all schools, public, private, and parochial, must join with community groups and private clubs, the private sector and public agencies, colleges and universities, and the clergy because the task is a communitywide responsibility. The Superintendent, Dr. Crosby Copeland, Jr., created a community advisory committee to help plan and conduct programs and activities for cross-cultural and interracial contact (*Desegregation Plan for Educational Excellence*, Revised, 1986, pp. 23-24).

The home and school link was also addressed by two additional projects; improvement of cross-cultural communication and Parent Effectiveness Training. Additions to staff included a Teacher Specialist to assist in districtwide desegregation coordination and a half-time Desegregation Community Relations Specialist. The district's newspaper, *Trenton's Education News* devoted a column exclusively to desegregation. To further encourage family involvement, a parent survey of attitudes on desegregation implementation and school improvement was scheduled for May, 1987 (*Desegregation Plan for Educational Excellence*, Revised, 1986, pp. 24-25).

Initially, at least, the 1985-90 plan was more successfully carried out by the Trenton Board of Education, and that implementation was greeted with far more enthusiasm by the New Jersey State Department of Education. Dr. Copeland even thanked the State Department for having "pushed the district" to develop and implement the plan. During 1986-87, the term "Integrated Quality Education (IQE)" was coined to describe the integration efforts in the participating schools. In its evaluation of Trenton's desegregation efforts for 1987-88, the State Department recognized the achievement of a full day kindergarten, computer/language arts magnet programs, joint assemblies of racially isolated schools, and staff development programs (Letter of July 29, 1988, Barbara Anderson, Director, OEEO to Dr. Crosby Copeland, Jr.; July 29, 1988 Observations and Recommendations, Barbara Anderson to Mark Raivetz, Trenton Desegregation Coordinator).

The 1988-89 plan was intended to continue the apparent spirit of cooperation of the year before. Districtwide focus was the primary objective, and regular planning sessions were scheduled for the principals of the eight schools targeted for inclusion in the IQE program. However, as the implementation stage of the program began, it was discovered that there were more fifth and sixth grade students than initially anticipated and than the receiving schools could accommodate. When the Trenton Desegregation Coordinator brought this to the attention of the State OEEO Director, both sympathy and additional funding were in short supply. The city felt that the state should have been more understanding; the state felt that the city should have been better prepared (Letter, Mark J. Raivetz to Barbara Anderson, September 30, 1988; interview with Mark Raivetz; interview with Marcellus Smith).

The report of monitoring visits held during October and November of 1988 noted insufficient compliance with the agreed-upon plan. The recommendation to "Adjust program to meet requirements or provide alternatives," offered no suggestion as to where the funding for these programs or alternatives should originate. Based on the first two months of the school year, the Trenton school system was found to be non-compliant with respect to Element 9-Equal Educational Opportunity/Affirmative Action. The state feared that based on IQE

hours in September and October, there would be an insufficient total
of hours by the end of the school year (Interoffice Memorandum, Rae
C. Roeder, OEEO Coordinator, to Barbara Anderson, December 6,
1988; Letter, Mark J. Raivetz to Barbara Anderson, December 6,
1988).

Once again, the Trenton schools felt betrayed by the State
Department of Education. In a nine-page letter, Mark Raivetz
described how the system was attempting to meet the demands of
the State Department despite overwhelming difficulties. He argued
that the first two months were not necessarily representative of the
entire year and that it was unfair to conduct what was in effect an
end-of-year evaluation so early. He delineated the activities planned
and noted how the district intended to increase the IQE hours for the
remainder of the 1988-89 school year   (Letter, Raivetz to Anderson,
December 6, 1988).

Marcellus Smith, of the State Board's OEEO, in an annotated copy
of Raivetz's letter, indicated his concern regarding Trenton's ability to
fully implement the IQE. Despite the length of the letter, Smith
determined a lack of detail and specificity. Raivetz, himself, on page
seven of the letter, while lauding the program as allowing "the
district the peaceful opportunity to develop real desegregation
opportunities for the first time in its history," at the same time
admits that "it is a model, however, that may be reaching its
maximum   potential in Trenton."   Raivetz continues that
"desegregation within a school district must be considered a regular
component of the instructional process. Given the present IQE model
in Trenton, that will probably never be the case." While arguing that
the district has complied with the State's order, Raivetz admits that
even with that compliance, the desegregation desired by everyone
may not come to pass (Letter, Raivetz to Anderson, December 6,
1988).

In his letter, Raivetz contends that the state monitoring process is
to a great extent to blame for the situation, since it "makes far more
demands upon urban districts than it does upon non-urban districts.
The main reason for this may be less a function of poverty or race
and more a function of size. The larger the district, the more schools,
the more obligations, and the more opportunities to fail." Raivetz
continues by pointing out that "all urban districts are required to
have desegregation plans" [while] "most suburban districts are not."
Of those children within Mercer County who are eligible for public
assistance, 93 percent attend Trenton Public Schools. "New Jersey
places the burden of school desegregation on those districts which
have the least resources to implement it" (Letter, Raivetz to
Anderson, December 6, 1988, pp. 7-8).

Student enrollment continued to decline, and the proportion of
white students declined even faster. Between 1980 and 1988
enrollment dropped by over 2800; the white population declined by

20.6 percent to 10.6 percent of the total student enrollment. "Without adequate numbers of [white] students, desegregation becomes increasingly more difficult." The intent to expand the IQE for 1989-90 was expected to enhance permanent desegregation through grade reorganization. The district's desire to provide "better opportunities for our children" was reiterated, and two days later Superintendent Copeland received word from Barbara Anderson that she "accepted the district's desegregation plan modification . . . based on the understanding that the 1988-89 desegregation plan is a 'transitional' plan to be in effect for the 1988-89 school year only, because a districtwide reorganization" would begin on December 1, 1988. After the reorganization, it was expected that the IQE would be expanded and enhanced (Letter, Barbara Anderson to Dr. Crosby Copeland, Jr., December 8, 1988).

The 1989-90 "Desegregation Expansion & Continuation" Plan had as its objective to provide "the maximum reasonable and feasible desegregation opportunities to our children within the geographic, demographic, and political constraints of the City of Trenton." The plan declared its commitment to maintaining OEEO approval by promising to implement all approved activities, support these activities and their transportation needs through funding from the district's operating budget and Chapter 2, complying with OEEO dates and timelines, continuing to employ the Teacher Specialist for Desegregation on a full-time, year-round basis, and providing monthly reports on events and activities related to desegregation (*Desegregation Expansion and Continuation Plan, 1989-90*, pp. 2-4).

The district pledged to offer both traditional (full-time reassignment) desegregation programs as well as its more innovative IQE programs. Self-contained seventh and eighth grade classes in four schools were to provide specialized programs in math and science, fine and performing arts, and computer education. These traditional magnet programs would be augmented by multicultural enrichment experiences for staff and students, and the district promised to "continue to move forward in its plan for districtwide grade reorganization" (*Desegregation Expansion and Continuation Plan*, 1989-90, pp. 4-5).

The IQE programs for fifth and sixth graders established in 1986 and 1987 in computers, art, and languages in eight schools as well as the joint assemblies and performances in the same schools would be continued. The plan noted its expectation that students in the IQE program would outperform non-participants in the California Achievement Test and would be less likely to be retained at the end of the year. Further, they were expected to demonstrate greater appreciation of cultural differences, and their teachers were to express higher expectations of them (*Desegregation Expansion and Continuation Plan*, 1989-90, pp. 5-7).

The district would also continue its commitment to maintaining an integrated instructional staff in all schools. Teacher rosters for each school, identifying instructional staff by race and origin, were also to be submitted to OEEO during the fall of 1989 for the 1989-90 school year (*Desegregation Expansion and Continuation Plan*, 1989-90, p. 6).

The most significant component added to the 1990-91 desegregation plan was a foreign language magnet program. Virtually all of the programs begun or maintained in 1989-90 were to be continued.   Districtwide reorganization was again promised. Multicultural education was to be infused into the curriculum to embody an overall perspective. Students were to become aware of their own perspectives to better deal with the cultures of others (*Outline for Trenton Public Schools 1990-91 Desegregation Program*, pp. 1-6).

Since the proportion of white students in the Trenton system has diminished to such a significant extent, black/white integration is not really possible. However, the predominating groups, African-Americans and Hispanics, tend to live segregated from each other as well. While, ideally, there should be a mix of all groups, programs that encourage integration of different minority groups also serve a valuable function. The Trenton Board of Education determined that the IQE programs offer the greatest possibilities for meaningful interaction among the different groups that make up the city's school population (Letter, Jilda L. Rorro, Acting Director, OEEO, to Dr. Crosby Copeland, Jr., September 6, 1989, pp. 1-2; interview with Marcellus Smith, March 5, 1992).

In 1988-89, the IQE standard set for the eight participating elementary schools was 75 hours of integrated instruction per student per year. Those standards were exceeded by 45 hours in two schools and by 14.5 hours in three others. However, in three schools only 16.5 hours of integrated instruction was provided. In continuing its monitoring of the district's desegregation efforts, the State Board also chastised the district for putting popular full-day kindergarten and self-contained seventh and eighth grade classes in neighborhood schools rather than in magnet schools where they would be more likely to advance desegregation efforts (Letter, Rorro to Copeland, September 6, 1989, p. 2).

At the conclusion of the 1989-90 school year, the district surveyed students, teachers, and principals regarding desegregation. The majority of fifth, seventh, and eighth grade students indicated pleasure in meeting new people and going to another school for special classes. The greatest complaint was riding the bus. The students suggested that additional trips and cultural activities be included. More than two-thirds of the students wanted to be in the program again the following year and would recommend it to friends; they liked being in classes with students from other parts of the city and felt that they learned about "people from other cultures and races who are different from me; their parents almost unanimously wanted them to be in the program" (*Desegregation Student Survey Results*, August, 1990).

Teachers and principals were somewhat less satisfied. While approximately half thought the program was at least partially successful and two-thirds felt that multicultural materials were "being infused into the curriculum," most also felt that the staff needed increased awareness training and more planning time. At least half of those responding deemed services and programs to be inequitably distributed among the schools, and transportation and materials were cited as needing improvement. Some suggested that it was only "a band-aid approach" and should be eliminated (*Desegregation Teacher and Principal Survey Results*, August, 1990).

As Trenton moved into the 1990s, changes were at best incremental. While white and Hispanic enrollments increased marginally in 1990-91, the number of white students dropped just slightly more in 1991-92, while Hispanic pupils decreased in proportion while increasing a bit in absolute numbers. Total enrollments dropped 1.1 percent in 1990-91 and increased, for the first time since 1982, in 1991-92, by 2.7 percent. Despite years of desegregation efforts and a total schoolwide white population of only 8.8 percent, three of 17 elementary schools in 1991-92 had white populations in excess of 60 percent, and one at almost 30 percent, while six of the 13 other elementary schools each had less than one percent whites. Further, by the time students reached high school only 3.8 percent of those attending Trenton public schools were white (*Trenton Districtwide Enrollment*, 1990-91, pp, i, 1; 1991-92, pp. i, 1, 5-8, 14).

The district has been somewhat more successful in the racial balancing of teachers. By 1986, the teaching staff had gone from primarily white to 50 percent white, 48 percent African-American, and 2 percent other; administrators were represented in approximately the same percentages. In 1991, 10 percent of the professional staff was Hispanic, with the remainder being divided between whites and African-Americans (Interview with Mark Raivetz and Phyllis Langford).

There are no real villains in the recounting of Trenton's attempt to desegregate its schools. Those interviewed agreed that political groups played a minimal role in the effort. Only a few whites joined the community group, Save Our Schools, trying to avoid desegregation, while the NAACP was active both on the streets and in the courts to promote it. The Trenton Public Schools both encouraged and controlled community participation by making community relations a consistent part of its desegregation plans. For example, the 1989-90 plan included seven community relations activities, including a telephone hotline, a speakers' bureau, and a directory of those involved in the system reorganization (*Reorganization Task Force Meeting Minutes*, December 12, 1988, p. 3; interviews with Fred Burke, Mark Raivetz, Jilda Rorro, Marcellus Smith).

Views on which administrators helped and who hindered depend upon where one's affiliations lie. Those who work for the state, such as Jilda Rorro and Marcellus Smith, feel that the State Department of Education enforced the law and held the districts accountable. From Mark Raivetz's perspective, the state made too many demands and offered too little support. Fred Burke's tenure as Education Commissioner received universal praise; he was lauded for bravely making the case for the need to desegregate in a way that helped it become acceptable to both blacks and whites (Interviews with Fred Burke, Mark Raivetz, Jilda Rorro, Marcellus Smith).

The state as the most active participant in the desegregation effort was seen as being the most constuctive element in the effort by all of those interviewed while also being cited by some as being counterproductive when its actions became heavy handed. The situation itself, with a dearth of whites going to school in the city, creates the greatest difficulty. Mark Raivetz noted in his interview that "desegregation plans are usually white family retention plans." (Interviews with Fred Burke, Mark Raivetz, Jilda Rorro, Marcellus Smith).

In offering advice to another community, Mark Raivetz warned that "people must feel that they have control." Ask people what they want, but do not raise expectations so high that it is impossible to succeed. Marcellus Smith advocated that emphasis should be on academics and the social development of the children. There must be mutual respect and respect for multiculturalism. Smith agreed with Raivetz on the importance of including parents and the community in the formulation of plans, as did Jilda Rorro. Both Rorro and Smith stressed establishing an aura of cooperation and maintaining high standards (Interviews with Fred Burke, Mark Raivetz, Jilda Rorro, Marcellus Smith).

During the summer of 1991, Dr. Bernice A. Venable became Superintendent of the Trenton Schools. The system once more promised the State Board of Education that its IQE activities would enable its staff to provide equality in its educational programs. Those coordinating the desegregation efforts were most enthused about The Princeton University Art Museum Project, which was to be implemented early in 1992. Art was to be the vehicle to enable 75 sixth grade pupils coming from three different elementary schools--one predominantly white, one predominantly black, and one mixed--to achieve seven goals. According to the project outline the students would, for example, "acquire tools for interaction with works of art through sharpened observation; experience success within a diverse group; recognize how art reveals the common threads in all cultures and times; and become comfortable in a museum and university setting" (*Trenton Times*, March 6, 1992; *Art Museum Project Guide*, January 15, 1992).

The State Board found the Princeton Project as well as the National Dance Institute Program, in its third year, to be "both innovative and substantive." However, in its conditional approval of the 1991-92 plan the OEEO repeated concerns similar to those voiced earlier relevant to the number of students to actually benefit from the various programs, the amount of time the students would participate, the training received by staff, and how the program could be appropriately evaluated. A new and improved plan was requested for the 1992-93 school year that would include more than the 60 percent participation of sixth graders included in the 1991-92 plan. Even the most enthusiastic and optimistic participant in Trenton's desegregation efforts would admit that the system still has a long way to go (Letter, Jilda L. Rorro to Dr. Bernice A. Venable, January 8, 1992).

During the 20-year period that Trenton has actively engaged in attempting to desegregate its schools, numerous elements of progress can be recorded: several new, innovative programs have been developed and implemented, the relations between the city's administration and those at the State Board of Education offices have grown more cordial, and educational opportunities for the students within the system have been, to at least some extent, equalized. In interviewing the participants, both in the local and state offices, one cannot help being impressed with their good intentions and commitment to the children of Trenton. However, with a school population that is two-thirds African-American, one-quarter Hispanic, and less than one-tenth white, the schools have not been and really cannot be desegregated without expanding the district to include other parts of Mercer County.

By late 1994, New Jersey had ceased its efforts to require Trenton to formally institute a desegregation program in the district. The city was required only to prepare a statement of assurance of non-discrimination. Middle schools had been semi-magnetized and included two emphasizing performing arts and two specializing in science, but desegregation was not their principal goal. Relations with the State Education Department, downsized under the administration of Governor Christine Todd Whitman, "was no longer a battle but just a wimper." Trenton's four major suburbs, Hamilton, Ewing, Lawrence, and Princeton, have seen some increases in their minority enrollments, in the order listed. Hamilton, with 15 percent minority population, has been required, since 1991, to create a desegregation plan (Interview with Mark Raivetz, November 15 and 22, 1994).

Chapter 5

Wilmington

While the section of the court decision in *Evans v. Buchanan* (379 F. Supp. 1218, 1974) that ultimately desegregated almost all of New Castle County, Delaware was not determined until 1978, the efforts to desegregate the Wilmington schools actually began as part of that most famous 1954 Supreme Court decision, *Brown v. Board of Education of Topeka, Kansas* (347 U.S. 483, 1954).

The public schools and their racial composition must be seen in the context of the city itself. Wilmington, at the beginning of this century, was a middle-sized city located in the Delaware River Valley, which, by virtue of its location at the confluence of waterways and railroads, had become a thriving manufacturing center (Hoffecker, 1983, p. 3).

Initially, it had the same mix of founding and fabricating industries as its urban neighbors in New Jersey and Pennsylvania. However, the decision of E.I. du Pont de Nemours & Company, in 1802, to begin to manufacture gunpowder on the Brandywine River near Wilmington determined the direction of the city a century later when heavy industry began a steady and irreversible decline (Hoffecker, 1983, pp. 3-4).

In 1906, the Du Pont Company began the construction of a large office building in downtown Wilmington that was to become its corporate headquarters. It pioneered modern business organization by employing professional managers and eschewed the general trend of locating its central offices in New York City (Hoffecker, 1983, pp. 4-5).

Among the important results of this decision was the entry into the Wilmington area of a corps of highly educated and trained middle- and upper-income managers, scientists, and technicians and their families. A new social structure emerged, and there was strong support, and the financial resources, for making and keeping the

5.1 Wilmington SMSA (Delaware), 1970

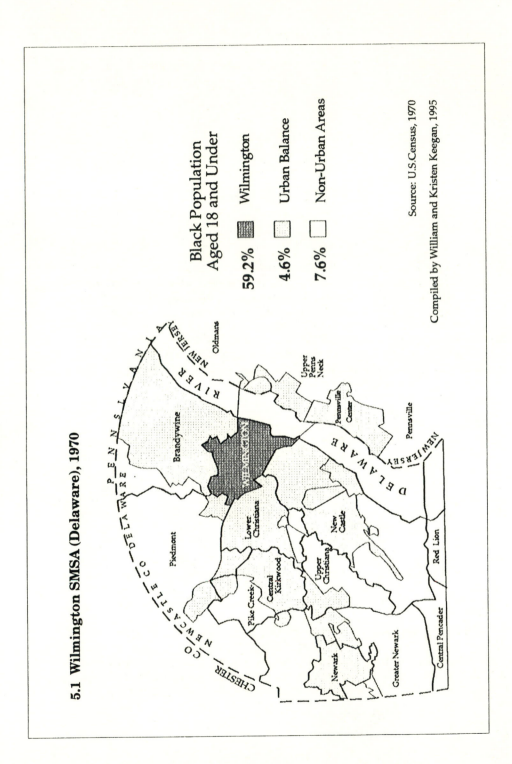

Black Population
Aged 18 and Under

59.2% ▓ Wilmington

4.6% ☐ Urban Balance

7.6% ☐ Non-Urban Areas

Source: U.S.Census, 1970

Compiled by William and Kristen Keegan, 1995

Wilmington public schools academically strong. Pierre S. du Pont was particularly instrumental in these efforts to improve educational opportunities in the area. Between 1918 and 1827, he generously financed the Service Citizens of Delaware, a reform organization based on business principles. By 1924, P. S. du Pont had spent over three million dollars building consolidated schools throughout the state. He also spoke at public meetings, urging the reorganization of the state's 424 separate school districts and was to a great deal responsible for the Delaware legislature's adopting a highly controversial school code in 1919 that raised school taxes throughout the state (Wolters, 1984, p. 176; Hoffecker, 1983, pp. 77-79).

The schools in Wilmington were specifically excluded from the most significant changes in the law, and the poorer districts in the southern part of the state were more affected than the towns in the north. However, the suburbs around Wilmington were influenced by the new law's emphasis on consolidation of rural districts, the creation of a dependable tax-based income for education, and the inception of "special districts," in which citizens could vote to raise taxes to provide additional revenues for school purposes (Hoffecker, 1983, pp. 80-82).

Although, at this time, the Wilmington schools were the best in the state, they were severely deficient by national standards. While the School Board responded to public pressure and had at least one building in each of the city's 14 wards, these structures suffered from the Board's unwillingness to raise sufficient taxes to maintain them properly. The majority of the schools were old, overcrowded, and lacked indoor plumbing; five of the 30 schools were built before the Civil War. Teachers were ill-paid, and the curriculum was inflexible. With per pupil spending at 30 dollars per year in 1917, Wilmington was investing only two-thirds as much as the average American city. Conditions in schools for blacks were even more deplorable (Hoffecker, 1983, p. 82).

Between 1925 and 1935, the Wilmington schools underwent a significant building program. The new school code provided state aid, and P. S. du Pont augmented those funds with generous contributions. The new buildings included rooms for physical education, vocational training, home economics, and assemblies, in addition to well-lit corridors, bathrooms, drinking fountains, and cafeterias. Most of the construction benefited the white students; however, in 1928 du Pont also donated 900,000 dollars to build a new Howard High School for black students (Hoffecker, 1983, p. 83).

Meanwhile, primarily because almost twice as many students were choosing to stay in high school until graduation as in the previous decade, Wilmington High School had become hopelessly overcrowded. In 1935, an elegant replacement, named against his will for the city's most prominent benefactor, was constructed for 1.8 million dollars of public funds. It featured an 1100 seat auditorium,

modern science rooms, gymnasiums for both girls and boys, and
various other specialized rooms. Some contended that during the
second quarter of the twentieth century, P. S. du Pont was "the finest
high school, public or private, east of the Mississippi River"
(Hoffecker, 1983, pp. 83-84; Wolters, 1984, p. 194; interview with
William B. Keene, June 19, 1991).

Prior to 1896, the only educational opportunities for black children
were those provided by the black community itself. Later, when the
state furnished public education for all children, it did so on a racially
discriminatory basis as sanctioned by the *Plessy v. Ferguson* decision.
Although separate was supposed to be equal, it was generally agreed
that the white schools were clearly superior. At the secondary school
level, Howard High School had an unusually competent and dedicated
principal in Edwina Kruse, who hired a faculty of outstanding merit,
including Alice Dunbar-Nelson, a gifted writer and teacher. The
school's classical curriculum reflected the fact that the city's
employers refused to hire vocationally trained blacks (Schmidt in
Green, 1985, pp. 37-38; Hoffecker, 1983, pp. 94-95).

As a border state, Delaware in 1950 exhibited a mixture of
northern and southern customs. While schools, restaurants, and
theaters were segregated, public "libraries, buses and trains were
not and blacks voted as freely as whites" (Wolters, 1984, p. 176).

Until the late 1940s, many suburban children attended
elementary school in their local districts and then came into
Wilmington for high school. However, as the suburbs became
increasingly populous, many of them chose to build their own high
schools. Districts could choose to subsist on state funds or to become
a special district and bond themselves to supplement the state's
school allowance. For example, the Mt. Pleasant Special School
District, which included the eastern portion of Brandywine Hundred
and was the residence of many scientists, engineers, and white collar
managers, developed a reputation for quality education when its
residents consistently supported extra bond issues to insure modern
schools and exemplary educational programs. In contrast, the
wealthy residents of Kennett Pike, who traditionally sent their
children to private schools, and the moderate income families south
of Wilmington were content to operate their schools on the state
appropriation (Hoffecker, 1983, pp. 121-22).

The suburban schools progressed from being inferior, to equal, to
generally superior to the city schools as the suburbs became more
populated. The trend was accelerated in the mid-fifties when the
Supreme Court ended racial segregation in the public schools.
Although school administrators worked diligently to dispel parental
fears as they reassigned students and teachers and sought to place
highly qualified black teachers in schools that had previously been
all-white, they could not totally stem the white flight of 5000 children
of middle-income families who could afford to move to the suburbs

during the five years immediately following desegregation (Hoffecker, 1983, p. 123).

Considering the present condition of Connecticut's cities, it is at the least ironic that, in the 1950s, Wilmington's leaders looked to New Haven in particular as a model of progressive urban development. Henry Belin du Pont, a nephew of Pierre, who spent a great deal of time pursuing his hobby of sailing off the Connecticut coast where his family had a summer home, was especially impressed with Mayor Richard Lee's dynamic policies, which galvanized business and political power to encourage the city's renewal (Hoffecker, 1983, pp. 129, 140, 172).

The history of the desegregation of the New Castle County schools is as long as that of any area in the nation. The first Delaware plaintiff was Mrs. Fred Bulah of the rural village of Hockessin, located ten miles to the west of Wilmington. In 1950, she wrote to state officials in an attempt to gain bus transportation for her adopted daughter, Shirley. The child attended a one-room black school with two teachers and 43 students, which was two miles from her home (Wolters, 1984, p. 176).

No transportation was provided to the black school, but the bus to the white school passed nearby. Mrs. Bulah was informed that the state did not operate the buses but provided students with an allowance that could be used to pay a private company. There were no buses for blacks because there were insufficient numbers of these students in the town and it was therefore not profitable for the service to be offered (Wolters, 1984, pp. 176-77).

At about the same time, eight black teenagers who lived in Claymont, a predominantly white suburb nine miles north of Wilmington, filed suit to attend their local high school rather than travel into Wilmington to all-black Howard High School to which they were assigned. The litigation for both suits was financed by the National Association for the Advancement of Colored People (NAACP) and the briefs were prepared by Louis L. Redding, a black graduate of Brown University and Harvard Law School. NAACP attorney Jack Greenberg stressed that separate could not be equal, and Redding made the case that the black facilities in Hockessin and Wilmington were inferior and therefore in violation of the equal protection as guaranteed by the Fourteenth Amendment (Wolters, 1984, p. 177; SANE Report, 1978, p. 33).

The case was heard by Chancellor Collins Seitz, who was sympathetic to the plaintiffs and their arguments but felt that the case should be decided by the Supreme Court. Seitz ruled that in both *Belton v. Gebhart* (Claymont) and *Bulah v. Gebhart* (Hockessin) the existing educational facilities were not equivalent for blacks and whites and ordered the immediate admission of the black children into the white schools. These two cases were later incorporated into

the 1954 *Brown* decision   (Wolters, 1984, p. 178; SANE Report,
1978, p. 33).

Opinions on the desirability of the suits were mixed on the part of
both blacks and whites. Some blacks felt that the higher standards
at Claymont and the reduced travel time for the black students more
than compensated for the loss of racial identity afforded by the
segregated schools. Some black teachers feared that their jobs would
become casualties of desegregation. Some black parents voiced
concern that the white teachers would not be as sympathetic to their
children and would not serve as positive role models. For whites,
who comprised more than 80 percent of New Castle County and who
stayed in their original schools, the change was less radical. On the
surface, at least, a cordial atmosphere prevailed (Wolters, 1984, pp.
179-80).

Blacks had been very gradually migrating into New Castle County
since the beginning of the twentieth century, with the pace increasing
rapidly after 1950. The two streams of migration into Wilmington,
from the North and the South, show the characteristics of the city: a
northern city in a border state. Whereas the blacks in the South
frequently resided in the rural areas, those dwelling in the North
were more likely urban. The Negroes moving into the county, as the
school enrollments demonstrated, were far more likely to become city
residents. In 1940, the 2433 non-white students in Wilmington
comprised 16.3 percent of total enrollment, while 952 non-white
students made up 9.2 percent of the enrollment of the suburban
schools; in 1960, 2638 non-white students were 6.8 percent of the
total suburban enrollment while the non-white city enrollment of
5889 pupils formed a far more significant 45 percent of the student
body (Tilly, 1965, pp. 9-10, 23).

The desegregation of Wilmington proceeded peacefully. Blacks,
who made up 27 percent of the student body, were moved into the
grammar schools in 1954, the junior high schools in 1955, and the
senior high schools in 1956. Seminars on race relations sponsored by
the National Conference of Christians and Jews and door-to-door
visits by the local Parent Teacher Associations (PTAs) encouraged
support, or at least acceptance, of the integration efforts. The state
police were advised that whatever their personal thoughts, the
preservation of law and order within the community was paramount.
In keeping with a two-decade-old policy, parents were allowed to
transfer their children to schools or classrooms other than the ones to
which they were assigned and this, without question, eased tensions
with respect to those parents most disturbed by the changes being
implemented (Wolters, 1984, p. 180).

The initial desegregration of the Wilmington schools worked well.
There was even hope that the ten-point disparity between average
white and black IQ scores would be diminished as a result of better
teaching in integrated schools. However, the superficially peaceful

response to the desegregation efforts masked a steady exodus of whites from the city. In 1954, school enrollments were 73 percent white and 27 percent black; in 1969, the proportion was more than reversed, and by 1976, less than ten percent of Wilmington's school children were white (Wolters, 1984, pp. 181-82).

It is not likely that this total reversal of racial majority was completely intended or solely the result of school desegregation. Whites throughout the nation were moving to the suburbs or to small towns outside central cities; similarly, the trend of Southern blacks to move northward in search of greater opportunities was not restricted to northern Delaware. Whatever the cause or the intent, by the mid-1970s, there was no doubt that the Wilmington schools had resegregated. Efforts to retain the more academically able students by further grouping by scholastic ability were unsuccessful, and while "there was no change in the range of ability, . . . there was a marked change in the frequency of distribution." Some students were able to succeed in the traditional college preparatory curriculum, but "a growing number needed to move at a slower pace." School officials devised special programs for both above-average and the increasingly more numerous below-average pupils (Wolters, 1984, p. 183).

Meanwhile, in other parts of Delaware, desegregation was proceeding neither peacefully nor successfully. In 1956, the suit *Evans v. Buchanan* was entered in District Court on behalf of five black students residing in the Clayton School District. The court action contended that black students were not admitted into the local schools on a racially non-discriminatory basis. In a 1957 continuation of the suit, six additional cases were consolidated with the Clayton plaintiffs. The Court found that insufficient effort had been made to comply with the *Brown* decisions of 1954 and 1955. The schools were "enjoined from refusing to admit black students and the State Board of Education was ordered to submit an overall desegregation plan" (*Fact Book*, 1978, p. 27).

An acceptable plan was presented in 1961 and, in 1965, the State Board of Education adopted a resolution that provided for the closure of numerous small schools and effectively ended *de jure* segregation. By June 30, 1967, the last black district was phased out and, during that year, the United States Department of Health, Education and Welfare praised Delaware for being "the first southern or border state to have dismantled its dual system of education" (*Fact Book*, 1978, p. 27).

In 1968, the Delaware Legislature passed the Educational Advancement Act to reorganize the school districts of the state. Consolidation resulted in 49 school districts being reduced to 26. Since no district was to have more than 12,000 students and Wilmington alone contained 16,000, Delaware's largest city was exempted from all of the provisions of the act (Wolters, 1984, p. 212).

The act was passed in a year of riots and National Guard patrols, at the "apogee of interracial tensions and fears in Wilmington." It did not appear that the omission of Wilmington from the act's provisions had any racial motivation, and while both blacks and whites were concerned about the progressive academic failure of the city's students, there was also a sense of satisfaction in the black community with regard to its growing civic power, most evident in 1970 when new school board appointments created the first black majority. City legislators, both black and white, voted for the act (Hoffecker, 1983, pp. 244-45).

While *Evans v. Buchanan* was initially concerned with black students gaining access to white schools in the rural town of Clayton in 1956, when it was resurrected in 1970, it was as much because white parents living within the city of Wilmington wanted access to the neighboring suburban schools for their children. P.S. du Pont High School no longer enjoyed its former reputation as the best in the state, and the schools in neighboring Mt. Pleasant and the Alfred I. du Pont Districts were now reputed to be "more orderly and academically enriched." Only a decade earlier, suburban students had been allowed to transfer into Wilmington when it was perceived that the city had the superior educational facility. White Wilmington parents were now supporting the five black plaintiffs and attempting to use the same arguments as blacks had to create more balanced educational opportunities for their children (Hoffecker, 1983, pp. 245-46; Raffel, 1980, p. 45).

What began as a primarily white neighborhood task force, established by Wilmington Mayor Harry G. Haskell in 1969, to provide two-way communication between the mayor's office and the citizens, became the spearhead of one of the most complicated and far-ranging legal cases in the history of desegregation. By the time the issue was resolved, virtually every person, jurisdiction, and organization that could possibly become involved was a participant-- including the City of Wilmington, the State Board of Education, the eleven other school boards in New Castle County, the American Civil Liberties Union, and the NAACP. The case was heard in two different federal courts, and a panel of three federal judges, two from Delaware and one from New Jersey, heard the case. The situation was a boon for almost all of the numerous legal firms practicing in Greater Wilmington (Hoffecker, 1983, pp. 247-48).

To achieve an inter-district remedy, which was what the plaintiffs desired, it was necessary that they show that the State had purposefully acted to maintain segregation. The plaintiffs cited the exclusion of Wilmington from the 1968 Educational Advancement Act as proof that the State had intentionally worked against the cause of desegregation, as the Wilmington schools were already more than

Table 5.1
Wilmington Population by Race: SMSA and City, 1970 and 1980; County and City, 1990

	1970		1980		1990	
	N	%	N	%	N	%
TOTAL CITY	80,386		70,195		71,529	
WHITE	44,901	56%	31,663	45%	30,134	42%
BLACK	35,072	44%	35,858	51%	37,446	52%
HISPANIC	N/A		3,424	5%	5,072	7%
SMSA OR COUNTY	499,493		523,221		441,946	
WHITE	436,405	87%	441,640	84%	355,399	80%
BLACK	60,896	12%	73,064	14%	72,834	16%
HISPANIC	N/A		8,517	2%	11,804	3%

Note: Categories may not total to 100% because of other groups and because Hispanics may also be listed as White or Black.

Source: U.S. Census, 1970, 1980, 1990.

half black in 1968 and 72 percent black by 1971 (Raffel, 1980, pp. 46-47).

The State's argument that 12,000 students was the "upper limit for efficient school district size" and that Wilmington was in itself beyond that limit did not convince the District Court. On July 12, 1974, the three-judge panel declared that despite Wilmington's adoption of racially neutral attendance zones, segregation within the system had never really been eliminated and that a dual school system still existed. The Court did not specify a remedy and reaffirmed the State Board's responsibility to provide for desegregation. It ordered the Board to submit a Wilmington-only and a metropolitan-inclusive plan (Raffel, 1980, p. 47).

On March 27, 1975, the District Court held that "an inter-district remedy would be appropriate, based on its findings that":

1. there had been a failure to alter the historic pattern of inter-district segregation in Northern New Castle County;
2. governmental authorities at the state and local levels were responsible to a significant degree for increasing the [racial]

disparity in residential and school populations between
Wilmington and the suburbs;

3. the City of Wilmington had been unconstitutionally excluded
   from other school districts by the State Board of Education,
   pursuant to a withholding of reorganization powers under the
   Delaware Educational Advancement Act of 1968. (44 F. Supp. at
   877)

On November 17, 1975, the United States Supreme Court
summarily affirmed the District Court ruling, and two months later it
denied the State Board of Education's petition for a new hearing. On
May 19, 1976, the District Court issued an opinion that "a
Wilmington-only plan would not significantly affect the present racial
identifiability of the Wilmington or suburban schools." Thus the
Court proposed a plan that would include all of the school districts in
New Castle County, with the exception of Appoquinimink and the
New Castle County Vocational School District. Appoquinimink is a
huge, sparsely populated, and integrated district (28 percent
minority in the mid 1970s) in the extreme southern part of the
county. Its inclusion would have added extensive traveling time for
county students without significantly altering the integration efforts
(*Fact Book*, 1978, pp. 28-29).

The inclusion of the City of Newark as one of the participating
districts came only after tremendous discussion and acrimony. As the
home of the University of Delaware and the Du Pont Company's
Engineering Department, its population included a high proportion of
people who "prized education to an unusual degree." The schools had
integrated the five percent of its student population that was black,
and the city itself was one of the larger municipalities in Delaware,
with its population of 21,000. Newark's residents argued
passionately to be excluded from the case and from the ultimate
metropolitan district (Hoffecker, 1983, p. 249).

However, the case made by the residents of the Mount Pleasant
District in Brandywine Hundred, the oldest, most settled suburban
region, proved to be the more convincing. If Newark were excluded it
appeared likely that "suburban settlement patterns would shift."
Those most concerned about property values and school quality
would gravitate toward Newark, which would be unaffected by
regionalization. The only way to minimize the impact on the
participating suburbs was to include them all (Hoffecker, 1983, p.
249-50).

Meanwhile, the subject of desegregation and the appropriateness
of inter-district remedies were issues in locations far beyond
Delaware. In Detroit, Michigan, courts heard a case that bore
similarities to that of Wilmington. The plaintiffs in *Milliken v.
Bradley* also sought a metropolitan resolution to racial imbalance
that had reached extreme proportions within the central city.
However, in that case, the court ultimately decided against a

metropolitan solution. The Supreme Court in its decision on July 25, 1974 determined that "it must be shown that racially discriminatory acts of the state or local school districts, or of a single school district have been a substantial cause of inter-district segregation" in order for an inter-district remedy to be imposed. The 1968 Educational Advancement Act in Delaware was seen to be support for segregation by the State of Delaware; no such complicity was felt, by the Supreme Court, to have been exhibited by the State of Michigan (*Fact Book*, 1978, p. 34).

On May 19, 1976, the District Court hearing *Evans v. Buchanan* reiterated its findings of an inter-district violation and therefore declared that the ten suburban districts were to be included in the remedy. Schools with enrollments in each grade of between 10 and 35 percent black would be considered to be *prima facie* desegregated. Secondary schools were to become desegregated in September, 1977, and elementary schools the following year (*Fact Book*, 1978, pp. 34-35).

Numerous attempts were made by the various suburban communities to have the order stayed in light of other court rulings decided in desegregation suits involving Washington, D.C., Texas, Illinois, Indiana, and Ohio. The three- judge panel in Delaware held firm. Meanwhile, an interim voluntary transfer program was instituted, and approximately 2000 students whose race was underrepresented in the transferee school participated in this program between 1976 and 1978 (SANE Report, 1978, p. 3).

On May 18, 1977, the United States Third Circuit Court of Appeals affirmed the District Court judgment with the modification that the 10-35 percent enrollment criterion be eliminated and that "no particular racial balance will be required in any school, grade, or classroom." The State Board of Education was to establish a five-member board to plan and initially operate the new unitary school system (SANE Report, 1978, p. 3).

Following the May 18 ruling, Judge Murray M. Schwartz became the presiding judge in the case, and he has remained so to this writing. Under his direction, the eleven districts in New Castle County were to become one district on July 1, 1978. His remedy order of January 9, 1978 finally took effect in September of that year. Its main provisions were:

1. A 9-3 concept: 9 years out of the home districts for Wilmington and De La Warr students and 3 years for students from the other districts (kindergarten, special education, and vocational students would be exempt).
2. Reassignment of faculty and staff in a non-racially identifiable manner.
3. In-service training programs for teachers, administrators, and other staff.
4. Human relations programs throughout the district.

5. Preservation of the bilingual education plan for Wilmington's Hispanic population.
6. An affirmative reading and communication program.
7. Curriculum offerings reflecting cultural pluralism and free of racial bias. (*Fact Book*, 1978, p. 5)

The pupil assignment plan was based on the predominantly black districts of Wilmington and De La Warr being assigned to the nine predominantly white districts for nine years. All students from the white districts were assigned to schools in Wilmington or De La Warr for three consecutive years. This inequality took into account the fact that there were approximately three times as many classrooms available in the predominantly white school districts as in those that had a majority of black children. The assignment of students was organized within four attendance areas:

Area I: Wilmington/ Alfred I. du Pont, Claymont, Mount Pleasant
Area II: Wilmington/ Alexis I. du Pont, Conrad, Marshallton-McKean, Stanton
Area III: Wilmington/ Newark
Area IV: De La Warr/ New Castle-Gunning Bedford

Students were to be assigned for all 12 years to schools geographically located within their respective attendance areas. As far as possible they were to attend school with children from their own neighborhood and with the same group of children in a feeder system. Grade centers were to be organized on the basis of three continuous grades: 1-3, 4-6, 7-9, 10-12 (*Fact Book*, 1978, p. 6).

As part of the reorganization, some buildings had to be downgraded from secondary to elementary schools. With the exception of Wilmington High School, which was maintained, and Conrad High School, which was converted to a junior high, all of the changed schools had been black. This antagonized many of the black families, but not nearly as much as the fact that inner city students, mostly black, were to be bused for three times as many years as suburban students who were mostly white (Raffel, 1980, p. 188).

The court order required the implementation of a number of programs that were designed to help blacks reach "the educational level they supposedly would have achieved if they had attended racially balanced classes." Almost 100 teachers were employed as human relations specialists, and 470 others were paid to attend summer workshops emphasizing race relations at the University of Delaware. Training was believed to be the key to successful school desegregation, especially for middle-class teachers who would need to improve their ability to resolve conflicts with disruptive students "whose values differed from their own" (Wolters, 1984, pp. 229-30).

In September, 1980, the white student population in the four districts varied from 66 to 73 percent, with the total student body being 70.7 percent white. All of the districts contained small numbers of Hispanics and Asians, while African-Americans comprised the greatest portion of the minority student representation. Ten years later, the four districts ranged from 64 to 70 percent white, the total enrollment had dropped to 67.1 percent white, with slightly more Asian and Hispanic students proportionate to African-Americans in the minority category (*Regulations for Reorganization*, 1980, Appendix B; July 19, 1990 Report of Suspensions and Expulsions).

Judging by the previously noted statistics, the court-ordered inter-district desegregation of New Castle County schools, including those of Wilmington, in at least some respects must be judged a success. For more than ten years, the proportion of white students to minority students has consistently remained extremely uniform throughout the four districts and well within an appropriate range relevant to the proportion of whites and African-Americans for the area as a whole. There has been some white flight to private schools, but the central city during the first three years of desegregation actually lost more black students to the suburbs than it did white students. In fact, the number of white students actually increased slightly (Klaff, 1981, p. 24).

Desegregation also resulted in positive and progressive changes in the rate of school tax assessments. In De La Warr and Wilmington, the new uniform tax rate of 1.875 dollars meant a school tax savings averaging two dollars in De La Warr and 80 dollars in Wilmington. In the affluent districts, tax increases ranged between 100 and 200 dollars; proportionately, the highest tax rate increase fell on white blue-collar districts. The new assessments were based more on the ability of those taxed to pay than the former tax plans and also moved in the right direction in making compensation for the effects of past racial discrimination (Raffel, 1980, p. 190).

In assessing proportionate responsibility for the successful desegregation of the New Castle County schools, the courts must be accorded a central role. Only the courts could declare with authority that Delaware's dual school system had never truly been dismantled and then require state officials to provide a suitable remedy. However, the messages emanating from the three levels of the judiciary were not always consistent, and frequently the orders were vague as well. This made things all the more difficult for the state and local officials responsible for creating the acceptable plan that was demanded (Raffel, 1980, p. 61; interview with Dr. Henry C. Harper, June 18, 1991).

The job of the governmental officials was not only to please the courts but also to be accountable to their constituents. While few officials were totally obstructionist, the majority were very sensitive to the lack of enthusiasm for desegregation that was felt by most people living outside of Wilmington and some residents of the central city as well. Some symbolic anti-busing legislation was offered and passed; the majority of the state legislators avoided taking a positive stand on desegregation when possible despite their realization of their responsibility to implement the law. By walking a fine line between acknowledging the courts' demands but not actually providing a plan for implementation, state legislators reflected the views of the majority of state residents (Raffel, 1980, pp. 118-19; interview with Dr. William B. Keene, June 19, 1991).

School officials felt equally responsible to their constituents. Those from the districts outside Wilmington were very much aware that desegregation seemed to offer little to white suburban residents and that many black suburban residents were unenthusiastic as well. Even many blacks from the central city were of mixed minds, as regionalization was certain to dilute their hard-fought-for power and authority, at least within Wilmington itself. However, once the court's decision was final, administrators worked together to create a viable system. At the present time, those responsible for operating the system take great pride in what, in their view, is a great success and a series of major accomplishments (Raffel, 1980, pp. 87-88; interviews with Dr. James Spartz and Dr. Jack Nichols, June 18, 1991; Harper interview).

No school system can be any better than the teachers who ultimately represent the schools' philosophy to the students and their parents. For the teachers of New Castle County, the period of judicial consideration and ultimate decision and implementation was one of great uncertainty and concern. For the majority, desegregation was uprooting, with many teachers being transferred on short notice so that the instructional staff as well as the student body could be integrated. While many rose to the occasion, many others found the changes so disruptive that their teaching and commitment to the students suffered (Keene, Harper interviews).

Union representation and financial equity were also issues of great importance to the teachers. Previous to the 11 district merger, suburban teachers were represented by the New Castle County Education Association (NCCEA), a National Education Association affiliate, while the central city teachers had a Wilmington-based American Federation of Teachers (AFT) organization as their bargaining agent. In the spring of 1978, the NCCEA defeated the Federation group by more than two to one. In-service training for teachers was implemented through the spring and summer, and contract negotiations were pursued as well. The latter were less successful than the former, for as school opened in September, there was still no contract between the teachers and the new Board of Education (Raffel, 1980, p. 80).

The subject of salaries presented a particular sticking point. City teachers were paid on a higher scale than those in the suburbs. Understandably, suburban teachers wanted an increase to parity, city teachers were opposed to a pay cut to achieve a single scale, and the Board was concerned about finding the 22 million dollars to eliminate the difference. Mediation through September and October was unsuccessful. The Board insisted that it needed three years to equalize salaries; the Association insisted that it be done in one. On October 16, more than 80 percent of the teachers began what became a 31-day strike (Raffel, 1980, pp. 190-92; Keene, Harper interviews).

While money was the major issue of contention, there was also a wide variety of working conditions to be resolved, such as the length of the school day. Since Wilmington teachers enjoyed the more favorable conditions, they had the least to gain and were the ones most likely to cross the picket lines. The Association, still undergoing pressure from the Federation, felt obligated to obtain a favorable contract to use in its next battle with the AFT (Raffel, 1980, pp. 192-94).

Pressure from parent groups, which at first supported the strike but then even more wanted the schools reopened to enable the education process to go forward, and intervention by the governor finally settled the strike on November 19. Parity would be achieved within a year and a half. The strike had not really been caused by the desegregation process but rather by the reorganization of the numerous school systems (Raffel, 1980, p. 194).

The strike was but the first instance of the teachers appearing to be negative forces in the desegregation efforts. White parents claimed that discipline was lax in the new integrated schools and that African-American students were left unpunished for inappropriate conduct. Parents of African-American students cited school records showing that black children were suspended at more than twice the rate of whites and argued that they were being discriminated against. Dr. Harper explains this discrepency by noting that the races exhibit different kinds of misbehavior; while white students may break rules against smoking, black students are more likely to be the ones found fighting. Academic-minded parents complained that standards were being lowered and the curriculum was being watered down. The results of at least some standardized tests seemed to support that contention (Raffel, 1980, pp. 194-95; Harper interview).

There is agreement that credit for the generally peaceful desegregation of the New Castle County schools was the result of many segments of the involved population working together. Perhaps most important were the community groups. Early in the desegregation efforts, Mayor William T. McLaughin of Wilmington established a Breakfast Group comprised of the Governor's counsel and his education assistant, the county executive's policy coordinator, the president of the school board, the deputy superintendent of the county school district, and the presidents or chairpersons of nearly every parent and community group in the county. During the implementation phase of the desegregation process, the group met twice a month. These meetings allowed people in the community to feel that they were being heard and enabled those implementing the desegregation efforts to explain the programs in their best light. As noted by Dr. Keene, "What people believe at the moment influences what ultimately happens" (Raffel, 1980, p. 120; Spartz and Keene interviews).

Those in the community opposed to busing and desegregation found a home in the ironically named Positive Action Committee (PAC). Begun in 1975, at its height, it claimed more than 10,000 dues-paying members. PAC's strong ideological stance narrowed its possible constituency but at the same time gave those most in opposition the feeling that their opinions were being heard. While, in the short run, the organization delayed and made the implementation of desegregation more difficult, ultimately, it helped the cause by channeling frustrated   feelings into peaceful, acceptable, and eventually, futile protest (Raffel, 1980, pp. 154, 172).

Studies in 1981, three years after the implementation of school desegregation, indicate that only minimal changes took place in both personal attitudes and academic achievement. Parents in all-white and mostly white neighborhoods maintained the least positive racial attitudes over the three-year period. Those in neighborhoods that were half-white and half-black became slightly more positive after the first year but then less positive during the next two years, while those in the all-black neighborhoods became more positive during each of the three years. Parents' attitudes toward perceived school quality followed racial attitudes except that, in the third year, all groups tended to be less positive. With regard to parental expectations of their child's performance, all but those living in the mostly black neighborhoods developed lower expectations (Darden in Green, 1985, p. 133).

Student attitudes proved to be very similar to those of their parents. Further, "school desegregation did not appear to be related to a reduction in the gap in student racial attitudes by neighborhood racial composition. After three years of desegregation, racial attitudes became less positive in all neighborhoods." Perhaps, what is most discouraging, "educational self-concept on the part of students in all neighborhoods also became less positive" especially in "mostly black neighborhoods where students' educational self-concept was most positive prior to desegregation" (Darden in Green, 1985, p. 135).

Although attitudinal changes were at best mixed, achievement changes while minimal were all positive. The greatest gains were made by students in the mixed and mostly black neighborhoods; the all-white neighborhoods exhibited the least change but still recorded the highest scores on national math and reading tests. While all students improved, the achievement gap narrowed by approximately ten percent (Darden in Green, 1985, pp. 139-40).

As in Rochester, New York, residents of New Castle County indicate great civic pride in the fact that desegregation was achieved peacefully. Even Jea Street, the charismatic and outspoken director of the African-American coalition that opposed the desegregation efforts and a staunch critic of the current system, was pleased not to be "another Boston" (interview with Jea Street, August 14, 1991).

However, Street remained extremely distressed by the current educational opportunities for African-Americans in New Castle County. He impassionately noted that "the 1978 reorganization was the worst thing that ever happened to little black children." He cited the 200 percent increase in black suspensions, the 75 percent increase in special education of black students, and that fewer black students are graduated from high school now than before desegregation. He claims that the increased suspensions and other negative situations are not the result of overt racism but rather of a more subtle form of discrimination (Street interview).

There is no disputing that New Castle County desegregated its public schools in 1978 and has maintained a desegregated educational system for more than ten years. There is less unanimity of opinion regarding whether it offers a quality, integrated education to its 48,000 students. According to Jea Street, black students at least were better off when they had the support of homogeneous schools in their own neighborhoods, staffed by predominantly black teachers. Dr. Spartz and Dr. Nichols concede that while the system is desegregated, that does not necessarily mean that it is integrated. Dr. Keene noted that desegregation is a mechanical process; integration is different and far more complex (Street, Spartz, Nichols, Harper, Keene interviews).

Early test results suggested that all children benefited academically, with white children who had previously attended predominantly black schools making the greatest gains. According to county and state educational administrators, the system is working well for the majority of students in the four districts. Judge Murray Schwartz notes that there are more blacks in the mainstream now than there were a dozen years ago and that education must be a component of this change. Perhaps, the question of whether desegregated education has been achieved, as well as the answer, requires refining (Schweitzer in Green, 1985, pp. 173, 183-84; interview with Judge Murray Schwartz, June 14, 1991).

In the interim to late 1994, there were few significant developments in the New Castle County schools. The State Board appeared satisfied that all desegregation requirements had been satisfied, and a petition was filed to declare unitary status on December 19, 1994. This action would relieve the districts from the court order they had been under, with the final ruling made in Spring, 1995. The proportion of white and minority students in the four districts remained relatively unchanged (Interview with Dr. Jack Nichols, November 15, 1994).

Chapter 6

Hartford

On April 26, 1989, 17 children, African-American, Puerto Rican, and white, 15 from Hartford and two from the suburb of West Hartford, sued the State of Connecticut, claiming that the schools, as they were currently organized, violated the constitutional rights of Hartford school pupils to equal opportunity and freedom from discrimination. The suit, known as *Sheff v. O'Neill*, does not suggest that the state intentionally created this condition; nevertheless, the plaintiffs contend that since these circumstances exist, it is the state's responsibility to correct them. "Although school desegregation battles traditionally have been fought in federal courts, this one will be fought in a state court--in a case similar to *Horton v. Meskill*, the long running legal battle for equal school financing in Connecticut." (*The Hartford Courant*, April 27, 1989, p. 1).

The *Sheff v. O'Neill* case is but the latest manifestation of differences of opinion as to the appropriate role that the State should play in the education of Connecticut's children since the colony was founded. During the past three and a half centuries, control and responsibility for the education of Connecticut's children has been uneasily shared between the towns and the state. Unlike the majority of states, Connecticut counties have never played a role (Interview with Christopher Collier, July 28, 1992).

If there had been less competition between the Reverends John Cotton and Thomas Hooker, the current City of Hartford would have had different and later English roots. However, the combination of theological controversy and infertile soil caused Thomas Hooker, in 1635, to lead six dozen men, women, and children from what was then Newtown, Massachusetts to the confluence of the Connecticut and Little Rivers, which the Indians called Sukiaug. The Newtown people were able to sell their former community to another group of Englishmen, who, the following year, had it renamed Cambridge; the new Newtown also underwent a name change to Hartford, in honor of

6.1 Hartford SMSA (Connecticut), 1970

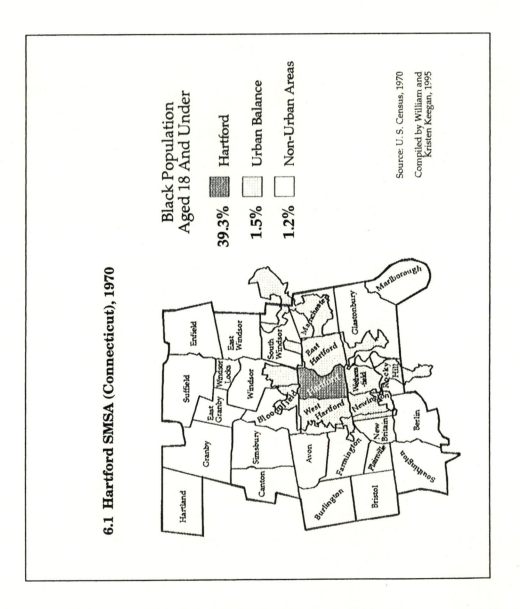

Black Population
Aged 18 And Under

39.3% Hartford

1.5% Urban Balance

1.2% Non-Urban Areas

Source: U. S. Census, 1970

Compiled by William and
Kristen Keegan, 1995

the English home of the Reverend Samuel Stone, Thomas Hooker's assistant. Settlements in Windsor and Wethersfield were occurring at the same time (Weaver, 1982, pp. 8-12).

The first white men had visited Connecticut in 1631 when the party of Governor Winslow of Plymouth explored the area for trade possibilities and returned to their more eastern settlements with hemp, furs, and deerskins and the knowledge that the area appeared hospitable to farming. They also noted that the resident Indians were friendly (Stuart, 1853, pp. 9-10).

Although there were probably provisions for education almost as soon as the colony was founded, the first direct notice regarding schooling in Hartford is dated 1642, when on December sixth of that year, "30 pounds are settled upon it." In 1643, it is directed that 16 pounds yearly should be paid to Mr. William Andrews as the town's first schoolmaster. The curriculum of the day included the alphabet, writing (penmanship), and arithmetic, as well as some religious instruction. The same act declared that "the Town shall pay for the schooling of the poor and for all deficiencies" and required that all families that were able contribute the equivalent of a quarter bushel of corn for the maintenance of the school (Stuart, 1853, pp. 161-63; Collier interview).

Hartford's first schoolhouse was most likely a shabby and hastily built affair, as by 1648 the Town was required to replace it with a new one. The Town made an appropriation of 40 pounds and requested that individuals contribute as well so that it could contain greater conveniences and comfort (Stuart, 1853, p. 163).

Between 1636 and 1650, the colonial government passed acts as needed relevant to the schooling of the childen of the colony. In 1650, for the first time, an actual code was compiled but even this existed only in "hand script" and was not published until the nineteenth century. This code required all towns to establish schools and further ordered that towns with more than 50 families were to establish "higher schools." In effect, the central government had mandated that education be made available to all of its children (Collier interview).

The Code of 1650, Conecticut's first school law, decreed that "all towns with 50 families should employ a teacher to instruct children to read and write." Initially, church societies played an important role in determining school policy, including the location of schools, the length of the school term, the choice of teachers, and the cost to the individual student. "Rotation of school location was not uncommon," and the amount of time assigned to a particular location was frequently dependent upon its wealth. While students could follow the school from one location to another, most only attended when it was nearby. By the middle of the eighteenth century, most church societies ended the rotation policy and established permanent schools; in 1795, "legislation terminated church control over education and placed it in the hands of school committees or

selectmen who tended to economize when making educational policy"
(Stave and Palmer, 1991, p. 96).

According to the Code of 1650, towns of 100 householders were
required to set up "a Grammar School whose Master shall be able to
to fit Scholars for the University" to be sure that men have "a
knowledge of the Scriptures" and that "Learning should not be buried
in the Graves of our Forefathers." A particular benefit of study of the
Scriptures was to insure against the influence of Satan; more
immediately, it would enable graduates to be eligible for the
fellowship to Harvard College, for which contribution was also
mandated. This special grammar school received a legacy of 400
pounds by order of Governor Hopkins, "in order that 'hopeful youths'
might be encouraged 'in a way of learning, for the public service in
future times.'" The "Hartford Grammar School" continued through
the nineteenth century as the primary high school for the City of
Hartford (Stuart, 1853, pp. 307-9).

Between 1650 and 1675, the Town also continued to maintain
its Common School. Parents were required to provide "either a little
load of wood or three shillings toward procuring it," rooms for
scholars were hired from John Church and others, and at least four
schoolteachers--William Andrews, Samuel Fitch, William Pitkin, and
a Mr. Davis--were placed on the payroll. Further, it was made a
duty of the Selectmen "to see that children and apprentices received a
proper education." To fulfill this responsibility, they were permitted,
if necessary, to remove the children from their homes, if their parents
had proven themselves uncooperative, and place the children in foster
homes until the girls were 18 and the boys 21. The children were to
be instructed so that "they might be fitted for 'some honest, lawful
labor or employment, and not become rude, stubborn and unruly.'" At
least once a week, this education was to include catechism and
principles of religion (Stuart, 1853, pp. 310-11).

Responsibility for education gradually shifted from towns to the
individual parishes within the town and, in 1712, parish control was
made statutory. These parishes or ecclesiastical societies were not
synonymous with the churches but rather were constituted as all of
the families that lived within that geographical area that had not
withdrawn from the church fellowship in order to join an Anglican or
Quaker church. All of the children residing within the district,
whatever their religion, were expected to attend the public schools.
Each parish constructed a school building that could house 40
students; as the population of the parish increased, it split into
districts so that each district would have one school. However,
parishes in sparsely populated areas might combine into one district,
and each parish would then have its own elected "visitor" who was
the equivalent of today's superintendent of schools or member of the
board of education (Collier interview).

Beginning in the late 1730s, as the result of the colony's selling seven northwestern Connecticut towns to private individuals and that money being put into a colony fund, the colonial government had the means to begin to offer financial support to the school districts, which had for most purposes superseded in importance the parish structure. The remainder of school funding came from a tax levied by the school districts on the residents of the district (Collier interview).

In the period before the Revolutionary War, the City of Hartford was both a bustling river port and an area with extensive farming operations. Geographically, its boundaries extended as far west as Farmington and to the east, across the Connecticut River, it included what are now the towns of East Hartford and Manchester. The total land area was 86 square miles, and the majority of its 5000 inhabitants were concentrated in the area between the west bank of the river and Asylum Hill (Grant, 1986, p. 9).

The War of Independence had a disastrous effect upon the city's economy. The troops of both General Washington and those of his French allies placed insatiable demands for provisions on the area while its port was commercially idle. The virtually impoverished state's merchants and sea captains wanted to restore the once prosperous maritime trade. Although they reopened their warehouses and readied their vessels, much of the trade had been taken over by foreign ships, and the British began to dump goods on the American market as part of their strategy to dominate overseas commerce. The War of 1812 subsequently created further havoc with shipping and trade (Grant, 1986, pp. 9, 12).

The inefficiency of the local government exacerbated the economic difficulties. Police protection was insufficient, and the streets, highways, and wharves were in need of significant repair. Business leaders determined that the only solution was "to obtain control of the situation by petitioning the Legislature for incorporation as a city." The well-known schoolmaster, Noah Webster, was an ally in the cause, while the farmers of the community felt the idea offered no benefit to them. In December of 1783, incorporation proponents were encouraged when East Hartford separated into a new township; rural opposition was now significantly weakened (Grant, 1986, p. 9).

In the May, 1784 session of the Legislature, Hartford, as well as Middletown, New Haven, New London, and Norwich, were granted city charters. Hartford's new boundaries covered only the areas already settled and were reduced to 1700 acres. "Until 1896, Hartford operated with two governments--one for the city and one for the town" (Grant, 1986, p. 10).

The first ordinances enacted by the new city were directed at "keeping livestock from roaming the muddy streets untended" and granting permission for "a lottery to erect new wharves at the foot of State Street." Hartford's wealthiest merchant and most influential citizen, Jeremiah Wadsworth, spearheaded the city's return to prosperity. In 1788, he served as the principal organizer of the Hartford Woolen Manufactory, the first mill of its type in the United States. Although the quality of its goods was not competitive and the factory survived for only seven and a half years, it was an important milestone in the development of the city. Wadsworth also promoted Hartford's first banking institution and engaged in an insurance partnership, the beginnings of the city's preeminance as a financial center (Grant, 1986, pp. 10-12).

In 1795, the State sold the Western Reserve (which became the State of Ohio in 1803) for $1.2 million, enabling the State of Connecticut to provide far more monies to the local school districts. At about this same time, because numerous Baptists, Quakers, Methodists, and Anglicans (who were now called Episcopalians) had joined the Congregationalists in the State, there was objection to the Congregationalist ecclesiastic societies operating the schools. In response, their title was changed to school societies; their functions and geographic districting remained the same, as did their direct relationship to the state government. The Constitutional Convention of 1818 disestablished the Congregational Church and allowed other Christian churches to flourish, although anti-Catholic sentiment prevailed through much of the nineteenth century; Jews were granted similar privileges in 1842 (Collier interview; Grant, 1986, p. 13).

In 1819, the port city of Hartford had somewhat more than 6000 inhabitants living on 38 unpaved streets. The city limits were extended four times between 1820 and 1850 and the population doubled to 17,500. When the city was then divided into six wards, the influence of the new and numerous Irish immigrants increased significantly. When elections had been at-large, the native-born population, which outnumbered the foreign-born by four to one, had prevailed. With the ward system, an alderman and four councilmen were elected from each of the six wards, and the Sixth Ward in 1851 elected the first Irish councilman. In 1853 and 1854, Irish voters helped the Democrats capture the mayoralty (Grant, 1969, p. 15; Grant, 1986, p. 14).

West Hartford became a separate town in 1854, and Hartford achieved its present size of 18.4 square miles, slightly larger than Bridgeport but smaller than New Haven. Thomas Seymour was chosen as mayor, a post he held for 28 years, the longest term in the city's history. During that period, he also served first in the lower and then in the upper house of the State Legislature and as chief judge of the Hartford County Court (Grant, 1986, p. 10).

The first half of the nineteenth century witnessed a flood of immigration and the arrival of the railroad. Hartford's business community recognized the opportunity for the city to become an important manufacturing center. The Jewell Belting Company opened in 1845, and by 1860 it was the leading industrial-belting producer in the world. Bidwell, Pitkin & Company, manufacturers of boilers, steam engines, feed-water heaters, and building heating equipment, was established in 1849. Sharps Rifle Manufacturing Company set up shop the following year and ultimately produced 140,000 rifles for the Union Army. By far the largest pre-Civil War industrial operation was the Colt Patent Firearms Manufacturing Company which, after a failed start in Paterson, New Jersey in 1836, moved first to Hamden, next to Pearl Street and then to Grove Street in Hartford before finally establishing permanent quarters in the South Meadows. The plant, which Samuel Colt constructed in 1855 to produce the revolver he invented two decades earlier when he was 21, was at the time probably the largest individually owned factory in the world (Weaver, 1982, p. 78).

The end of the Civil War marked a time of growing prosperity for Hartford's business community. Of its population of almost 40,000, half were employed in one of several hundred factories. The city bustled with carriages and horse cars, and numerous smokestacks gave evidence of its productiveness. In 1868, the tanneries and hovels surrounding the Park River were replaced by Bushnell Park. When Mark Twain made his first visit to the city that year, he was so impressed with this city that enjoyed the highest per capita wealth in the United States that he noted, "I think that this is the best built and handsomest town that I have ever seen. They call New England the land of steady habits, and I can see the evidence about me that it was not named amiss. . . . This is the centre of Connecticut wealth" (Grant, 1986, p. 16).

Hartford's power structure was dominated by insurance industry leaders, such as James G. Batterson, president of The Travelers Insurance Company, and Morgan G. Bulkeley, head of Aetna Life. The city's reliable name in the insurance industry was the result of its good fortune in having insured only a small portion of those suffering casualties in fires in New York City in 1834 and again in 1845 and in Chicago in 1871. Companies responsible for greater numbers of policies were unable to honor their commitments, and the Hartford carriers looked very good in comparison. Life insurance followed fire insurance and, a century later, Hartford was home to 39 companies with worldwide assets of 46 billion dollars (Grant, 1986, p. 16; Weaver, pp. 84-89).

Beginning in 1701, Hartford and New Haven alternated as the site of Connecticut's annual legislative sessions. Hartford was eager to become the sole capital and in March, 1872, the city purchased the Washington Street campus of Trinity College for $600,000 and offered the state a half million dollars toward the construction of a new capitol. The following year, the state's voters approved a constitutional amendment making Hartford the permanent capital. Although construction of the building took significantly longer and cost infinitely more than was originally planned, when the capitol finally was ready for occupancy in 1879, the public's reaction was ecstatic (Grant, 1986, pp. 18-19).

Between 1795 and the 1850s, the school districts had achieved statutory existence. They became the corporate entities recognized by law and the repositories of school administration for the State, which controls and has responsibility for the education of its children. Although the districts were not legally autonomous, *de facto* they became so and the courts recognized them as carrying out these functions and having the responsibility to do so. Rather than contacting the school societies, the State sent its directives to the district. This would occur when a district did something opposed to State regulation, but more likely when it did not fulfill its obligations (Collier interview).

From 1830 to 1850, reformers had attempted to consolidate districts in the hope of improving the quality of education. According to Christopher Collier, the Connecticut State Historian, while prior to 1830 Connecticut was looked upon as a leader in public education, after that time, "it was a disaster." Local autonomy enabled those areas unenthusiastic about raising taxes to grossly underfund their schools, and those who served as visitors could employ nepotism in the selection of teachers. Wealthy parents sent their children to private school, and at one point in many areas more children were enrolled in the private elementary schools than in those that were public; secondary schools were almost exclusively private (Collier interview).

While some who advocated for public schooling had an educated citizenry as their goal, others, such as the preacher Horace Bushnell and *The Hartford Courant* editor Theodore Dwight, saw the public schools as the best way to absorb "the foreign-born into the Anglo-Saxon culture through a Protestant-based curriculum." The Catholics responded by setting up their own schools; by 1854, almost 700 Catholic boys were students at St. Patrick's free school and two others in Hartford. When John M. Niles founded *The Hartford Times* and used his position to promote the Democratic Party and defend new immigrants, battle lines were drawn between the two major political parties, the two most popular religions, and the two city newspapers. With Niles' support, the Democrats in Connecticut nearly tripled their membership (Grant, 1986, pp. 13-14).

The year 1882 marked the apex of immigration of northern and western Europeans to Hartford. Seven years later, the Connecticut Bible Society and six students from the Hartford Theological Seminary documented the city's ethnic composition at the end of the nineteenth century. The city's total population was found to be 48,179. Of that number just under half, 23,154, were noted as "American," of that number 1191 were reported to be colored; the Irish numbered 15,757; Germans, 3060; English, 1676; Scotch, 804; French, 798; Italian, 614; Swedish, 444; Danish, 367; Russian, 278;

Polish, 65; Chinese, 31; Romanian and Bohemian, 22 each; and Swiss, Norwegian, Hungarian, Spanish, Austrian, Portuguese, Greek, Welch, Indian, Bulgarian, Hindu, Maltese, and Hollanders totalled 85. More than a dozen religious beliefs were represented as well, of which 25,011 were Protestant, 19,309, Catholic, and 1158, Jewish (Grant, 1986, p. 69).

Italians outnumbered all other immigrant groups during the first quarter of the twentieth century, and they concentrated their residence in the areas of Market Street and the South End. They worked in factories and as stonemasons, bricklayers, shoemakers, bakers, and "mom and pop" restauranteurs. Many families whose men began as laborers progressed to become owners of heavy construction businesses. Similar success stories were replicated among other immigrant groups (Grant, 1986, pp. 72-73).

In the mid-1850s, the State passed permissive legislation that allowed districts to consolidate within towns if all were agreeable, but few so chose. In 1866, the State went a step further by allowing towns to consolidate if a majority of districts within them were agreeable. Some towns did in fact reorganize, but, until the end of the century, when approximately half the towns in the State had consolidated, as elections changed town officers, towns might go back and forth depending upon the mood of the voters and taxpayers. In the case of Hartford, there was never a firm decision to consolidate. When West Hartford consolidated, the Prospect district continued to have children from both that community and Hartford (Collier interview).

In the case of Hartford, as with the other major cities in the State, high schools, although situated in a district, were run by special high school committees. Students might come from as far as 30 miles away, and some might board with friends or relatives during the week. At first, out-of-town students had to pay tuition. By the beginning of the twentieth century, however, when high school attendance became compulsory, if a town did not have a high school, it was required to pay the tuition for the out-of-district students (Collier interview).

In 1909, all but 15 of the larger towns were required by the State to consolidate. Each consolidated town now had a school committee or board of education. Towns such as Hartford, which did not consolidate until 1940, or Middletown, which was the last town to do so, in 1950, continued to have a visitor or a board of visitors. At that point, Hartford had three school committees: one for the high school, one supervised the districts, and one served the school in the Prospect Street area. Originally, there had also been one for black students, but that committee had been eliminated after 1868 "when the Legislature finally passed a law requiring all children to attend their own district school regardless of race" (Collier interview; Grant, 1986, p. 60).

Although all of the students residing in Hartford were supposed to go to Hartford schools, many went to schools in other towns if they were closer, and students from other towns went to school in Hartford for the same reason. Parental preferences played a role as well, and tuition exchanges were made where appropriate. By the 1940s, parents paid the tuition charges if the towns were unwilling (Collier interview).

Vastly greater participation in secondary education began to take place at the beginning of the twentieth century, as well. In 1935, legislation was passed to allow for the first regional high school. Previously, the State had mandated that the towns provide transportation to a high school and pay the tuition for that school. Now, rural areas were permitted to build their own high schools and the tuitions would be paid by the town; the State was to reimburse the transportation costs (Collier interview).

At the same time, and especially after World War II, there was a tremendous increase in the amount of State involvement in the day-to-day administration of the schools. Prior to the early 1900s, teacher certification was voluntary and could be done by the same school committee that hired the faculty members. Subsequently, certification requirements became much more stringent. Graduation from normal school, the first of which was established in New Britain in 1849, was desirable (Collier interview).

Beginning in the 1880s, the State added drug and alcohol education to the requirements that schools teach reading, writing, and arithmetic. At the turn of the century, with an increasing influx of non-English speaking immigrants, the State began mandating the Americanization of civics, Connecticut history, celebration of Arbor Day and Flag Day, and the care of animals. In addition, regulations were enforced regarding the number of hours of the school day as well as the number of school days in the year. Henry Bernard, education theorist and administrator, who served as a Whig representative in the State Legislature, spearheaded the reform movement, which was effected in 1837 but then dismantled by the Democrats two years later when they achieved majority status. When the Whigs returned to power at the next election, Barnard's reforms were reinstituted. By the late nineteenth century, the State Board of Education was recommending legislation, supervising requirements, and bringing suits against districts that were not fulfilling their mandates, such as the provision of transportation to regional high schools (Collier interview).

Until the 1940s, the black presence in Connecticut was very limited. A column in the weekly *Connecticut Courant* during 1784 noted that the General Assembly had provided for the gradual emancipation of the 6500 slaves then in the state, although the ten dollar reward for the capture of a runaway slave was not addressed. The black population peaked at approximately three percent around

1820 and slowly diminished until about 1940, when there was an exponential leap during the next 20 years. Despite the small number of blacks statewide, there was a presence felt in the cities, since approximately 90 percent of those blacks lived in less than half a dozen of Connecticut's urban areas. Blacks were not permitted to purchase land, which made it virtually impossible for them to own farms. Thus, the jobs available encouraged them to congregate in cities. They became teamsters, and riots resulted when the Irish determined to take over those jobs. Many blacks also became sailors, frequently on whaling vessels. They congregated in port cities such as New London, Norwich, and New Haven. Primarily, they were involved in service occupations, especially as domestic servants (Grant, 1986, p. 10; Collier interview).

Hartford's first black residents had all been slaves who originally lived with their owners, either in the same house or in a small servants' building adjoining the main house. As Connecticut's "gradual emancipation" laws went into effect, the freed blacks had to find other accommodations. Most, having little skills and even less funds, found cheap rentals in the least desirable parts of the city: on an east-side industrial street, near the tanneries, or in other small, emerging ghettos. The neighborhoods, which became known as "Hardscrabble," "New Guinea," and "Sinking Fund," had an excess of population and a shortage of sanitary facilities and pure water (Weaver, 1982, p. 90).

By the 1820s, black-owned tailor and cobbler shops were located in the Talcott Street section and on South Green. Thirty years later, they had been joined by scores of similar businesses, and the area was home to those blacks who enjoyed relative prosperity. The Hartford city directories reflected the segregation of the time. While the black businesses were listed in the white directories, the residences, which frequently were at the same address, were listed in a separate black section. The lack of enfranchisement and the prohibition regarding securing employment in government service further emphasized the segregation of Hartford's African-American residents (Weaver, 1982, pp. 90-91).

While anti-slavery sentiment had been considerable in Hartford from the time of the Revolutionary War, the city was not particularly hospitable to blacks. Churches enforced segregated seating; blacks were so uncomfortable in white schools that they requested schools of their own; and although Hartford participated in the underground railway, it was to help blacks continue on to Canada or return to Africa. The intent was not to make them feel at home in Connecticut (Weaver, 1982, pp. 91-92).

The low status of blacks continued into the twentieth century, when their numbers doubled to nearly 30,000 in the state between 1910 and 1930, with Hartford and New Haven having the greatest proportion. Employment opportunities primarily remained relegated to servant and laborer positions. No matter how excluded and despised immigrants might feel, for insecure whites, blacks remained available to be seen as being a notch or two lower (Jeffries, 1979, p. 13).

With the beginning of World War II, more blacks came north to work in the defense industries. While "firms still did not train, place, pay, or promote blacks on an equal basis with whites, especially in skilled positions . . . black men and women did get more 'dirty, heavy, hot jobs' on the production lines." In 1941, a large interracial group was established in Hartford "to combat discrimination in housing, employment and job training." Blacks attempted to initiate a "Double V" theme, connecting victory over the Axis powers abroad with victory over racial discrimination at home. Church organizations, federal agencies, and some state labor and political leaders joined blacks in campaigning against job discrimination (Jeffries, 1979, pp. 111-12).

Early in 1943, the Reverend Dr. John C. Jackson, pastor of Hartford's Union Baptist Church, was attacked and beaten by two white men while traveling on a train in Alabama. Despite wide press coverage, the U.S. Justice Department took no action. In the summer of 1943, just before the Harlem riots, when 20 blacks assaulted a white policeman in Hartford for apprehending an African-American, the local CIO decided it was time to sponsor a bi-racial conference on racial problems. The meeting urged the mayor to "establish a commission to study the causes of racial friction and to propose ways to eliminate tension and to prevent further outbursts." In the charged atmosphere, then Mayor Dennis O'Connor was more receptive than his predecessor Tom Spellacy to establishing an Inter-Racial Committee. On June 29, the Connecticut Civil Rights Commission was created. It was the first in the nation, and Dr. Jackson was appointed a member (Grant, 1986, p. 78; Jeffries, 1979, pp. 152-56).

In 1944, the Hartford Common Council, following the much-publicized strike of white transportation workers in Philadelphia who objected to black promotions, "adopted companion resolutions condemning the strikers' anti-Negro motivation and urging the Hartford Police Board to immediately consider the appointment of six blacks." The Police Board evaded the proposal, and a 1944 study by the National Urban League showed with "depressing clarity" that Hartford was rife with discrimination in public and private employment and in public and private housing, and that the frightful conditions in the North End ghetto were the result of "the unwillingness of official and civic leadership to recognize the existence and urgency of problems facing the community." (Jeffries, 1979, pp. 152-56).

Blacks were always permitted to go to district schools. There were no whites-only schools; however, those blacks who attended the district schools were generally treated extremely poorly. They were ostracized, and being seated next to them was used as a form of punishment for white students. In the early nineteenth century, black parents requested that there be special black schools, and, by 1830, such schools existed in Hartford and New Haven to which white students could not go and for which black teachers were hired. However, since the district schools were almost always closer, the children frequently preferred to go to them, and the black schools ultimately failed. The issue was totally laid to rest when, in April, 1868, the Hartford Town Council passed an ordinance requiring all black children to attend the black school; when the General Assembly met the following autumn, it voided that ordinance, and, from then on, it has never been permissible to establish separate schools on the basis of race (Collier interview).

While the State forbid towns to set up special schools for blacks, it indirectly encouraged separation of the races by supporting the building of regionalized suburban high schools. Suburban students, who had previously attended high school within the city, were removed from the urban facilities when two or three towns ringing the city, with state assistance, built a new inter-district high school in one of their own towns. When the State operated its own regional technical schools, they encompassed much greater geographical areas, generally including a central city (Collier interview).

By 1970, 45 percent of Hartford's school children were black, and the city's black residents were able to exercise some political power. This was particularly evident in 1981 with the election of Thurman L. Milner as mayor, the first black to achieve that position in New England. The Urban League, the NAACP, and the West Indian Social Club were particularly influential in advancing blacks economically and politically (Grant, 1986, p. 78).

Between 1973 and 1983, black elementary students decreased from 46.8 percent to 42.1 percent of the total, while black high school students increased only slightly from 48.9 to 49.5 percent. However, in the ten years after 1975, the total number of black students in the Hartford system decreased by ten percent, while the contiguous suburb of Bloomfield saw its minority student population reach 65 percent. Meanwhile, Hispanics from Puerto Rico, Cuba, and Central and South America had been migrating to Hartford since the 1940s to neighborhoods in both the North and South Ends. Between 1973 and 1983, Hispanic elementary school students increased from 25.8 percent to 42.6 percent of total enrollment, while high school students rose from 18.3 percent to 36.1 percent. By 1986, about 20 percent of Hartford's residents were Hispanic (Grant, 1986, pp. 79-80).

The first Puerto Rican family arrived in Connecticut from New York in 1844 and settled in Bridgeport. It is not known why the

Table 6.1
Hartford Population by Race: SMSA and City, 1970 and 1980;
County and City, 1990

	1970		1980		1990	
	N	%	N	%	N	%
TOTAL CITY	158,017		136,392		139,739	
WHITE	111,862	71%	68,603	50%	55,869	40%
BLACK	44,091	28%	46,186	34%	54,338	39%
HISPANIC	N/A		27,898	20%	44,137	32%
SMSA OR COUNTY	663,891		726,114		851,783	
WHITE	10,041	92%	634,985	87%	711,315	84%
BLACK	50,518	8%	61,892	9%	87,255	10%
HISPANIC	N/A		34,207	5%	71,575	8%

Note: Categories may not total to 100% because of other groups and because Hispanics may also be listed as White or Black.

Source: U.S. Census, 1970, 1980, 1990.

wealthy sugar plantation owner Jose de Rivera and his family left Puerto Rico and then New York, why they chose Bridgeport, or where they went when they sold their house in 1855. After 1917, when Puerto Ricans first became American citizens, "they began to migrate to the mainland in large numbers." The Puerto Rican population in Connecticut increased dramatically between 1960 and 1970 and subsequently. In the former year, there were 15,247 Puerto Ricans in the state, ten years later the number was at least 88,361. By 1990, the number was at least 147,842, an increase from 2.8 to 4.5 percent of the population. Puerto Ricans currently comprise approximately two-thirds of the Hispanic population of the state (Glasser, 1992, pp. 1-4).

Hartford has consistently had the largest Puerto Rican population in Connecticut, both in absolute numbers and in proportion to other residents. Referred to in a 1954 *Hartford Courant* article as the "last migration," Puerto Ricans in Hartford numbered 24,615 in 1980 and 38,176 in 1990, increasing from 18.4 to 27.3 percent of the city's population. One of the most prominent Puerto Ricans has been Maria Sanchez, who, in 1954, came from Comerio, as did a disproportionate number of Hartford's Puerto Ricans. She worked for

14 years in a meat-packing plant in New Britain before opening a newsstand in the Clay Hill neighborhood. "She was instrumental in getting a Spanish-speaking priest for the Sacred Heart Church, and helped establish many of Hartford's Latino organizations." In 1973, Maria Sanchez became the first Puerto Rican to be elected to the Hartford Board of Education. "At the time of her death in 1989, Sanchez was, along with Juan Figueroa, one of the first Hispanic state representatives from Hartford" (Glasser, 1992, pp. 5, 33, 40-41, 43-44; *La Genta/La Casa*, undated, p. 1).

The dramatic advance in Hartford's Latino population coincided with an overall population decline in the city. Hartford's 177,136 residents in 1950 had diminished to 136,392 by 1980. "While the white population increasingly moved out to the suburbs in this period, Puerto Ricans migrating in found themselves sharing living space, jobs, and schools with African-Americans migrating up from the southern United States, other United States urban areas, and the Caribbean." Puerto Ricans originally settled in the Clay Hill area, "a neighborhood of older housing bounded by railroad lines and major transportation routes. As the population grew in the 1960s and 1970s, it spread out beyond the 'tunnel' to the South Green area, on the southern edge of downtown." Redevelopment of the area, in 1973, forced residents to reluctantly relocate, primarily to Frog Hollow. The loss of 10,000 of the city's 56,000 housing units between 1970 and 1980 further exacerbated the situation (Glasser, 1992, pp. 50, 53, 54, 55).

The Puerto Rican community has established a number of non-profit organizations, including the Community Renewal Team, begun in 1964, to provide social services that were felt to be insufficiently available through the government. The issue of bilingual education was of particular concern during the early 1970s. Although a 1968 federal law enabled schools to begin to establish bilingual programs, the Hartford school system was resistent. A class action suit, *Ramos v. Gaines*, brought by the Puerto Rican community in 1976, finally compelled the Hartford Board of Education, in 1978, to implement the program that ultimately became a model for the entire country. Gladys Hernandez, a teacher at the Ann Street School, was particularly instrumental in developing the program, as was Edna Soler, the program's first director (Glasser, 1992, pp. 58-59; La Genta/La Casa, 1992, p. 4).

In the 1960s, the Greater Hartford Chamber of Commerce was the spearhead for Hartford's power structure when an attempt was made to find a regional solution to the city's problems. The organization, Hartford Process, was formed and funded by a consortium of Hartford businesses. In the mid-1970s, its development arm, Devco, attempted to create a new town in the eastern Connecticut town of Coventry. However, the rural community was totally lacking in enthusiasm to become a part of the solution to the city's problems, and the likelihood of a long court battle coupled with a declining economy discouraged the developers from pursuing the project (Grant, 1986, p. 21; Stave and Stave, unpublished paper in possession of author).

The discourse regarding integrated education was energized when Gerald Tirozzi was appointed State Commissioner of Education in 1983. Dr. Tirozzi, who began his career as a teacher in the West Haven school system, subsequently served as teacher, principal, and guidance counselor in New Haven before becoming superintendent of that system. His most dramatic contribution at the state level, during his eight-year tenure, was to draw attention to the increasing segregation of Connecticut's schools (Interview with Dr. Gerald N. Tirozzi, September 29, 1992).

Three reports particularly significant to the question of integrated schools were prepared during Dr. Tirozzi's commissionership. The first, *A Report on Racial/Ethnic Equity and Desegregation in Connecticut's Public Schools*, was presented to the Connecticut State Board of Education in 1988. The major premise of this report, submitted by the Committee on Racial Equity, was that "segregation is educationally, morally and legally wrong." The report went on to detail the extent of segregation within Connecticut's schools, noting that while "minorities constitute 11% of Connecticut's population at large," they "constitute over 21% of the state's student enrollment. As these children become adults, the growth in the minority population will accelerate." The report continued that "over 60% of the minority students are enrolled in the five largest school districts," and that at that time Hartford, Bridgeport, and New Haven's minority enrollments exceeded 80 percent. The report noted that "the state's minority population [was] growing by 1.5% each year, with the Hispanic segment increasing the most rapidly" (Connecticut State Department of Education, January, 1988, pp. 1-2).

The Committee on Racial Equity presented four recommendations for action:

1. That the state through administrative and legislative means, endorse the concept of 'collective responsibility' for desegregating the public schools of Connecticut.
2. That the state, through the State Board of Education, make available substantial financial incentives to school districts that plan and implement voluntary interdistrict programs and advance desegregation, racial balance and integrated education in Connecticut's public schools.
3. That the State Department of Education provide technical assistance to school districts in the development and implementation of plans to achieve and maintain desegregated schools.
4. That the State Department of Education undertake broad-based planning with other agencies concerned with housing,

transportation and other factors that contribute to segregation
in the public schools, to find ways to counter adverse influences
on integration. (*Report on Racial/Ethnic Equity*, 1988, pp. 11,
18-19)

In discussing how these recommendations should be implemented,
the report advocated the concept of voluntary desegregation. Citing
the research of Christine Rossell in *The Carrot or the Stick in School
Desegregation Policy*, the report argues that states that desegregate
will be better positioned to meet the demands of the next century.
Additionally, according to Rossell, voluntary desegregation is more
likely to result in "interracial exposure" rather than merely "racial
balance." Voluntary magnet schools were also praised as effective
agents for desegregation (*Report on Racial/Ethnic Equity*, 1988, p.
21).

The January, 1988 report was followed in April, 1989 with a
further study entitled, *Quality and Integrated Education: Options for
Connecticut*. This document was designed to further emphasize the
theory of the earlier report by declaring that "a multicultural
environment is an irreplacable component of quality education." It
described activities taking place at that time as well as other
initiatives proposed to further that goal. Among the former was the
Interdistrict Cooperative Grant program, begun in 1985, to address
the impact of declining school enrollments and the economic benefits
of voluntary collaboration among school districts. In 1988, the
program's emphasis was refocused on quality, integrated education
and had spread a minuscule $239,000 among 60 participating
districts. The "Next Steps" advocated increased funding, creating a
corporate component, and facilitating student and teacher exchanges
between cities and suburbs (*Quality and Integrated Education:
Options for Connecticut*, 1989, pp. 1, 8-11).

Other options noted as "Promising Beginnings" included using
remedial summer school programs as means for integration at 47
sites serving urban and suburban students from 64 districts,
developing curriculum initiatives that promote a respect for
differences among people and recognize the pluralistic nature of
society, and expanding professional development "to prepare
educators to respond constructively to students with diverse cultural
orientations and different learning styles." Vocational-technical
schools were identified as being among the first magnet schools, "the
state's first public 'schools of choice,'" by having "a specific program
emphasis unlike other public high schools" and by "draw[ing]
students from a number of school districts." In 1989, there were 22
such schools covering 44 occupational fields (*Quality and Integrated
Education: Options for Connecticut*, 1989, pp. 14-22).

One of the earliest and most enduring programs has been Project
Concern. In operation since 1966, it "is often cited by researchers as

one of the more successful integration efforts in the country."
According to statute, this intercommunity program for disadvantaged
children is designed to "improve or accelerate the education of
children for whom educational achievement has been or is being
restricted by economic, social, or environmental disadvantages."
Hartford students, when they begin school, can volunteer to be a part
of the pool from which participants are randomly selected for the
program; those chosen are then educated in a neighboring suburban
community, and federal, state, and local monies combine to pay for
tuition, transportation, and administrative costs (*Quality and
Integrated Education: Options for Connecticut*, 1989, p. 12).

At its peak in the late 1970s, 1500 students representing 13
communities and six non-public schools were participating. Suburban
receiving towns benefited by being able to provide their students
"with a multiracial and multicultural environment." The program
was the first response to the 1964 Harvard Report, which stated that
"Hartford could no longer solve its educational problems alone but
must look toward 'metropolitan cooperation' if children were to
receive quality education" (*Quality and Integrated Education: Options
for Connecticut*, 1989, p. 12).

According to Mary Carroll, who began her career as a fourth grade
teacher in South Windsor in 1964 and who has been with the
program since its inception two years later (when she had two of the
first Project Concern children in her class), the design is vital to
preparing children for an integrated life in the twenty-first century.
Evaluations of the program, done between 1976 and 1980, describe
a number of benefits in both academic achievement and social and
academic attitude. Significant reading growth was noted, particularly
at the second, fourth, and sixth grade levels, and children and
parents perceived a friendly relationship between the urban and
suburban students in the classroom, although these friendships
might not extend out of the classroom. By the 1988-89 school year,
the number of participating students was halved to 747 in 12
communities; West Hartford, with 253 Project Concern students, had
the largest program (Interview with Mary Carroll, October 6, 1992;
Iwanicki, 1976, pp. 73-76; *Quality and Integrated Education: Options
for Connecticut*, 1989, p. 12).

The 1989 *Quality and Integrated Education* report praised the
"Promising Beginnings" of programs already underway or well into
the planning phase and advocated their continuation and/or
expansion. It then noted that new initiatives were needed and
suggested three: "the development of more magnet schools,
interdistrict collaboration in building new schools and renovating
existing buildings for joint use, and a campaign to recruit more
minority teachers and paraprofessionals." It was suggested that
magnet schools expand to include instructional as well as curricular
innovation. Incentive plans should be developed to fund the magnet

schools, and the creation of a Blue Ribbon Task Force was advised to develop ways to promote the schools (*Quality and Integrated Education: Options for Connecticut*, 1989, pp. 23, 26).

The Educational Equity Study Committee advocated that "the school construction grant program provide incentives for collaborative building projects between city and suburban districts." It called for a comprehensive study of enrollment patterns to relate students' economic and racial backgrounds to the locations selected for new school construction. Cost effectiveness and the promise of advancing quality and integrated education would be the two criteria for the selection of new school sites (*Quality and Integrated Education: Options for Connecticut*, 1989, p. 31).

Sensitive to the fact that, in 1989, only six percent of Connecticut's full-time professional staff was minority while one-quarter of its student body was so designated, recruitment of minority teachers has been seen as an important goal. Appropriate role models are desirable for students, while diverse colleagues enrich the majority teaching staff as well. The centerpiece of this proposal was to "pair two paraprofessionals, each of whom would work in a school one-half year and take courses in a teacher preparation program for the other half-year." Both private and public funding would be sought to enable them to remain on full salary while taking courses, so that there would be no financial burden on the paraprofessional. In Hartford, 80 percent of its paraprofessionals are minority and most live in the community; therefore, it was the Committee's assumption that there would be a high probability that many would remain in the same neighborhood once their training was completed. However, almost two years later, in the *Report of the Governor's Commission on Quality and Integrated Education*, the shortage of minority faculty continues to be noted. "Minority group members represent 6.3 percent of the certified school staff, compared to almost 25 percent of the student enrollment, and that gap, too, has been increasing. At the same time, 'minority teachers are more heavily concentrated in the five large cities than minority students are. The large cities employ 70.6 percent of the minority group teachers; the small towns, just over one percent.'" (*Quality and Integrated Education: Options for Connecticut*, 1989, pp. 32-33; *Crossing the Bridge to Equality and Excellence*, 1990, p. 6).

The Committee on Quality and Integrated Education noted that their document of April, 1989 was a report and not a plan. All actions recommended were to be voluntary and incremental. Equally important was the need to continue and accelerate the dialogue currently in process. The next step in this dialogue was the establishment of the Governor's Commission on Quality and Integrated Education on September 20, 1989. A membership of 28, representing all facets of Connecticut leadership, was charged with preparing a report by the end of 1990 that would review the

demographic trends responsible for the racial, ethnic, and economic
makeup of Connecticut's public schools; evaluate programs that
foster racial and economic integration in public schools in Connecticut
and other states; identify changes in the current school construction
laws and regulations that would foster integration; "develop
proposals to recruit and retain minorities in the teaching profession";
develop proposals for both intradistrict and interdistrict programs
that promote quality and integrated education; and review current
state funding programs relevant to support proposed integration
programs (*Quality and Integrated Education: Options for Connecticut*,
1989, p. 34; *Crossing the Bridge to Equality and Excellence*, 1990, pp.
2, 35).

The Commission, co-chaired by David G. Carter, President of
Eastern Connecticut State University, and Attorney James P.
Sandler, determined that its first task was to define "quality and
integrated education." There was agreement that early desegregation
efforts, which emphasized physical desegregation, did not always
provide "a quality and integrated education for all students." It was
also agreed that what has come to be called "second generation
programs," which focused on "equal treatment and equal access
within schools," were frequently also deficient. Ultimately, the
Commission defined a quality and integrated education as one that
"should expose students to an integrated student body and faculty
and a curriculum that reflects the heritage of many cultures. It
should also provide all students with equal opportunities to learn
and to achieve equal educational outcomes" (*Crossing the Bridge to
Equality and Excellence*, 1990, p. 3).

The Commission then "set out to determine whether Connecticut
students have the opportunity to obtain a 'quality and integrated
education.'" It was found that growing racial isolation blocked this
goal. "Over 80 percent of the state's minority students cluster in just
16, or 10 percent, of the districts. Seven of these districts
accommodate over 60 percent of our minority students while 140
other districts are more than 90 percent white." Five other factors
were cited as also impeding the goal. These are: lack of minority
faculty, the need for a multicultural curriculum, unequal educational
opportunites, a gap between non-minority and minority achievement
scores, and public attitudes toward integration in public schools
(*Crossing the Bridge to Equality and Excellence*, 1990, pp. 3-10).

In its final report, the Commission developed six findings:

1. Educational opportunity cannot be addressed in isolation and
   every aspect of public policy in every region of the state should
   be linked in the cooperative enterprise of removing barriers to
   achievement and of promoting the common ground that
   strengthen us all as a society.

2. A quality education requires an integrated student body and faculty and a curriculum that reflects the heritage of many cultures.

3. Every student can learn at high levels from a quality and integrated education.

4. A need exists for communities to appreciate and support public education, and for family members and others in the community to involve themselves in the education of Connecticut's youth.

5. Every educator must be trained to teach both a diverse student population and a curriculum that incorporates and honors the diverse cultural and racial heritages.

6. Connecticut needs to attract and employ minority educators. (*Crossing the Bridge to Equality and Excellence*, 1990, p. 12)

While the Commission advocated that work begin immediately to implement its recommendations by having "communities in each and every region of the state . . . join in a cooperative effort over the next year to identify and assess present barriers such as poverty, education, employment, housing, health and transportation which perpetuate inequality, isolation and the lack of greater integration," and then "develop and commit to a cooperative plan of community and regional action," such activity has not yet begun (*Crossing the Bridge to Equality and Excellence*, 1990, p. 12).

Commenting on the committee and its work in an interview on December 2, 1992, President Carter had high praise for the members of the group and for the report that they prepared. He emphasized the committee's preference for voluntary actions, but stated that a mandatory plan should be implemented if such voluntary actions did not occur. President Carter was disappointed that the report's recommendations had not been implemented, but felt that this was the result of fiscal constraints and not because the Governor and the Commissioner of Education lacked commitment to the cause. He noted that "there is a difference between being content and accepting reality. I know that the Governor is committed to eliminating inequities" (Interview with David G. Carter, December 2, 1992).

Although the state did not then formally mount a concentrated effort to pursue integrated education, various programs were undertaken by individual communities working together. The Connecticut Association of Boards of Education compiled an annotated list of such programs in May, 1989, and the Capitol Region Educational Council (CREC) created a similar document in June, 1990. At that time, CREC reported that 15 types of projects were being implemented within the region. Frequently, these activities were taking place in several locations throughout the area, likely with varying degrees of success. For example, the Sister School Project, which "is designed to bring together students and staff from diverse communities" and "through educational encounters . . . share ideas, skills, and experiences . . . to gain an understanding of each

other as well as the material studied," takes place in at least 15
elementary school pairs and five pairs each at the middle and high
school levels (*Creative Approaches for Reducing Racial/Economic
Isolation in Connecticut Schools, PAQIE Inventory of Progress to Reduce
Racial Imbalance*, 1990, pp. 1-9).

Other programs noted in the inventory include those that
concentrate on summer studies and those that emphasize language,
science, or multicultural curriculums. Programs are available for early
childhood and continue through elementary, middle, and high school,
including preparation efforts for students applying to the state
university (*PAQIE Inventory of Progress to Reduce Racial Imbalance*,
1990, pp. 10-25).

It appeared likely that, due to either the *Sheff v. O'Neill* court
action or as the result of other initiatives, more comprehensive
desegregation efforts would be undertaken, and, if so, a broad
spectrum of Connecticut citizens would be involved. Attempting to
assess how such a sample of these likely participants would view the
situation at that time, more than two dozen officials and other
interested parties were interviewed during September and October,
1992 and a few others later in the year. The questionnaire used
appears in Appendix B. Interviewees included the then current and
past State Commissioners of Education, plaintiffs and counsel in the
Sheff v. O'Neill court action, superintendents and other professionals
from local and regional school systems, and representatives from
business and government. A complete list of those surveyed and the
dates of their interviews appear in Appendix D.

There was a widely varied perception regarding the state of race
relations in the Hartford area. While many respondents, including
Bloomfield Superintendent of Schools Paul Copes and Hartford
Superintendent T. Josiha Haig, agreed with former State Education
Commissioner Gerald Tirozzi that these relations "mirrored the rest
of the nation," few identified the situation as being positive. A few
specific areas were singled out for commendation. Eugene Leach,
parent and *Sheff* plaintiff, praised the situation in West Hartford.
Jane Barstow, a Hartford parent, spoke favorably of Hartford's West
End. East Hartford Superintendent Sam Leone felt that race
relations were good in the schools but less so elsewhere in the
community. The State Department of Education's Elliott Williams
concurred for some schools as well.

However, Elizabeth Sheff, mother of the lead plaintiff in the
desegregation suit, categorized race relations in general as "divided
and divisive" and blamed much of the "deteriorating" situation on the
Reagan and Bush administrations, which "made it acceptable to
raise stereotypes and push selfishness over the edge." Linda
Seagraves of Aetna saw relations in Hartford as being "primitive" in
comparison with other parts of the country, such as Atlanta, the
District of Columbia, and California. Other adjectives offered

included "strained" by Manchester Superintendent James Kennedy, "tense" by former Hartford Superintendent Hernan LaFontaine, and "difficult" by Project Concern administrator Mary Carroll.

Opinions were divided as to whether conditions have improved or deteriorated during the past 20 years. While twice as many interviewees felt that things have gotten better rather than worse, others felt that the issue could not be so easily described. Cora Hahn, Trinity Professor of Education and of Korean ancestry, concurred with Mary Carroll that relations between the races had been getting better but then worsened. Professor Hahn agreed with Elizabeth Sheff that the Reagan-Bush presidencies were significantly responsible. She noted that it was not unheard of for Asian-Americans to be the victims of racist remarks on the Trinity campus.

Susan Davis, Vice-President of the Hartford Federation of Teachers, noted that, while there was more discussion of racial matters, there has been little real progress. Professor Edward F. Iwanicki, of the University of Connecticut, who has performed several evaluations of Project Concern, and Mildred Torres-Soto, Director of Planning and Development at Casa de Puerto Rico, each pointed out that the racial makeup of Hartford and especially its schools has been changing. They noted that Puerto Ricans will soon be the most populous group in the city. The high proportion of Latinos in Hartford make the city highly unusual for the northeast where, in general, the largest minority tends to be African-Americans.

Respondents were looking forward to the *Sheff v. O'Neill* court action, which finally came to trial on December 15, 1992. While a fifth of those interviewed were unwilling to profess an opinion as to the outcome, most of the remainder anticipated that, whatever the court finding, the case would be appealed to the State Supreme Court by the losing side. However, it was assumed by more than half of the total that eventually some kind of regional solution would be implemented.

A significant breadth of opinion regarding community reaction was offered by respondents. Most pessimistic was T. Josiha Haig, who predicted that even the hearing of the case would divide the community. Gerald Tirozzi opined that if desegregation was mandated there would be an "exodus" of white families. Susan Davis expected "chaos." On a more positive note, Mary Carroll suggested that the court action will "raise consciousness," and Hernan LaFontaine felt that it will "force a solution." Whatever the outcome, Sam Leone was fairly certain that East Hartford would not be affected, since approximately one-third of the students from within his town's borders are already from minority groups. Linda Seagraves argued strongly that the situation would have to be forced: "integration will not occur voluntarily because housing patterns are too ingrained." She noted that if she had a child attending Hartford schools, she would try to bus him or her out. "Separate but equal cannot exist."

Opinions were equally wide-ranging on the subject of other forces operating to encourage desegregation. Both former Commissioner of Education Tirozzi and then State Education Commissioner Vincent Ferrandino were cited by several respondents as praiseworthy for their efforts on behalf of desegregation. The State Department of Education, itself, was mentioned, as was the regional state education organization, the Capitol Region Education Council (CREC), and its director, John J. Allison, Jr. Also viewed as having an effect on desegregation were the economy; making cost-saving regionalization efforts appealing; and the deteriorating condition of the city and fears for safety, which makes regionalization appear more problematic. Echoing the sentiments of Superintendent Leone of East Hartford, Superintendent James Kennedy of Manchester noted that the rapidly increasing proportion of minorities in his system would soon make it less appropriate for Manchester to participate in regional desegregation programs, asking how worthwhile it really is "to integrate Hartford African-Americans with those from Manchester."

In answer to the question "How important a component of quality education are integrated schools?" most respondents sought to distinguish between offering students the opportunity to acquire academic information and skills and to prepare them to live and work in a diverse and multicultural world. The majority of interviewees felt that knowledge could be transmitted in any well-funded and supplied institution of learning whatever the makeup of the student population; however, to prepare children to function and interrelate with diverse others it was absolutely necessary that schools be integrated. Both John Allison and Eugene Leach used the word "redundant" in discussing the phrase "quality integrated education"; for them and several other respondents, integration is required for a school to be considered of high quality.

Various emphases were projected when respondents were asked to define "integrated schools." While Hernan LaFontaine advocated that a specific numerical mix be required, Gerald Tirozzi was equally insistent that numbers could not be the primary basis for measurement. Elizabeth Sheff offered one of the more comprehensive definitions, suggesting that there must be "opportunities for people of all races and classes to interact, a teaching staff that also reflects the same diversity," and activities that have children interrelating and "not just sitting together." Lloyd Calvert, who has held important positions in several area systems, including Windsor, Hartford, and West Hartford and is currently serving as a consultant to the Attorney-General's Office, added that the term should mean "an acceptance of differences." He continued that a sign that schools have truly been integrated will be "when we don't talk about it anymore."

Continuing the discussion, Linda Seagraves noted that integration must include a mixture of minority and majority cultures. "But, just mixing blacks and Puerto Ricans is not integration." She added that "if blacks and Puerto Ricans didn't feel so bad about themselves, it wouldn't matter if schools were integrated." She stated further that "socio-economics are as important as race and that people value themselves by measuring their financial worth. Blacks can be just as discriminatory as anyone else regarding geographic origin or economic class." Superintendent Kennedy felt that "a feeling of comfort on the part of all students" was also required, as was a need for "all students to feel that their contributions were equally valued."

Susie Hinton, for several years principal of Hartford's Noah Webster School and currently principal of the SAND Everywhere School, attended segregated schools in her native South Carolina, where she felt that she received a good education. According to Ms. Hinton, "integrated schools are not just people." Equally important are "curriculum, approaches, and the whole process of education." During her segregated, southern education, she "developed self-esteem" because despite "inferior resources and supplies, the teachers were caring and committed to the children." T. Josiha Haig was even more vehement about emphasizing the child almost to the exclusion of school organization. He declared that integration "is not the number one criteria. Number one is to focus on the child. A program must be conceived for each child. When this is done, integration will follow."

Opinions were very mixed on the subject of how desegregation should be accomplished, although at least half of the respondents felt that some kind of regionalization would be required considering the overwhelming proportion of minority students in the Hartford schools. Some, such as Eugene Leach, were sure that only mandatory desegregation had a chance of success, while others, such as Lloyd Calvert, citing the work of James Coleman, were equally assured that only a voluntary approach was likely to be acceptable to the surrounding suburbs. Linda Seagraves proposed a novel approach: that people who work in the central city be required to live there and have their children educated within the city's boundaries. She argued that currently there was little within Hartford that encouraged people to come into the city voluntarily.

Gerald Tirozzi pointed out that one hundred Connecticut communities are already working together to accomplish some aspect of desegregation. To further the effort, he suggested major planning grants to increase the number of students crossing town lines, more school construction grants, more magnet schools, a new school equalization formula to increase funding for education and perhaps to fix the per pupil expenditure money to the individual child, rather than having it go to the school system in the town in which the student resides. Tirozzi, noting the research of Christine Rossell, agreed with Lloyd Calvert that mandating desegregation would not succeed.

Mary Carroll suggested that the magnet schools be placed at the edge of the city to minimize the amount of traveling children would have to do. Cora Hahn emphasized the importance of workshops to sensitize and inform teachers and other school professionals about diverse cultures.

Mildred Torres-Soto, Susan Davis, and Edward Iwanicki stressed that school desegregation was not the real issue, and that it was instead segregated housing patterns. If communities had more affordable housing units and people were more accepting of differences, neighborhood schools would be naturally integrated. T. Josiha Haig and Susie Hinton went even further in arguing that it was the program and the child that should be at the center of consideration and that school desegregation was irrelevant.

Respondents' views on the factors most important in providing quality integrated education ranged as widely as the scope of the question allowed. Haig and Hinton returned to the tight specifics of a child-centered curriculum; Seagraves expanded the sphere to a "global village," including along the way "an integrated teaching staff and administration, quality materials and methods of teaching, opportunities for role modeling and building self-esteem, creating a community of learners, and establishing an environment that appreciates both similarities and differences."

Lloyd Calvert's list was equally comprehensive. He stressed that "integration had to be voluntary or it would be inconsistent with what was sought to be the ultimate outcome of the experience, that children have to go in both directions, that efforts should have a clear educational purpose and not be just for mixing, that there must be intensive staff development, that parents and the community must undergo intensive preparation as well, and that there must be continuing on-going evaluation regarding both the children and their parents."

Jane Barstow, a resident of the West End of Hartford, whose two daughters attended Hartford schools, emphasized the need for sensitive teachers and an inclusive curriculum. She also noted that "gender should be as important a consideration as race." Her husband, Norman, who teaches in Simsbury, cited many of the factors already named and added a concern for safety, appropriate class size, and strong parent involvement. Paul Copes argued that the commitment of school staff is more important than that of parents because "you cannot control parents. If you believe that you can make a difference, then you can make that difference." He noted that administrative vision and leadership were also qualities that had tremendous effect. Mary Carroll was another respondent who felt that teachers exerted the greatest influence on the success of the endeavor. Elliott Williams joined Jane Barstow in including gender with race in considering equity, and added national origin as well.

There was some agreement and much disagreement regarding which groups and institutions are most instrumental in bringing about the kind of change being discussed. There was general consensus that the courts should not be the body to make policy regarding school desegregation, but that frequently it falls to the judicial system since other, more appropriate, agencies do not act. While agreeing with *Sheff* attorney and University of Connecticut Law School Professor John Brittain, Eugene Leach, and Elizabeth Sheff, that the courts should enforce constitutional rights and promote and maintain racial justice, most respondents, such as Norman and Jane Barstow and Linda Seagraves, hoped that the courts would pressure other institutions to act rather than be themselves the agent of change. Paul Copes was in the minority in feeling that by interpreting the Constitution, the courts should also prescribe a remedy. Susan Davis expressed concern that if the courts declared a remedy but did not provide "accompanying lubricants, chaos will be created." Maria Torres-Soto regretted that "too many issues have to be decided by the courts. People should not have to file a lawsuit to get a quality education."

The Legislature was seen by most respondents as the prime source of funds and the most appropriate body to develop the policy necessary to implement desegregation. However, many of those interviewed were not confident that legislators would fulfill this responsibility. Representative Nancy Wyman, then Co-chairman of the Education Committee, was herself of mixed mind on the issue. While agreeing that funding was a legislative responsibility and that there was an obligation to advocate desegregation, she noted that there was hardly overwhelming support for desegregation from her constituents in northeastern Connecticut or even from residents of Hartford itself. She saw the Legislature's primary role as one of oversight.

Among those who felt that the Legislature has the authority to develop a solution was Commissioner Ferrandino, who wanted the Legislature to "establish a fair and equitable system of access." However, he was less than confident that these representatives would take the initiative in this regard. John Allison, James Kennedy, and Linda Seagraves shared the Commissioner's concern, the latter feeling that it is "not in the self-interest of legislators to press for desegregation." Susan Davis found the "totally political nature of the Legislature frightening" and felt that they are "hostages to the voters." Professor Iwanicki shared the views of Seagraves and Davis. John Brittain advocated that legislators "abolish district boundary lines and abandon the myth of local control." Hernan LaFontaine hoped that after the litigation was completed, the legislature would "play a leadership role."

6.2 Hartford SMSA (Connecticut), 1990

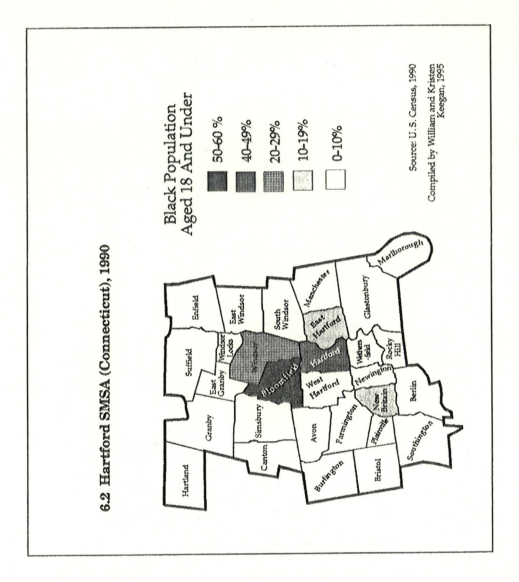

Black Population
Aged 18 And Under

50-60 %

40-49%

20-29%

10-19%

0-10%

Source: U. S. Census, 1990

Compiled by William and Kristen
Keegan, 1995

Not everyone was in favor of the Legislature's determining integration policy. Former Vernon Superintendent of Schools Albert Kerkin wanted legislators to provide funds but stay out of policy creation. Carroll, Tirozzi, and Williams also emphasized the necessity for the Legislature to allocate sufficient funds. Gene Leach hoped that the Legislature would "get out of the way of the courts," although he felt they would "eventually become a player" after desegregation was mandated. Elizabeth Sheff contended that since "doing the right thing is often unpopular" and "politicians tend to govern to get reelected and they do what makes them electable," as a result, "politics sucks."

In general, there was more enthusiasm for the State Board of Education. Sam Leone felt they were "excellent regarding publicly supporting desegregation and with respect to funding." Eugene Leach saw the Board as "less political." While Albert Kerkin thought that the Board was "overregulating," most respondents desired the Board to assume an active role. Commissioner Ferrandino felt that the State Board should be the policy-setting body, but that it cannot act alone and should function closely with the Legislature. Lloyd Calvert saw the role of the State Board as proposing policy to the Governor and Legislature and wanted to see it involved with moral suasion as well. The most active role was envisioned by Hernan LaFontaine, who advocated that the Board could "draw new lines and change district boundaries."

Respondents were very much aware that however the policy is made or modified, ultimately implementation will have to be conducted at the local level. In the words of Eugene Leach, school administrations have "the most intimate role in implementation." Most respondents hoped that administrators would offer leadership in the task of implementation rather than just "going along." James Kennedy saw the opportunity for those at the local level to "express the legitimacy of desegregation and integrated education and to be the marshalling force of local resources." Elliott Williams felt assured that those at the local level are sincere in recognizing the need for desegregation but are dependent on external funding to pursue interdistrict efforts. Professor Iwanicki was relatively alone in feeling that local systems have not done enough, although he singled out Peter Relic, formerly of West Hartford, for praise. Mary Carroll represented majority feeling in advocating that "superintendents have been right out in front serving as knights in shining armor." She had particularly positive words for Lloyd Calvert.

For those who view school as the place to train for later life and work, integrated schools are the appropriate and logical location to prepare for functioning in an integrated work place. Eugene Leach spoke for James Kennedy and Paul Copes as well when he noted that "it is in the best interest of business that desegregation occur." Leach continued that business had so far not participated as fully as it might in bringing desegregation about. John Allison felt that business should "convince its workers that diversity is good." Commissioner Ferrandino concurred that business would benefit from a work force prepared for desegregation in the schools and should support initiatives to that end. Lloyd Calvert referred to businesses as "stakeholders" in the process and was "troubled by the degree to which we look to economic needs to determine educational policy." Susan Davis and Mary Carroll felt that business should be doing more; Sam Leone cited partnerships through the Connecticut Business and Industry Association (CBIA) and the Connecticut Public Expenditure Council (CPEC) involving tutorials and mentoring as the beginning of the types of programs that are needed.

At least equally "pivotal," according to Linda Seagraves and others, is the community-at-large. Most respondents agreed that the community must "be involved" (Kerkin, Brittain), "be receptive" (Wyman), "be supportive" (J. and N. Barstow, Davis, Tirozzi, LaFontaine), and "be willing to change" (Sheff). Commissioner Ferrandino felt that the community must "face up to the fact that there are inequities in how children are educated, that the suburbs must realize that they have a role to play, and that the remedy must include regionalization since the city of Hartford is more than 90 percent minority." Paul Copes contended that "it is in the best interest of everyone to advocate for quality, integrated education as it is a quality-of-life issue for all. Everyone should have equal access and equal ability to participate whether in education, running the government, or with regard to opportunities for employment. There are tensions for all when there is an underclass." James Kennedy hoped that the community would not "buy the lies of demagogues" and that desegregation could be accomplished "without quotas."

Several of those interviewed indicated regret that the religious community, in recent times, has not played the role that it did in the 1960s. James Kennedy attributed this to the rise of evangelicalism among the Protestants, creating a "different agenda, more concerned with the hereafter, while the Catholics became more involved with the abortion issue." Edward Iwanicki contended that the recent reticence of the church has financial overtones. The archdiocese has not taken a leadership role in issues such as supporting the integrated South Catholic High School, which was poor, while it helps to bolster more middle class programs. T. Josiha Haig also felt that there was a place for more involvement by the church. Mary Carroll blamed the press for creating exclusive editions of *The Hartford Courant*. "Suburban editions do not cover the city," and discourage those living outside the city to feel a part of what is occurring there. Gerald Tirozzi felt that colleges and universities through their teacher preparation programs have the opportunity to assist with the desegregation effort.

The final question of the survey sought to discover what perceptions respondents had regarding obstacles to the success of desegregation. While racism, in its many aspects, was cited by more interviewees than any other answer as an obstacle to success, it was not the sole reason given. And, while racism among whites was mentioned more often than the same emotion existing among people of color, those who discussed the subject acknowledged that no single group had a monopoly on the feeling. Lloyd Calvert summed up the other qualities most mentioned, "inertia, self-interest, and fear of change." Jane Barstow noted others that are obviously pervasive: "fears for safety relating to crime, violence, and the existence of an underclass."

Linda Seagraves defined the problem as "parochialism that cripples, doing things as they've always been done, seeing yourself as different, lacking empathy, and divorcing yourself from the city's problems." She hoped that others would share her personal sense of mission and identification with children. One who has is Superintendent Kennedy. His definition of the problem sounded very much like Ms. Seagraves as he spoke of the "minds of men and of the economic and geographic isolation of the races." He blamed much of people's attitudes on the institution of slavery and the very different history of the African-American. Elliott Williams and Vincent Ferrandino placed the greatest blame on the Legislature. According to the Commissioner, constructive proposals have been put before that body and have not been funded. The legislators' feelings of obligation to their constituents have blinded them to the need to act for the common good.

The idea of regionalization, accepted by most of those interviewed, proposed by both former Commissioner Tirozzi and then Commissioner Ferrandano, was also considered by the Hartford Board of Education in 1988, during the superintendency of Hernan LaFontaine. Referring to the January, 1988 Tirozzi Report, a report prepared by G. William Saxton, Senior Assistant to the Superintendent, for the Hartford Board of Education, he noted the imbalance of the races within the schools of the state and the ineffectiveness of efforts to redress the situation based on "legislation, financial aid and incentives, program initiatives, and monitoring for racial balance." Saxton's report reiterated the reference to recent case law, which "holds states as well as local education agencies responsible and accountable for the occurrence and for the alleviation of racial segregation," and the need for legislation and a "firm and stated commitment by officials and decision-makers to eliminate racial/ethnic isolation" (*Background and Discussion Paper on School Racial/Ethnic Balance*, Hartford Public Schools, April, 1988, pp. 1-2).

Saxton's report continues with a discussion of the ten-volume study conducted by the Institute for Public Policy Studies of

Vanderbilt University and concentrates on the first volume, which details strategies for effective desegregation. The Vanderbilt report includes 17 recommendations among which are:

- desegregation should begin at the earliest possible age,
- voluntary desegregation is ineffective except in districts with small minority enrollments,
- one-way busing plans are not harmful to minority students and result in less white flight than two-way busing,
- magnet schools as part of a mandatory plan can reduce both flight and racial isolation but may, unintentionally, stigmatize non-magnet schools as inferior,
- it is better to enrich the curriculum of all schools rather than provide magnet programs,
- schools in poor physical condition contribute to parents' reluctance to the reassignment of their children,
- different minorities must be treated as discrete groups in determining desegregation plans,
- a critical mass of between 15 and 20 percent of any ethnic group is necessary to promote security,
- a critical mass of students who do well academically is necessary to increase the likelihood that all students will continue to achieve, and
- there is little evidence that bus riding has a negative effect on children. (*Background and Discussion Paper on School Racial/Ethnic Balance*, 1988, pp. 8-10)

The next section of Saxton's report described four scenarios for desegregating the Hartford schools. These included massive busing from city to suburbs, from suburbs to city, and in both directions at once. Using 1986 figures, it was noted that it would take a 1000 pupil exchange to reduce the minority population within Hartford schools by 4.1 percent. Hypothetical distributions of pupils were made, with Hartford and Bloomfield as the core communities, and the nine contiguous and 12 adjacent communities with white majorities being proportionally distributed. The total region would have approximately 127,000 students and a minority pupil population of 29.7 percent (*Background and Discussion Paper on School Racial/Ethnic Balance*, 1988, pp. 11-15, tables I-III).

An update of the 1988 report was prepared by Jeffrey L. Forman in April, 1990. In addition to detailing nine interdistrict cooperation programs with school systems either contiguous or adjacent to Hartford and Bloomfield, the 1990 report revised the population figures for the core communities and for the region as a whole. The report indicated that it was of particular note that "the population of minority youngsters in the region ha[d] gone from 29,269 in 1986 to 30,526 in 1988 or 29.7 percent to 33.8 percent." In the core cities, Hartford's minority student population was 91.3 percent, while that of Bloomfield was 73.9 percent (*Background and Discussion Paper on School Racial/Ethnic Balance: Update*, 1990, introduction and p. 11).

A January, 1992 study prepared by the Capitol Region Strategic Assessment Task Force for the Capitol Region Council of Governments (CRCOG) buttressed the regional approach suggested by the Hartford school board during Hernan LaFontaine's superintendency. Among its more than two dozen findings, it noted that "the region faces a profound challenge: to eliminate the educational disparities between students in the region's core and the surrounding towns. This is critical to the future health of the regional economy because young people from the heart of the region will make up a growing percentage of the region's work force growth" (*Where We Stand, Part 2*, p. 93).

However, the emphasis shifted considerably when T. Josiha Haig became superintendent of the Hartford Public Schools in August 1991. The *Vision of Excellence*, the annual report of the Hartford Public Schools for 1991-92, prepared under Dr. Haig's direction, did not discuss desegregation. Instead, in the message from the Board President, Carmen M. Rodriguez, emphasis was placed on nurturing "the individual capacity for growth" and "the worth of each child as a human being" (*Vision of Excellence, 1992-1993*, Hartford Public Schools, introduction).

Superintendent Haig declared this as his goal: "By the Year 2000, we envision that the Hartford Public Schools will serve as educational institutions that ensure that all students as well as all staff are committed to lifelong learning for the purpose of maximizing the probability that they will actualize their potential." To develop and disseminate this vision, three-hour workshops have been held every month for all administrators. Principals and program managers have been directed to draft vision statements, and those within the system "will work together towards turning the vision into reality, regardless of the organizational or environmental constraints" (*Vision of Excellence, 1992-1993*, p. 1).

Part of this vision is the 204.5 million dollar building plan to construct eight schools and renovate four others, which was approved as a bonding issue on November 3, 1992. An editorial on April 2, 1992 and two articles by Don Noel on April 3, and May 20, 1992 in *The Hartford Courant* pointed out that in light of possible court or state-imposed desegregation actions, this plan "asked voters to build schools that may be obsolete before they're ready for occupancy" (pp. D14, D13, B13).

As one looks toward the future, another factor that requires serious consideration is the already significant and growing proportion of Latino students in Hartford's schools. In October, 1991, Hispanics at 48.9 percent held the plurality of ethnic groups; majority status in the very near future is assumed (*Vision of Excellence, 1992-1993*, p.6).

Extended family relationships, easy and inexpensive air passage, and their parents' search for better employment cause many of Hartford's Puerto Rican students to travel back and forth between Connecticut and the island attending school for relatively brief periods of time in each place. In 1991, of Connecticut's 12,578 Hispanic pupils who were eligible for enrollment in bilingual programs, 40 percent, or 5,098, were from Hartford (*Vision of Excellence, 1992-1993*, p. 7).

Irregular attendance caused by frequent moves makes a consistent educational experience difficult to achieve and retards the learning of both English and Spanish. While schools in Puerto Rico are required to provide at least one hour per day instruction in English, a visit in January, 1993, to both an elementary and a middle school in suburban San Juan demonstrated that only students who had spent significant periods of time on the mainland were capable of truly understanding and speaking English. This observation was all the more disappointing in consideration of the high level of competence in spoken English shown by the teachers of these children. On the other hand, administrators pointed out that students who spent long periods of time on the mainland often had difficulty with Spanish upon their return to the island (Interview with Norma Cruz de Cima de Villa, January 14, 1993; interview with Elba Diaz, visits to Luis Muniz Marin Elementary School and Rene Marques Middle School, Carolina III District, January 15, 1993).

Other observations made during classroom visits were equally discouraging. While teachers and administrators showed great love and concern for their students, teaching programs appeared to lack educational rigor in comparison with those in Connecticut. To a great extent, this may be due to a paucity of educational materials. Few books and instructional aids were found in the classrooms; only 80 cents per student was budgeted annually for such supplies by the Commonwealth of Puerto Rico (January 14 and 15, 1993 interviews).

Two factors are likely to have the greatest effect on the desegregation of the Hartford schools: the ultimate outcome of the *Sheff v. O'Neill* trial and the Legislature's response and willingness to make significant financial commitment to the Governor's call for the desegregation of the State's schools through a process of regionalization. The court case testimony concluded at the end of February, 1993. Briefs were originally due in early spring of 1993, and summations for the two sides was then expected to be scheduled for mid-May (Conversation with John Brittain, March 22, 1993).

The trial lasted 11 weeks; testimony from 54 witnesses was heard. More than one thousand documents were introduced as evidence. The plaintiffs argued for a ruling that would "force the state to provide more money for Hartford's struggling, mostly black and Hispanic schools, and develop a school desegregation plan linking the city with its more affluent and mostly white suburbs." The state, on the other side, contended that "it had already spent millions of dollars attacking urban school problems, that school desegregation has failed elsewhere and caused whites to flee the cities, and that the social ills afflicting city schools are too complex to be cured by a court order. The state also has argued that the legislature, not the courts, should address the problem" (*The Hartford Courant*, February 28, 1993, p. 1).

The State Legislature was faced with a difficult choice. As Representative Nancy Wyman, Co-chairman of the House Education Committee, noted, "We have this court case hanging over our head. . . . People feel we have to do something." The possible "something" included acting on the Governor's plan to create six regions, each of which would have been responsible for designing a desegregation plan for its area and would likely include magnet schools and cooperative programs between towns. Republican leaders proposed a school choice plan that would provide $2500 vouchers to assist poor children to attend private schools. The Education Committee's other co-chair, Senator Kevin Sullivan, sponsored a bill that would allow regional charter public schools free from state mandates governing other state accredited educational facilities (*Willimantic Chronicle*, March 31, 1993, p. 1).

On April 12, 1993, the State Legislature's Education Committee put its own stamp on the Governor's desegregation proposal before sending the bill to the Appropriations Committee. The plan, which was approved by a vote of 21-6, increased the number of regions from six to ten and exempted 29 towns located in the northeastern or northwestern part of the state because they are "too far from any of the state's major or small cities" (*Journal Inquirer*, April 13, 1993, p. 3).

Senator Kevin Sullivan, co-chair of the Education Committee, said that "the regions were redrawn to reflect a more logical relationship between the cities and towns." Sullivan also pointed out that "the bill approved by the committee places a greater emphasis on high-quality education, rather than on desegregation." The University of Connecticut's Institute for Public Service would replace the Commissioner of Education as the administrator of the forums to be conducted by the regions. Magnet schools, regional agricultural and vocational schools, school choice, summer school, and extra-curricular programs were among the measures that could be employed to achieve compliance (*Journal Inquirer*, April 13, 1993, p.3).

While school superintendents in Somers and Stafford voiced relief at being excluded, Killingly Superintendent David Kressy did not. He noted that his town is "racially isolated" and felt that "all towns" should participate in desegregation efforts. In addition, he was concerned that Killingly would lose out on the state funding that participation would ensure (*The Hartford Courant*, April 14, 1993, p. B9).

When Public Act 93-263 was put into final form, effective July 1, 1993, all of Connecticut's 169 towns and all of the state's 167 school districts had been assigned to one of 11 regions. By April, 1994, each town was to set up a committee to meet and discuss what desegregation efforts were already in place in their district and what additional steps they were willing to undertake (*the Chronicle*, July 8, 1993, p. 5) . An Englehart cartoon reflected the feelings of many when it suggested that the legislation was designed to bury the issue under a mantle of planning (*The Hartford Courant*, July 1, 1993, p. B12).

While some communities embraced the legislation as a n opportunity to dream about educational enhancements, others, such as Tolland, 15 miles northeast of Hartford, saw the process as a possible threat to local control of its schools (*The Hartford Courant*, September 25, 1993, p. B2). State Commissioner of Education Vincent Ferrandino toured the state, attempting to quell concerns by explaining the legislation and emphasizing its voluntary nature (*the Chronicle*, September 30, 1993, p. 3), while *The Hartford Courant* joined with the Study Circles Resource Center and The University of Connecticut's Institute of Public Service to sponsor regional discussion programs on the topic "Quality Education and School Integration in Connecticut" (Studies Circles Resource Center, 1993). However, a University of Connecticut School of Social Work professor who surveyed nearly 200 Hartford residents found that those who would be most affected by the desegregation case seemed to know the least about it. Professor Julio Morales also discovered that Hispanic parents were as worried about the safety of their children on buses that would take them to the suburbs as Caucasian parents are about sending their children to urban schools (*UConn Advance*, November 12, 1993, p. 1).

Meanwhile, Superior Court Judge Harry Hammer scheduled final arguments in the *Sheff v. O'Neill* trial for December 16, 1993, the date of the trial's first anniversary. It was nine months since testimony had been concluded, and it was hoped that a decision would be reached by the following April (*The Hartford Courant*, November 9, 1993, p. C9). Those who hoped that the judge's decision would be affected by the state legislature's initiative were disturbed to learn that state budget experts estimated that it would cost more than half a billion dollars a year to implement that law. State Senator Kevin B. Sullivan of West Hartford, a key sponsor of the desegregation legislation, predicted, "There is no way on Earth that amount of money will be available" (*The Hartford Courant*, November 23, 1993, p. A1).

While court case and legislation were predicated on the demographics of the 1980s, as time passed, the issue has become further complicated by population changes in both the city and its suburbs. During the 1980s, Hartford became the first Connecticut city where whites are not a majority of the population; the white population shrank by 18.6 percent to 55, 869 people, while the city's black and Hispanic population increased by 17.7 percent and 58.2 percent, respectively. "While the majority of the region's blacks and Hispanics lived in Hartford in 1990, the majority of the regions Asians lived in the suburbs. The 1990 census counted 11,792 Asians in the Capitol Region, 9,768 of them outside of Hartford" (*The Hartford Courant,* December 12, 1993, p. H1).

Although the majority of blacks and Hispanics remained in the city, significant numbers moved out into the suburbs. "The '70s and '80s were the first two decades in which black population grew faster in the suburbs than in the city. In 1970, 87 percent of the region's blacks lived in Hartford; by 1990, only 67 percent of the region's blacks were city dwellers." The suburban black population grew by 74 percent during the 1980s, and while the suburban Hispanic population grew by 127 percent, even faster than that of blacks, the the rate of growth in the city was even faster (*The Hartford Courant,* December 12, 1993, p. H10).

During the 1980s, already heavily black Bloomfield saw 2881 new African-Americans join its ranks, while 2265 blacks moved to East Hartford and 993 moved to Manchester. West Hartford's black population increased by 627, Enfield's by 603, Vernon's by 316, Wethersfield's by 167, and Newington's by 153. Hispanic population growth in the suburbs was led by 1760 to East Hartford, 1092 to West Hartford, 706 to Manchester, 591 to Windsor, and 573 to Enfield. The smaller and more remote towns were not exempt: Bolton received 23 blacks and 48 Hispanics, Canton 26 and 43, respectively, and Somers 239 and 151 (*The Hartford Courant,* December 12, 1993, p. H10).

The population figures above demonstrate that while the plaintiffs in *Sheff v. O'Neill,* the City of Hartford, and the citizenry of Connecticut awaited the outcome of the court action and while the State Legislature acted to hold off substantial judicial redress, blacks and Hispanics were desegregating the suburbs without waiting for either judicial or legislative actions. In October, 1992, minority students in the towns surrounding Hartford made up 83.5 percent of the enrollment in Bloomfield, 38.1 percent in East Hartford, 36.9 percent in Windsor, 17.2 percent in West Hartford, 8.3 percent in Glastonbury, 7.6 percent in Newington, and 6.7 percent in Wethersfield (*The New York Times,* December 12, 1993, p. CN14).

Those who hoped that the legislative initiative would influence Judge Hammer's opinion were heartened when the judge determined on December 16, 1993 that, instead of presenting final arguments, the attorneys for the plaintiffs and the defense should instead argue the merits of the justiceability of the case and whether he had jurisdiction to make a decision in light of the legislative initiative. Although both sets of attorneys agreed that the case was not influenced by the legislature's action and the subsequent local and regional meetings, the judge determined to delay further action on the case until this new issue had been resolved to his satisfaction. Briefs related to the issue were to be presented to the court by mid-January (Superior Court, Vernon, December 16, 1993).

Crowded court calendars caused postponement of the January date with only occasional status conferences taking place until a new date of May 11, 1994 was finally set. There was shock throughout the state when, on April 28, just two weeks before the trial was finally to resume, the defense's highly regarded chief counsel, John R. Whelan, committed suicide. The case was once more delayed to allow the defense team time to regroup (*The Hartford Courant*, April 29, 1994, p. D1).

The court finally reconvened on September 28. The judge again surprised both participants and spectators when he further postponed both the issue of justiceability and the closing arguments to discuss whether or not the City of Hartford should be joined as a party in the case. Again attorneys for both sides were in agreement that the city had no desire to be included. However, it took more than an hour for the judge to be convinced, and then not until John Brittain, one of the plaintiff attorneys, assured the judge that he would secure a letter to that effect from the Hartford Corporation Counsel, Pedro Segarra (Superior Court, Vernon, September 28, 1994; *The Hartford Courant*, September 29, 1994, p. A3; *the Chronicle*, September 29, 1994, p. 1).

Meanwhile, there was increasing dissatisfaction with Hartford School Superintendent T. Josiha Haig. On January 15, 1994, *The Hartford Courant* editorial board, anticipating the action of the school board a few days later, wondered what would happen to the superintendent's strategy for change if his contract, due to expire at the end of June, was not renewed. The editorial, while applauding "his commitment to reform," noted with regret that he often spoke in "incomprehensible jargon," seemed detached during a protracted school budget battle between teachers and board members, and chose to visit Eastern Europe at the end of a school year instead of attending graduation ceremonies (p. B8).

On January 18, the Hartford Board of Education voted not to renew Haig's contract. The ouster of the superintendent came just shortly after the departure of the city's police chief, fire chief, and city manager. While some came to the defense of the departing superintendent, the overwhelming sentiment appeared to be relief that he would be leaving. Some board members even commented openly that they hoped that he would leave even before his term expired (*The Hartford Courant*, January 19, 1994, p.1; January 20, 1994, p. B1).

There was far less enthusiasm when State education Commissioner Vincent L. Ferrandino announced the following month his intention to resign in August "to become chief executive director of the prestigious accrediting agency New England Association of Schools and Colleges," a job that carried "less challenge but more security." While there had been significant concern two years earlier at the appointment of the superintendent from one of the smallest and wealthiest communities in the state, Ferrandino quickly showed he could not only understand the problems of urban school systems but make integration plans seem somewhat less threatening to suburban constituencies. It was he, who, in the summer of 1993, broke an impasse between Hartford's teachers and their school board that threatened to keep the schools from opening in the fall (*The Hartford Courant*, February 18, 1994, p. B10).

But perhaps the most unsettling event of all was the arrival on the scene of Education Alternatives, Inc. (EAI) of Minneapolis. Executives from the company began meeting with city leaders at the end of March, 1994, promising that it could offer Hartford "millions of dollars more for city classrooms, better schools, and improved student performance" (*The Hartford Courant*, March 22, 1994, p. D1). Frustrated with insufficient funds to adequately provide textbooks and supplies as well as teachers for the system's 25,000 students, the Hartford Board of Education, bitterly divided six to three, decided to hire EAI to manage its 32 schools, becoming the first community in the nation to entrust all of its schools to the private company. EAI promised that it would "find enough savings within Hartford's $171 million annual budget not only to finance physical and academic improvements but also to make a profit" (*The New York Times*, July 23, 1994, p. 24).

After three months of debate with the City Council and against the very vocal wishes of the teachers' union, the Hartford Board of Education voted to hire EAI on October 3. Hartford's Corporation Counsel Pedro E. Segarra, siding with the Council, refused to sign the agreement. The contract called for the company to manage the schools for five years, make recommendations on hiring, firing, and other personnel matters, participate in collective bargaining, provide staff training, improve student achievement, and invest more than $20 million in the schools over the life of the contract. If profit could be made it was to be divided equally between the company and the city (*Journal Inquirer*, October 4, 1994, p.3).

One month after the beginning of school, the private company was finally hired although the teachers' union was still protesting the action, claiming that it violated their contract by unilaterally changing the conditions of their employment. The teachers threatened to take the issue to court (*The Hartford Courant*, October 13, 1994, p. B9).

Meanwhile, with perhaps greater enthusiasm and sincerity than expected, the eleven districts created to prepare diversity plans proceeded with their meetings and on schedule presented their reports to Acting Commissioner of Education Theodore S. Sergi. Magnet schools featured in many of the reports, and the Department of Education requested $27 million for diversity programs and $50 million for capital funding to build magnet schools. Increased use of educational technology, minority staff recruitment and retention, partnerships with business and community agencies, developing common school calendars, increased parental involvement, early childhood education, and increased instructional time were mentioned in many of the regional reports. One state board member, reflecting the feelings of many, stressed the need for the process to be voluntary. The next steps were the holding of public hearings on the plans and then votes by each municipality (*Journal Inquirer*, October 6, 1994, p. 6; Letter to Steering Committee, Regional Forum 4 from Acting Commissioner Theodore S. Sergi, October 18, 1994, pp. 5-6).

However, not everyone was enthused about the regional efforts. Kenneth W. Rodgers, a consultant working with the 23 Hartford area towns, warned that similar attempts in other areas had failed. Others voiced concerns that the plans would result in a lowering of standards and a polarization of the community once serious discussion of plan implementation began (*Journal Inquirer*, October 4, 1994, p. 16). The issue had provoked so much interest that *Harper's Magazine* featured an essay by James Traub on the subject in its June, 1994 issue. While Traub sympathized with the difficulties inherent in the Hartford schools, he was pessimistic that there would be "enough good will to go around" to enable voluntary actions to make significant changes (pp. 36-47).

As 1994 drew to an end, two long-awaited events took place. Judge Harry Hammer heard the final arguments in the *Sheff v. O'Neill* case on November 30, 1994, only one day before local communities were required to report their votes of approval or disapproval of their region's proposed plan. The summations and questioning by the judge took an entire day and even brought out the newly reelected Attorney General Richard Blumenthal to speak for the state. On December 1, Acting Commissioner of Education Theodore Sergi announced that only three of the 11 regions had voted in support of their districts' plans. All but the northeastern, southeastern, and Greater Hartford regions had voted to oppose any further participation. Meanwhile, EAI was finally getting into Hartford's schools. However, all was less than agreeable as the private company proposed to install a controversial computer software package instead of the Apple Macintosh computers, which were preferred by most of the teachers in the system (*The Hartford Courant*, November 2, 1994, p. A3; November 5, 1994, p. A3; December 1, 1994, p. 1; December 2, 1994, p. 1).

The situation facing Judge Hammer was very different from that of five and a half years previous when the *Sheff* case was first filed. Hartford's minority population had become less black and more

Hispanic, and its first ring suburbs were far more integrated than in 1989. In fact, by Spring, 1995, East and West Hartford had sufficient minority population, unequally dispersed, so that both were out of compliance with the State's "racial imbalance law- - more than two decades old- -which requires that the percentage of minority enrollment in any school come within 25 percent of the district composition overall for that grade" (*The Hartford Courant,* December 11, 1994, p. D1; *Journal Inquirer,* March 14, 1995, p. 17).

In late March, Judge Hammer requested and received a two-week extension to further review and edit his decision. Finally, on April 12, 1995, Judge Hammer ruled for the defendants, determining that the state is not required to desegregate its schools because it was not state action that created the segregation. Plaintiffs were disappointed with the ruling and vowed to appeal the decision. However, even many of those who were pleased were surprised that the Judge had based his decision on the minority opinions of U.S. Supreme Court Justice William O. Douglas. They found it odd that the decision for a case based on state law was decided on federal law and federal cases (*Journal Inquirer*, March 29, 1995, p. 20; *The Hartford Courant*, April 13, 1995, p. 1).

On April 27, as expected, the *Sheff* plaintiffs filed their formal appeal. A week later, the state Supreme Court, the state's highest court, indicating a desire to accelerate the appeal process, asked Judge Hammer to rewrite his decision being sure to "address all of the issues raised in the landmark case." A few days later, the Supreme Court asked the attorneys for both sides "to submit by May 25 a list of facts on which they agree, along with each side's proposed findings." The Court indicated its intention to hear arguments in the fall (*The Hartford Courant*, April 28, 1995, p. A8; May 9, 1995, p. A12; *Journal Inquirer*, May 12, 1995, p. 25).

The role of EAI in the administration of the Hartford schools also remains uncertain. Challenged all year by teacher and parent groups, the private company initially had the support of two-thirds of the nine member school board. However, recent criticisms regarding monies spent for travel and housing for EAI employees, as the private company advocated substantial reduction in teaching jobs, led the school board to reduce EAI's focus from all 32 of the city's schools to only five during the next academic year (*The Hartford Courant*, June 20, 1995, p.1). The future direction of the Hartford schools is still far from predictable.

Chapter 7

Conclusion

Whether one examines judicial decisions, reviews the literature created by experts in the field, or investigates the programs that have been or currently are being implemented in school systems throughout the nation, one rapidly becomes aware that there is little agreement on the "best way" to approach or decide whether, and if so how, school desegregation should proceed. While first granting constitutional protection to deliberate segregation in *Plessy v. Ferguson* (163 U.S. 537, 1896), "[t]he Court began assuming a progressively more affirmative role in matters of race and public policy," when, in *Buchanan v. Worley* (245 U.S. 60, 1917), it "struck down a municipal ordinance requiring residential segregation in Louisville."

Although the opinion in *Brown v. Board of Education of Topeka, Kansas* (347 U.S. 483, 1954) that state-sanctioned segregation in public education created schools that were inherently unequal was the watershed decision to be rendered on the subject, making segregation illegal did not concomitantly make it nonexistent. Segregated housing patterns in the North guaranteed the maintenance of *de facto* if not *de jure* separation of the races in public schools, while in the South, active hostility to the Court decision was manifested in continued dual school systems. A dozen years after *Brown*, 95 percent of African-American school children still attended segregated schools (Metcalf, 1983, p. 10).

Cisneros v. Corpus Christi Independent School District marked the political institutionalization of busing. When the defendant school board claimed that "dire effects" would result from the transportation of white students, the judge responded that "the children who are being bussed now make no such claims, nor have I been shown any harmful effects on the individual children that will outweigh the harmful effects on the Negro or Mexican-American child who is in a segregated and dual system" (324 F. Supp. 599, S.D. Tex. 1970). In

Swann v. Charlotte-Mecklenburg Board of Education, a year later in 1971, the Court while conceding the desirability of the neighborhood school, nevertheless declared that for a time "awkwardness" and "inconvenience" might be necessary to implement desegregation and that "walk-in schools" might have to be foresaken (402 U.S. 1, 1971).

Magnet schools first became a court-supported means of desegregation in 1970 in the case of *United States v. Board of Education, Independent School District No. 1, Tulsa* (429 F.2d 1253, 10th Cir. 1970). Magnet schools "draw students on a voluntary basis by offering educational innovations which are attractive to parents. They appeal to many educational constituencies by simultaneously creating desegregation without mandatory busing" and frequently "blow a fresh breeze of educational innovation into city school systems" (Metz, 1986, p.1).

While decisions ordering the creation of magnet schools achieved some success in Tulsa, and perhaps in Houston, they were far less effective in New York, where an insufficient number of white students applied; in Baton Rouge, where although the court so ordered, they were never actually implemented; in Chicago, where only four percent of the students participated; and in Missouri, where the state refused to pay transportation costs for students who were to travel outside of their districts (*Hart v. Community School Board of Education, New York School District No. 21* (512 F. 2d 37, 2nd Cir. 1975); *Davis v. East Baton Rouge Parish School Board* (F. Supp. 869, M.D. La. 1981); *United States v. Chicago Board of Education* (554 F. Supp. 912, N.D.Ill. 1983); *Liddell v. State of Missouri* (717 F.2d 1180, 8th Cir. 1983)).

Once northern school districts were subject to the same scrutiny as those of the South, it took only a year for the Court to progress from allowing lack of intent to permit continued segregation in New Jersey in *Spencer v. Kugler* (404 U.S. 1027, 1972) to ordering the desegregation of the Denver schools despite the absence of a history of legislated dual school systems in *Keyes v. School District No. 1 of Denver, Colorado* (413 U.S. 198, 1973). These cases proved to be the turning point for judicial decisions, the emphasis changing from *de jure* to *de facto* segregation. This resulted in a series of cases that ordered the desegregation of Northern schools. The desegregation arena expanded from the South and border states to the entire country, reflecting the nation's changing demographics as well.

Later in the 1970s, in decisions such as *Milliken v. Bradley* (418 U.S. 717, 1974) involving Detroit, Boston, and Minneapolis, when metropolitan plans were not feasible, the Court ordered enriched educational components that emphasized reading and communications, multicultural and bilingual education, staff training, and school-community relations (Vergon, 1990, pp. 32-33).

By the 1970s, the Court was prepared to demand a metropolitan solution when the original desegregation plan for Wilmington,

Delaware was no longer feasible, as the white population of that city continued to diminish. The Court could distinguish the justification of this action from prior contrary decisions by pointing to the city's previous *de jure* segregation (*Evans v. Buchanan*, 379 F. Supp. 1218, 1974). An interdistrict remedy was also deemed to be appropriate in Jefferson County, Kentucky, which includes Louisville, where the Court ordered county-wide desegregation. When the Louisville system protested the decision and then lost in the district court, it voted itself out of existence. According to state law, this automatically transferred authority to the county, and the metropolitan remedy was realized (*Newburg Area Council v. Board of Education*, 421 U.S. 931, 1975). In Indianapolis, the Court's remedy was to transport black students from the city center to the white areas in the outer fringes of the city. This decision has been widely criticized by desegregation planners because no transportation was required in the other direction (*United States v. Indianapolis Board of School Commissioners*, 573 F.2d 400, 7th Cir. 1978). Opposite determinations were made in the cases of Dallas, where the courts refused to even consider a metropolitan remedy (*Tasby v. Estes*, 517 F.2d 92, 5th Cir. 1975, cert denied, 423 U.S. 939, 1975), as well as in Boston, Dayton, Columbus, and Birmingham (Gordon, 1989, pp. 206-8).

A case heard before the Southern District Court of Ohio has particular relevance to Connecticut, where Governor Lowell Weicker in 1993 called upon the Legislature and the general population to voluntarily desegregate Connecticut's schools by having the state divide into six regions and then have each district devise its own desegregation plan. In the case of *Mona Bronson et al. v. Board of Education of the City School District of Cincinnati et al.* (Case No. C-1-74-205; 640 F. Supp. 68, 1984), Judge W.H. Rice found the Cincinnati School District in compliance with some provisions of a school desegregation consent decree but not in compliance with others. The original decision was historic in allowing the school district charged with promoting or allowing unconstitutional segregation to choose for itself the means of arriving at desegregation goals. As incremental success was achieved, the Court removed jurisdiction over those areas, maintaining control only over areas that were still in non-compliance.

While few of those who study the issue of school desegregation would disagree that its implementation is highly desirable, there are almost as many views as to how this desegregation should be accomplished as there are educational theorists. Gary Orfield is convinced that mandatory desegregation is the only effective method (1978); Robert Crain is equally supportive of the goals and benefits of desegregation, such as in Project Concern, the city-to-suburb desegregation program begun in the Hartford area in 1966, but less certain as to the best means to accomplish that end (Crain, Mahard, Narot, 1982).

Charles V. Willie advocates controlled choice (1991), while Christine H. Rossell, who began her career as a supporter of mandatory desegregation, now argues that only voluntary measures will achieve true integration and interracial exposure (1990). Meanwhile, David J. Armor, who agrees with Christine Rossell on the desirability of voluntary as opposed to mandatory desegregation (Stephan & Feagin, 1980, p. 225) further contends that desegregated schools have demonstrated no significant effect on the achievement of black children (*The Hartford Courant*, December 16, 1992).

Case studies of five discrete communities that have experienced or are undergoing desegregation efforts offer an opportunity to assess the issue from different vantage points. Granting that every region is somewhat unique, these communities nevertheless have significant parallels. All five are areas with increasingly large, poor, minority populations in their central cities, which are surrounded by mostly white, generally affluent suburbs. All five are mid-sized urban communities with standard metropolitan statistical areas of less than one million inhabitants, and all are located in the northeastern quadrant of the United States.

Based upon these studies, several factors that influence the success or failure of desegregation programs emerge. Committed and charismatic leadership, civic pride and community involvement, strong educational components to encourage participation, a constructive and positive working relationship between city and state, and the creation of districts too large to enable easy white flight are elements that will make any specific desegregation plan more likely to be successfully implemented.

For the purpose of this study, desegregated schools are defined as having a student population that comes close to reflecting the ratio of the population of the area, while integrated schools assume that this mixture of students actually relates with each other in classrooms, lunchrooms, and during other activities. In order for integration to be able to occur, desegregation must first take place.

The desegregation of the Dayton, Ohio Public Schools was the result of a court mandate. Lead plaintiff Mark Brinkman was joined by black and white parents representing their minor children and others similarly situated.   The National Association for the Advancement of Colored People (NAACP) joined as a party plaintiff to the suit, which was known as *Brinkman v. Gilligan*. Defendants included Ohio's Governor and Attorney General, the Ohio State Board of Education, the Superintendent of Public Instruction of the Ohio Department of Education, the Dayton Board of Education, its individual members, and its superintendent (503 F. 2d 684 (1974)).

The Court's finding for the plaintiffs noted that the city's schools had remained officially segregated even after Ohio law, in 1887, mandated an integrated school system. Despite protests from the NAACP and other groups, the State of Ohio continued to contribute to Dayton schools even after the *Brown* decision, which meant that after 1954 federal as well as state law was being ignored (*Brinkman v. Gilligan*, 689-90).

The Dayton Board finally admitted its guilt in these matters in April, 1971, when it appointed "a broadly representative committee to evaluate and advise it on plans to reduce racial isolation and improve educational opportunities." The committee report prompted the Board to pass three desegregation resolutions in December of that year. These resolutions, however, were short lived when those Board members were voted out of office and the new Board rescinded the actions of its predecessor. The *Brinkman v. Gilligan* suit was a response to that recision and was filed on April 17, 1972 (691-93).

The District Court found for the plaintiffs the following year and ordered desegregation activities involving both students and faculty. However, the plaintiffs felt that the ruling did not go far enough. The United States Court of Appeals, Sixth Circuit agreed and, in 1975, ordered a systemwide plan for the 1976-77 school year. The Board's appeal to the Supreme Court in 1977 was at first successful, but when the Court of Appeals reheard the case in 1978 and it was returned to the Supreme Court in 1979, the plaintiffs ultimately prevailed (*Dayton Board v. Brinkman*, No. 76-539, 420; Goodman in Yarmolinsky, 1981, p. 53; Metcalf, 1983, pp. 261-62).

Desegregation in Dayton has included the use of magnet schools, school pairing, and a freedom of enrollment policy to improve racial balance. School administrators encouraged community involvement at every juncture of planning and implementation. Civic and business groups, parents, and the press were courted as well. Finally, the commitment and enthusiasm of the school superintendent cannot be overstated. As one listened, in 1992, to James Williams describe his hopes and expectations for the Dayton school system, its pupils, and its teachers, one felt oneself to be in the presence of a charismatic leader who was truly dedicated to the cause of quality integrated education (*Dayton Cares for Kids: From Court Order to Implementation*, 1977, Kirby interview, Williams interview, Williamson interview).

The decision of Rochester, New York to desegregate its schools in 1969 was not in response to outside pressure or judicial decree. Although only 32 percent of the city's students were minority, their distribution throughout the system was very uneven. Six of the city's 45 schools had minority populations of more than 90 percent (*U.S. Census; Grade Reorganization and Desegregation of the Rochester Public Schools*, 1969, p. 18).

In 1950, the first Puerto Rican families arrived in Rochester, and five years later their numbers had swelled to 3000 (McKelvey, 1961, pp. 242-43). At the same time, blacks were moving up from the South and city residents were moving to the suburbs. Rochester's population, which peaked at 332,488 in 1950, dropped by 16,000 in the 1950s and 25,000 in the 1960s. Meanwhile, the non-white population tripled through the 1950s and increased by 110 percent in the next decade (McKelvey, 1973, pp. 240-42).

A 1963 directive from the New York State Commissioner of Education prompted Rochester to address the growing racial imbalance in its schools. An open enrollment plan was implemented to allow students from six inner-city schools to attend classes in any of 18 receiving schools elsewhere in the system. Summer programs allowed inner-city Rochester students to attend classes in Brighton and other suburbs, and regular school year transfers enrolled 25 first grade pupils each year from an inner-city school to suburban West Irondequoit, where it was intended that they would complete their school careers (*Grade Reorganization and Desegregation of the Rochester Public Schools*, 1969, pp. 9, 11; McKelvey, 1973, pp. 250-51).

However, not all of the residents of Greater Rochester were favorably disposed. Some parents of West Irondequoit instituted legal suits to safeguard their schools from "a black invasion," and this act understandably affronted the black community. Whites were discouraged from membership in the NAACP. Most white Rochesterians, who took pride in their city's reputation for tolerance and humanity, were bewildered and disturbed by this rebuff. They were even more astonished by the rioting that began in July, 1964 (McKelvey, 1973, pp. 250-52).

Once order was restored, the Rochester City School District Board explored a variety of desegregation plans. Concomitantly, a Student Union for Integrated Education was formed, as well as various school advisory committees, which grouped together as Project Unique. Strong educational components were added to the Rochester school system, including the highly regarded World of Inquiry School (*Desegregation of the Elementary Schools*, 1967; *Grade Reorganization and Desegregation of the Rochester Public Schools*, 1967, p. 13; McKelvey, 1973, pp. 264-65).

Although there were some setbacks between 1969 and 1971, the mid-1970s saw a re-activation of parent and neighborhood groups, especially the Nineteenth Ward Community Association and the Citizens for Quality Integrated Education. The magnet programs, which are still operating, were begun, and racial balance was gradually implemented. Enrollment in magnet schools is voluntary but may not negatively affect the racial balance of the student's neighborhood school. An unfortunate effect of this regulation is that only students who form part of the majority group in their neighborhood school may apply to attend a magnet school (Reid, 1984, p. 2; *CQIE Newsletter*, April, 1972; Rochester City School District Magnet Schools, *1989-90*; *Magnet Schools: Elementary Programs*, p. 3).

Of the five cities included in this study, Rochester is the only community to voluntarily implement its desegregation program. School officials, parents, and community representatives were uniform in their pride that Rochester had chosen to desegregate on its own rather than being pressured to do so by outside agencies. It is generally agreed that a fortuitous combination of dedicated and capable administrators and vigorous community support was responsible for the ultimate success of the desegregation efforts of the Rochester school system. The strong educational components, particularly the magnet school concept, offering an appealing choice of programs including foreign languages, technology, computer sciences, and the performing arts, made compliance all the more appealing (*Magnet Schools: Elementary Programs; Selections*).

Through much of the nineteenth century, public education in Trenton, New Jersey was viewed "not as a right, but a privilege." Further, despite the Board of Eduction's Rule Number 17, which required children to attend the school nearest to their home, Trenton's schools remained effectively segregated until 1944 (Washington, 1990, pp. 49-51). These attitudes and circumstances prove to be an unfortunately appropriate beginning for a desegregation effort that has made little progress subsequently as well.

By 1970, the city's population, which had reached 128,009 in 1950, was reduced to 104,638, of which 37.9 percent were African-American. The previous year, the State Board of Education had passed a resolution to determine which school districts in the state had racially imbalanced schools and to "undertake such steps as . . . necessary to correct such conditions of racial imbalance as may be found" (*Questions and Answers on Commissioner Marburger's Trenton Decision on Desegregation*, 1970, p. 6).

The assassination of Dr. Martin Luther King, in April, 1968, brought to a head the frustrations of both blacks and whites in Trenton. Whites were angered by a loss of job security and falling property values as the city's industry continued to decline; blacks, "having endured years of discrimination and humiliation," saw the whites remaining in the city as the cause of their distress. The schools, in the hands of a primarily white school board, which disregarded the increasing number of black students, reaped the bitter harvest of this mutual disdain (Cumbler, 1989, pp. 174-76).

Finally, in reaction to the riots after Dr. King's death and a directive by the State Board of Education's newly created Office of Equal Opportunity, an attempt was made to begin to correct the racial imbalance of the city schools. Busing was instituted between predominantly minority and mostly white schools. The whites responded with rioting, including overturned buses, and a lawsuit. Even the State Commissioner, who also serves as an officer of the court, in deciding for the plaintiffs, agreed that the plan was poor. He cited its counterproductivity, its lack of educational goals, and the absence of community involvement in its planning and development (*Trenton Plan for Educational Excellence, 1984*, p. 1; interview with Marcellus Smith; *Questions and Answers on Commissioner Marburger's Trenton Decision on Desegregation*, 1970, pp. 1-2).

Trenton's inability to satisfy the State Board and the Commissioner in the late 1960s and early 1970s set the pattern for relations between the city and the state that have continued to at least some extent up to this writing. Like Hartford, Trenton is the state capital and therefore particularly visible to state agencies. Whatever occurs, or what does not occur when it should, becomes immediately apparent. During the past 20 years, a variety of plans have been proposed, modified, implemented, modified, found insufficient or ineffective, and ultimately superseded by a new proposal. Meanwhile, during that time, making the issue infinitely more complicated, the proportion of black and Hispanic students has risen, while those who are white diminished. By 1990, the district was just over 90 percent minority: 69.7 percent African-American, 19.8 percent Hispanic, 9.9 percent white and 0.6 percent other minorities (Interview with Mark Raivetz, *Trenton Demographic and Geographic Considerations*, 1986, p. 6; *Trenton Public Schools, Districtwide Enrollment*, 1990-91, p. i).

The situation in Trenton is particularly discouraging because while there are no villains, circumstances have not allowed either for heroes. Intelligent and committed people are working for both the city and the state, but poor communications and apparent lack of trust have resulted in a minimum of constructive action. The citizenry is frustrated because it feels powerless. The demographics will allow for desegregation only if the district is permitted to move into the suburbs of Mercer County, and this seems unlikely, at least at present. Trenton provides a sad lesson of how good people with good intentions working at cross purposes are unlikely to achieve desired results.

While the section of the court decision in *Evans v. Buchanan*, which ultimately desegregated almost all of New Castle County, Delaware, was not determined until 1978, the efforts to desegregate the Wilmington schools actually began as part of that most famous 1954 Supreme Court decision, *Brown v. Board of Education of Topeka, Kansas*. As a border state, Delaware, in 1950, exhibited a mixture of northern and southern customs. While schools, restaurants, and theaters were segregated, public "libraries, buses and trains were not and blacks voted as freely as whites" (Wolters, 1984, p. 176).

Wilmington has the distinction of having experienced both *de jure* and *de facto* segregation. When, in 1950, Mrs. Fred Bulah protested the lack of bus transportation to the black school her adopted daughter attended, while the bus to the white school passed nearby, it was *de jure* segregation that was opposed and eliminated. However, when in 1968, the Delaware Legislature passed the Educational Advancement Act, to reorganize school districts in the state, and exempted Wilmington from all provisions of the act because its 16,000 students exceeded the 12,000 student maximum provided for by the act, those who protested did so on the basis of *de facto* segregation (Wolters, 1984, pp. 176-77; Hoffecker, 1983, pp. 244-45).

Wilmington schools were more than half black in 1968 and 72 percent black by 1971. The new plaintiffs contended that by exempting Wilmington from the 1968 act, the State had intentionally sought to maintain the city's segregated schools and that only an inter-district remedy would achieve meaningful desegregation (Raffel, 1980, pp. 46-47).

The District Court and the Supreme Court agreed and in May, 1976, the Court proposed a plan that would include almost all of New Castle County. The school district of Appoquinimink was excluded because it was huge, sparsely populated, and integrated to the extent that it was 28 percent minority. Located in the extreme southern part of the county, its inclusion would have added extensive traveling time for county students without significantly altering the integration efforts (*Fact Book,* 1978, pp. 28-29).

The 11 districts of New Castle County became four attendance areas within one district in 1978. Students in Wilmington and De La Warr (a Wilmington suburb but overwhelmingly minority, similar to the situation of Hartford, Connecticut's suburb, Bloomfield) were to spend three years in their home district and nine years in a suburb; the suburban students would be away for three years and home for nine. As far as possible children would go to school with others from their own neighborhood and with the same group of children in a feeder system. Grade centers were organized on the basis of three continuous grades: 1-3, 4-6, 7-9, 10-12 (*Fact Book,* 1978, pp. 5-6).

In September, 1980, the white student population in the four districts varied from 66 to 73 percent, with the total student body being 70.7 percent white. All of the districts contained small numbers of Hispanics and Asians, while African-Americans comprised the greatest portion of the minority student representation. Ten years later, the four districts ranged from 64 to 70 percent white, and the total enrollment had dropped to 67.1 percent white with slightly more Asian and Hispanic students proportionate to African-Americans in the minority category

(*Regulations for Reorganization*, 1980, *Appendix B*; *July 19, 1990 Report of Suspensions and Expulsions*).

If the current system is to be judged by numerical proportions, then the desegregation of New Castle County's schools should be declared a success. While there has been some white flight, the absolute number of white students actually increased, and the proportion of white to minority students has remained consistently uniform over the past ten years (Klaff, 1981, p. 24).

The Courts must be deemed most responsible for the implementation of desegregation in New Castle County. Only they had the authority to impose a remedy that would create a system so different from what had previously existed. In so doing, the Court made the desegregation district so large that white flight was made extremely difficult. Parents and students therefore had to give the new system a chance, and once they did, resistance significantly diminished.

When the suit known as *Sheff v. O'Neill* was filed under provisions of the Connecticut State Constitution rather than the federal, on April 26, 1989, it brought into sharp focus a situation that had been incrementally deteriorating over a prolonged period of time. While the plaintiffs conceded that neither the State of Connecticut nor the City of Hartford had consciously or purposely allowed the city's schools to become overwhelmingly minority, nevertheless, at the time the case was brought, whites comprised barely more than one-tenth of Hartford's school population, and that proportion has since diminished (*The Hartford Courant*, April 27, 1989, p. 1).

Blacks were always permitted to go to district schools, although during the nineteenth century, their treatment was frequently poor. And, while the State did not actively seek to separate the races, it encouraged that effect by supporting the building of regionalized suburban high schools after World War II. Suburban students, who had previously attended high school within the city, were removed from the urban facilities when, with state financial assistance, two or three towns ringing the city built a new inter-district high school in one of their own towns. In those rarer instances when the State operated its own regional technical schools, they encompassed a much greater geographical area, which generally included a central city (Collier interview).

While the first Puerto Rican family arrived in Connecticut in 1844, this group, which now comprises the overwhelming proportion of Hartford's Hispanic population, remained quite small for the next hundred years. Numbers increased slowly until 1960, but subsequently, migration has been far more intense. Hartford has consistently had the largest Puerto Rican population in the state, both in absolute numbers and in proportion to other residents.

Puerto Ricans now outnumber African-Americans in Hartford's schools (Glasser, 1992, pp. 1-5).

The discourse regarding integrated education was energized when Gerald Tirozzi became State Commissioner of Education in 1983. With experience in the suburbs and city, as teacher and administrator, Dr. Tirozzi was very familiar with Connecticut education. His most dramatic contribution at the state level, during his eight-year tenure, was to draw attention to the increasing segregation of Connecticut's schools (Tirozzi interview).

Three reports exploring the question of integrated schools were prepared during Dr. Tirozzi's commissionership. They documented his concerns and called for the state to accept responsibility for desegregating Connecticut's public schools through administrative and legislative means using voluntary desegregation (*A Report on Racial/Ethnic Equity and Desegregation in Connecticut's Public Schools*, 1988; *Quality and Integrated Education: Options for Connecticut*, 1989; *Crossing the Bridge to Equality and Excellence*, 1990).

Over the years, several integration programs have been implemented in the State. One of the earliest and most enduring has been Project Concern, which has been in operation since 1966. A one-way program, which at its peak in the late 1970s sent 1500 students to 13 suburban communities and six non-public schools, it also offers children in receiving towns an opportunity to go to school in a multiracial and multicultural environment (*Quality and Integrated Education: Options for Connecticut*, 1989, p. 12).

More recently, various programs have been undertaken by individual communities working together. The Connecticut Association of Boards of Education compiled an annotated list of such programs in 1989, and in 1990, the Capital Region Educational Council created a similar document (*Creative Approaches for Reducing Racial/Economic Isolation in Connecticut Schools*, 1989; *PAQIE Inventory of Progress to Reduce Racial Imbalance*, 1990, pp. 1-9).

Interviews conducted with more than two dozen individuals, employed at or otherwise involved in Hartford area schools, conducted for this study, indicated general support for the concept of desegregation but less unanimity regarding the proper method of implementation. Even more concern was elicited with respect to how the wider community would respond to such an effort. This concern was shown to be justified when eight of 11 regions, created by the State Legislature in 1994 to consider voluntary integration efforts, voted against continuing the planning process after the initial set of meetings.

When the issue of desegregation is raised, the Greater Hartford community, like people everywhere, elicit concerns for safety and the highest quality of education for its children.   If the schools of the Hartford area are to be desegregated with the support of parents and pupils, assurances of safety within the schools and in the surrounding neighborhoods will be necessary. Concomitantly, suburban parents are not alone in demanding a safe environment for their children. Inner-city parents seek it as well, and inner-city children are equally entitled to a safe educational experience. If a school is not deemed to be safe for a suburban child, it should not be considered appropriate for any other child. It is understandable that white and minority parents, city and suburban parents, would resent news reports that many public officials have chosen to educate their children in private schools.

Well-reported parental resistance to busing as a means of promoting desegregation must be separated from the issue of transportation. Ninety percent of the children in Connecticut live too far from their school to walk and are therefore transported to school on a bus. Few, if any, parents have been quoted as wishing to become responsible for this duty. Many other children travel longer distances when their families decide upon a private or parochial education. When children are going to a school that is seen to be desirable, the discussion is about transportation; it is only when they are to be sent somewhere deemed undesirable that "busing" becomes an issue.

It is a mistake to diminish the importance of self-fulfilling prophesy. With schools, as with many other entities, perception frequently influences reality. When those connected to a school--administrators, teachers, students, parents--believe in the superiority of that institution, that presumption is the beginning of that reality. It is not unreasonable for parents to want good schools for their children. Wherever schools are located, the highest quality of education must be the goal. This does not always require extensive financial outlay. In many highly regarded schools, it is the attitude of those involved, more than extravagant facilities, that makes the school desirable.

However, this should not be taken to mean that spending for education is either unnecessary or excessive. It is less expensive and infinitely more productive to suitably educate a child to qualify for a productive life than to have to incarcerate an anti-social and marginally skilled adult. Further, it is a delusion that children with impoverished home lives and complex needs can be educated for the same amount of money as those children who are fortunate enough to live in a home and community where much more can be provided for their welfare.

Whatever plan is ultimately implemented for the Hartford region, based on the findings of this study, the following insights should be of value.

The circumstances that existed relative to the ultimate desegregation of the Dayton schools bear an important similarity to that of Hartford. In both instances, it was state as well as federal law that was being challenged. As is the case in Connecticut, the State of Ohio Department of Education strongly encouraged desegregation efforts.

Strong personal identity and commitment on the part of the system's superintendents has played an important role in the success Dayton has achieved in its desegregation efforts. When James A. Williams replaced Frederick L. Smith as Superintendent in 1992, he had been with the system for six years as its Deputy Superintendent; C. Benjamin Kirby, the Director of Magnet Programs, has been with the system since 1962. One senses that a strong feeling of personal involvement and dedication is required to create the kind of charismatic leadership that is necessary to encourage people on a path that traverses unknown, and therefore sometimes frightening, terrain.

The civic pride felt and frequently mentioned in Rochester, New York was the motivating force behind this city's determination to desegregate its schools without outside pressures or judicial decree. Numerous community groups were established to discuss and support desegregation efforts while already-existing organizations, such as the Nineteenth Ward Community Association, made the promotion of integration among their highest priorities. A Neighborhood Diplomatic Corps was instituted by the school system to formalize the home-school partnership and train those who would be serving as the diplomats. Rochester's experience demonstrates that community involvement is an integral ingredient in the implementation of peaceful and effective school desegregation.

To encourage the amount of student participation necessary to make voluntary desegregation work, improved educational components were provided and a sense of ability to choose was created. Myriad magnet programs were conceived and offered at all levels. Elementary schools feature bi-lingual and bi-cultural opportunities, as well as specialization in science, computers, technology, and the performing arts. At middle and high schools, these programs are continued and augmented by specialties in the natural sciences and the liberal arts as well as the School Without Walls and the Academy of Excellence. If parents perceive an opportunity for superior education and feel that they can play an active role in determining how their children will be educated, those children will be encouraged to attend even non-neighborhood schools willingly.

Like Hartford, Trenton, New Jersey is the state capital, and its problems become immediately visible to those engaged in running the state's business. Since the 1960s, the state and the city have operated at cross purposes while ostensibly attempting to achieve the same objective: quality, integrated education for the students of the Trenton Public Schools. Goals are set, plans are proposed, reports are submitted, and the efforts are found wanting; the process begins again and again. Meanwhile, the schools of Trenton become less able to implement any meaningful desegregation as the white population shrinks to almost nonexistence. It is clear what Connecticut should learn from the unfortunate examples of New Jersey: when the plan for Hartford's desegregation is decided, those in the city, the region, and the state must work together cooperatively and effectively.

When the population of Wilmington, Delaware became so overwhelmingly minority that desegregation could no longer be effected within the city limits, the Courts called for a metropolitan remedy. At the time this study began, the population of the Wilmington area bore great resemblance to that of Hartford, since not only were the central cities' populations similarly primarily minority, but each had one suburb, De La Warr in Delaware and Bloomfield in Connecticut, which were also much more heavily minority than any other suburb.

By creating a district that encompassed almost all of New Castle County, white flight was effectively discouraged. People would have had to move beyond the point of convenience and thus were required to give the newly organized school district a chance. If a metropolitan solution is declared for Hartford, it is equally important that the district be made large enough to diminish the likelihood of white flight.

With the minority enrollment in Hartford's schools at 93 percent in 1994, only a metropolitan desegregation plan could be effective. Therefore, as much attention must be paid to Hartford's suburbs as to the city itself. Between 1989 and 1993, Hartford's minority enrollment increased by just three percent and actually dropped .6 percent during the last year, changes in the school populations of the suburban towns have been dramatic. In 1988, only two suburbs had minority enrollments that exceeded five percent; by 1992, only two towns had minority enrollments of less than five percent (See Table 7.1).

In 1993, in addition to Bloomfield at 83.5 percent, East Hartford reported 38.1 percent minority, an increase of 18.4 percent in just one year. Windsor, at 36.9 percent, increased only .1 percent in the last year, but still showed impressive minority proportions. Manchester and West Hartford were close to 20 percent, and Vernon was also in double digits. As Manchester's Superintendent James Kennedy noted, there is little benefit to integrating Hartford's minority students with those from Manchester.

Table 7.1
Minorities in Greater Hartford Public Schools, 1992

TOWN	NUMBER MINORITIES 1992	PERCENT MINORITIES 1992	PERCENT CHANGE 1991-1992
Avon	114	5.3	5.6
Bloomfield	2,060	83.5	4.0
East Hartford	2,353	38.1	18.4
Enfield	377	5.8	13.9
Farmington	204	6.6	9.7
Glastonbury	396	8.3	0.8
Granby	36	2.3	38.5
Hartford	23,628	93.1	-0.6
Manchester	1,383	19.0	22.9
Newington	287	7.6	9.1
Rocky Hill	172	8.3	-2.8
Simsbury	184	4.7	16.5
Vernon	492	11.6	16.3
West Hartford	1,345	17.2	8.9
Wethersfield	205	6.7	22.8
Windsor	1,594	36.9	0.1

Source: The Hartford Courant, March 23, 1993, p. B9.

In the same manner that desegregation has been required to progress from intra- to inter-city plans as city populations changed, a similar situation seemed to be developing in first-ring suburbs. While educators and politicians had been discussing if and how to desegregate the central city, African-Americans, Hispanics, and Asians were quietly desegregating the suburbs. Since this suburban activity did not change the population proportions of the central city and occurred in the Hartford area so recently and so rapidly, one is left with the same imbalance in the city, but with no readily accessible models elsewhere and fewer areas available around Hartford with which to interrelate.

While the majority of those interviewed for this study agreed that integrated schools were a necessity to properly educate children to function in the multicultural world that will exist in the twenty-first century, there was little agreement as to how this integration should be implemented. While at least half of the interviewees felt that regionalization would be required, the eight-to-three rejection of the regional forum preliminary reports as initiated by Governor Weicker and implemented by the State Legislature in its 1993 session has shown how difficult it will be to reach a consensus.

It is said that the only constant in history is change. Certainly the study of American school desegregation gives credence to this aphorism. Beginning with the decisions of the Supreme Court, we see segregation first as the law of the land in *Plessy v. Ferguson* in 1896, and then overturned in 1954 in *Brown v. Board of Education of Topeka, Kansas*. Subsequently, the Court slowed desegregation in *Brown II* (1955), and then hastened the effort in *Griffin v. County School Board of Prince Edward County* (1964).

Compulsory busing was ordered in *Cisneros v. Corpus Christi Independent School District* in 1970, but since that time, as in *United States v. Board of Education, Independent School District No. 1, Tulsa* (1970), the Court has frequently used magnet schools to make mandated busing unnecessary. While a regional solution was denied to the Detroit plaintiffs in *Milliken v. Bradley* in 1974, a metropolitan remedy was granted to the Wilmington plaintiffs in 1976 in *Evans v. Buchanan*.

Situations have remained relatively stable in Dayton, Rochester, Trenton, and Wilmington from 1991 to 1994 and seemed likely to continue unchanged in the years immediately following. However, in Hartford, the *Sheff v. O'Neill* court case and the legislative initiative appeared to guarantee that the issue would remain an unresolved matter of contention into the next century. Had this study been completed in 1989, recommendations based on the demographics of that year might have been made. As noted above, population shifts during the subsequent six years would have rendered any plan based upon those numbers obsolete. To be useful, specific recommendations will have to await a commitment, either by the courts or the legislature.

Thus, it seems wisest to concentrate upon those principles that are least likely to be subject to change.

- All parents seek a safe environment for their children. No child, urban, suburban, or rural, should be sent to a school that is not deemed to be safe. If city neighborhoods cannot be made safe, new school construction should be on the periphery of the cities or in the suburbs. By a margin of 3-2, non-whites have indicated a willingness to be bused out of their neighborhoods to achieve integration (*Journal Inquirer*, February 15, 1993, p. 14). While this may be cumbersome, and make parental participation in the schools all the more difficult, the advantages far outweigh the drawbacks.

- All children are entitled to the highest quality education. If all schools are viewed as offering an appropriately high level of educational opportunity, disagreements about location will be minimized. Parents transport their children great distances to private schools that they believe offer the quality of education that they seek. Public   education must be made to appear equally appealing and worthy of regard. Implementing this goal will be very expensive, but the alternative of an undereducated underclass will ultimately cost more.

• As the population statistics for Hartford and its suburbs demonstrate, we are rapidly becoming a multiracial and multicultural nation. Feelings of awkwardness and distrust diminish when people have real contact with each other. Sports teams appear to have little difficulty being integrated, as they must work together if they are to prevail. Spectators do not seem to discriminate between black and white players when the goal is to cheer on their alma mater or the group representing their municipality.   Patrons of amusement parks, movie theaters, and casinos comfortably coexist as they seek entertainment or instant wealth.

If children of varying backgrounds go to school together, they will find it easier to relate later in the workplace. Ultimately this familiarity may enable the integration of housing, and then school desegregation could occur naturally. Eventually, we might even be able to return to the much-beloved concept of the neighborhood school and at the same time achieve the goal of quality, integrated education.

Appendix A: Interview Schedule for Case Study Cities

1. What were the critical incidents that brought about the changes in your school system?

2. What was the racial composition of the schools and their general makeup previous to the change?

3. What are the major changes regarding race that have occurred within your school system since the critical incident?

4. What prompted these changes?

5. What legal issues and/or court decisions influenced the changes in your school system?

6. What effect did political groups have on the changes in your school system?

7. What effect did administrative actions have on changes in your school system?

8. What effect did community groups have on changes in your school system?

9. To what do you most attribute constructive actions toward desegregation?

10. To what do you most attribute counterproductive actions regarding desegregation?

11. What other factors were important in the desegregation of your system that we have not yet discussed?

12. Based on your experiences and/or your perceptions of what occurred in your system, what advice would you give to a metropolitan area about to embark upon an effort to desegregate its schools?

Appendix B: Interview Schedule for Hartford

1. How do you assess the state of race relations in your school district and elsewhere in the Hartford region?

2. Do you think race relations have improved or worsened in the past 20 years?

3. Have you been involved in any attempts to improve race relations in the schools in your district or anywhere else in the Hartford region?

4. How important a component of quality education do you think integrated schools are?

5. How do you define integrated schools?

6. What outcome do you anticipate from Sheff v. O'Neill?

7. What events besides the court case do you anticipate having significant effects on desegregation efforts?

8. How do you think desegregation should be accomplished?

9. With what desegregation models are you familiar?

10. What lessons do you think that they provide?

11. What factors do you think are most important in providing quality integrated education?

12. What groups and/or institutions in the region do you think are most instrumental in bringing about change?

13. What do you see as the role of the courts?

14. What do you see as the role of the legislature?

15. What do you see as the role of the State Board of Education?

16. What do you see as the role of the various school administrations?

17. What do you see as the role of business?

18. What do you see as the role of the community?

19. What other groups do you see playing a role?

20. What are the greatest obstacles to success?

Appendix C: Case Study Cities Interviewees

DAYTON, OHIO

Dale Frederick, Dayton Public Schools, June 23, 1991

C. Benjamin Kirby, Magnet Schools Director, Dayton Public Schools, June 24, 1991

Mary H. Moore, Assessment Director, Dayton Public Schools, June 24, 1991

Jane Rafal, Executive Assistant to the Superintendent, Dayton Public Schools, November 17 and 22, 1994

Mary A. Robinson, Assessment Evaluator, Dayton Public Schools, June 24, 1991

James A. Williams, Superintendent, Dayton Public Schools, June 23-24, 1991

Miley O. Williamson, Executive Secretary, Dayton NAACP, June 29, 1992

ROCHESTER, NEW YORK

Marie V. Andia, Magnet Schools Director, Rochester City School District, June 3, 1991

Nella Corryn, Magnet Schools Evaluator, Rochester City School District, June 3, 1991; November 15 and 22, 1994

Archie Curry, Former School Board Member, Rochester City School District, June 4, 1991

Lew Kiner, Rochester City School District Summer Lunch Coordinator, June 2, 1991

Marcia A. Reichardt, Recruitment Coordinator, Rochester City School District, June 3, 1991

Ben Richardson, Rochester City School District, June 3, 1991

Morley Schloss, Rochester City School District, June 3, 1991
Alfred J. Sette, Rochester City School District Parent, June 3-4, 1991

TRENTON, NEW JERSEY

Fred Burke, Former State Commissioner of Education, March 4, 1992
Phyllis Langford, Planning Assistant, Trenton Board of Education,
     June 17, 1991
Mark J. Raivetz, Director of Planning, Research, and Evaluation,
     Trenton Board of Education, June 17, 1991; November 15 and
     22, 1994
Jilda Rorro, Director, State Equal Educational Opportunity Office,
     March 9, 1992
Marcellus Smith, State School Desegregation Program Coordinator,
     March 5, 1992

WILMINGTON, DELAWARE

Ambrose Haggerty, State Department of Public Instruction, June 18,
     1991
Henry C. Harper, State Department of Public Instruction, June 18,
     1991
William B. Keene, Director, Office of School/University Partnerships,
     University of Delaware and Former State Superintendent, June
     19, 1991
Jack Nichols, State Department of Public Instruction, June 18, 1991;
     November 15, 1994
Judge Murray Schwartz, Presiding Judge *Evans v. Buchanan*, June
     14, 1991
James Spartz, Interim State Superintendent, June 18, 1991
Jea Street, Director of African-American Coalition, August 14, 1991

HARTFORD, CONNECTICUT

John J. Allison, Jr., Director, Capitol Region Education Council,
     September 17, 1992
Jane Barstow, Hartford parent, September 19, 1992
Norman Barstow, Hartford parent and Simsbury teacher, September
     19, 1992
Professor John C. Brittain, *Sheff* attorney, September 19, 1992
Lloyd Calvert, Former School Superintendent, West Hartford,
     September 19, 1992
Mary Carroll, Project Concern Director, October 6, 1992

David G. Carter, Co-chair, Governor's Commission on Quality and Integrated Education, December 2, 1992

Professor Christopher Collier, University of Connecticut, July 28, 1992

Paul Copes, Superintendent, Bloomfield, September 24, 1992

Donald Corso, Principal, McDonough School, November 14, 1994

Norma Cruz de Cima de Villa, Migrant Education Program Director, Puerto Rico, January 14, 1993

Susan Davis, Vice-President, Hartford Federation of Teachers, September 29, 1992

Elba Diaz, Carilina III, Puerto Rico, January 15, 1993

Vincent Ferrandino, State Commissioner, September 18, 1992

Professor Luis Figueroa, University of Connecticut, October 26, 1992

Cora Hahn, Professor, Trinity College, October 25, 1992

T. Josiha Haig, Superintendent, Hartford, September 29, 1992

Susie Hinton, Principal, SAND Everywhere School, October 2, 1992

Professor Edward F. Iwanicki, University of Connecticut, October 21, 1992

James Kennedy, Superintendent, Manchester, September 24, 1992

Albert Kerkin, Former Superintendent,Vernon, September 3, 1992

Hernan LaFontaine, Former Superintendent, Hartford, October 26, 1992

Eugene Leach, *Sheff* Plaintiff , September 15, 1992

Sam Leone, Superintendent, East Hartford, October 7, 1992

Jean Romano, Windham Schools Bilingual Program, November 10, 1994

Linda Seagraves, Aetna, September 23, 1992

Elizabeth Sheff, Plaintiff, September 9, 1992

Gerald Tirozzi, Former State Commissioner, September 29, 1992

Mildred Torres-Soto, Casa de Puerto Rico, October 22, 1992

Elliott Williams, State Department of Education, September 29, 1992

Nancy Wyman, State Representative, September 7, 1992

Bibliographic Essay: Cases and Sources

Although it speaks eloquently of such rights as freedom of speech, the press, assembly, and petition, the Constitution of the United States is silent on the subject of education. Therefore, by virtue of the Tenth Amendment, which states, "The powers not delegated to the United States by the Constitution, nor prohibited by it to the States, are reserved to the States respectively, or to the people," education is ultimately conceived to be the responsibility of the States. Thus, the contention that "the American system of jurisprudence, which ideally should have guaranteed equal educational opportunity for all children, actually has aided the cause of segregation by its hesitation . . . , its lack of clarity . . . , and its equivocation on many of the vital issues regarding the implementation of urban desegregation plans" becomes compelling when one examines judicial decisions rendered during the past century (Showell in Levinsohn & Wright, 1976, p. 104).

The Supreme Court first granted constitutional protection to deliberate racial segregation in *Plessy v. Ferguson* (163 U.S. 537, 1896). This "ultimate legitimation of segregation" occurred when the Court "upheld a Louisiana statute that mandated 'separate but equal' accommodations in railway trains for blacks and whites" (Meier, Stewart, Jr., & England, 1989, p. 42).

The Court found no violation of the Fourteenth Amendment, although the first section of that amendment states: "No State shall make or enforce any law which shall abridge the privileges or immunities of citizens of the United States, nor shall any State deprive any person of life, liberty, or property, without due process of law; nor deny to any person within its jurisdiction the equal protection of the laws." Judicial support for this separatist (and, indeed, racist) legal ideology was reaffirmed three years later in *Cummings v. County Board of Education* (175 U.S. 545, 1899). The Court declared that a white school board could decide to "close down

a Black school in order to use the money for a white school." Justice
Harlan's decision, which determined in essence that the Fourteenth
Amendment was irrelevant, permitted school boards to "deliberately
and systematically exclude Black children and provided additional
legal support for government and school-district policies fostering
racial isolation and subjugation" (Showell in Levinsohn & Wright, p.
104).

"The Court began assuming a progressively more affirmative role
in matters of race and public policy," when, in *Buchanan v. Warley*
(245 U.S. 60, 1917), it "struck down a municipal ordinance requiring
residential segregation in Louisville." Between 1930 and 1950, the
Court concentrated on a series of higher education cases brought by
the National Association for the Advancement of Colored People
(NAACP) (Vergon, 1990, pp. 23-24).

Thurgood Marshall was the principal attorney representing the
plaintiffs in these cases. In *Missouri ex rel Gaines v. Canada* (305
U.S. 337, 1938), "the NAACP won an appeal to the U.S. Supreme
Court which held that a black applicant to the University of Missouri
Law School had the same right to an opportunity for legal education
as whites within that state." The Court rejected the state's plan to
open a separate law school for blacks "whenever necessary and
practical" and "to provide scholarships for black students to attend
law school outside the state" (Meier, Stewart, Jr., & England, p. 44).

Law Schools were also the venue in the cases of *Sipuel v.
University of Oklahoma Law School* (332 U.S. 631, 1948), and
Sweatt v. Painter (339 U.S. 629, 1950), where the plaintiffs
successfully contended that a segregated law school could not
provide Ada Lois Sipuel or Heman Sweatt with educational
opportunities equal to those available at the law schools of the
University of Oklahoma or the University of Texas, respectively.

In *McLaurin v. Oklahoma State Regents* (339 U.S. 637, 1950), the
first case of pure segregation was argued. In this instance, McLaurin
was accorded "the same professors, books, and classroom
instruction"; however, "he was given a separate seat set aside solely
for his use in the classroom, library, and cafeteria." Attorneys in this
case argued persuasively that "the adverse psychological detriment . .
. that segregation inflicted on blacks . . . resulted in a denial of equal
education" (Carter in Bell, 1980, p. 22).

The same approach was adopted on May 17, 1954, in *Brown v.
Board of Education of Topeka, Kansas* (347 U.S. 483, 1954) when
plaintiffs contended and the United States Supreme Court agreed
that state-sanctioned segregation in public education was inherently
unequal. However, making segregation illegal did not of course
concomitantly make it nonexistent. In the North, segregated housing
patterns allowed for, and in some cases actually ensured, the
maintenance of *de facto* if not *de jure* separation of the races in the
public schools. In the South, active hostility to the Court decision was

manifested in continued dual school systems. Twelve years after *Brown*, 95 percent of African-American pupils still attended segregated schools (Metcalf, 1983, p. 10).

In his 1980 reassessment of the *Brown* case and his participation as a leading attorney in the litigation, Robert L. Carter reaffirms his belief in the need to have had state-enforced racial segregation outlawed; however, he suggests that "segregation was only a biproduct of society's commitment to white supremacy." Carter contends that "the real evil, white racism, will not easily succumb to innovative legal arguments," and that "there must be a greater emphasis on remedies designed to improve the caliber of education provided for black children" (Bell, p. 20).

The difficulty was primarily in the implementation of the 1954 *Brown* decision (*Brown I*) that "racial discrimination in public education is unconstitutional" and that "all provisions of federal, state, or local law requiring or permitting such discrimination must yield to this principle." This was especially so as the decision continued "there remains for consideration the manner in which relief is to be accorded."

Matters were further exacerbated when the Supreme Court a year later in *Brown v. Board of Education* (349 U.S. 294, 1955) (*Brown II*) decided to "apply the 1954 anti-segregation decree on a gradual basis." Many observers, including jurist Constance Baker Motley, viewed this decision as a "disaster" and a "promise of indefiniteness." "We cannot really know what would have happened if the court had said, 'Do it now'" (Showell in Levinsohn & Wright, pp. 105-6).

While *Brown II* required that children be assigned to school on a "racially nondiscriminatory basis," it also held that "this did not have to be done at once, or even within any specified time, but only 'with all deliberate speed.'" The Court purported to believe that this unprecedented permission to delay the enforcement of a constitutional right was required for administrative considerations; however, Washington D.C. and some of the border states by desegregating in the interim and before the *Brown II* decision demonstrated the fallacy of this argument (Graglia in Stephan & Feagin, 1980, p. 72).

If further proof of the Court's vacillation was needed, it was established three years later when in *Cooper v. Aaron* (358 U.S. 1, 1958) the Court again refused to order the immediate implementation of *Brown*, while it made clear that "violence was not a justification for delaying desegregation" (Crain, 1968, p. 229).

The Court appeared to take a step backward in *Shuttlesworth v. Birmingham Board of Education* (358 U.S. 101, 1958). In a *per curiam* decision (by the court, without a signed opinion), it upheld a lower court ruling permitting Alabama's pupil placement plan. "By the late 1950s, pupil placement plans had become the South's standard response to *Brown*. Under these plans, children were to be assigned to schools according to a long list of vague, ostensibly nonracial criteria. In practice, they were simply initially assigned by race as before, and the plan became operative only upon a pupil's request for a transfer." Administrative and judicial appeals and the vagueness of the criteria generally ensured that the applicant graduated before a transfer would take place (Graglia in Stephan & Feagin, p. 73).

Southern resistance to desegregation was ingenious and varied. On March 12, 1956, 96 Congressmen from Southern states "issued a manifesto in which they promised to use 'all lawful means' to maintain segregation and 'commended those states which have declared the intention to resist.'" New pupil assignment laws, "interposition" plans, and other creative schemes proved that as long as Southerners could legislate, they could continue to segregate. "A popular variation of pupil assignment laws was the 'minority to majority transfer' arrangement. After formally desegregating, a Southern school district would grant to any students who constituted a racial minority in their new school the option of transferring back to their old school in which their race were a majority." In the next signed opinion by the Court, in the case of *Goss v. Board of Education of Knoxville, Tennessee* (373 U.S. 683, 1963), the Supreme Court struck down such plans as a violation of *Brown*, stating that in this instance, "the right of transfer, which operated solely on the basis of a racial classification, is a one-way ticket leading to but one destination, i.e., the majority race of the transferee and continued segregation" (Kirp & Yudof, 1974, p. 307).

Ten years after the *Brown* decision, only 2.14 percent of Southern blacks were attending desegregated schools. However, the Kennedy-Johnson administrations of the 1960s caused an acceleration of desegregation activities, and by 1964 Congress had passed the Civil Rights Act "which forbade the use of federal funds in segregated institutions." The 1965 Elementary and Secondary Education Act reinforced that provision by "making considerable federal aid available but only to compliant school districts." Meanwhile, in *Griffin v. County School Board of Prince Edward County* (377 U.S. 218, 1964), the Court declared that "the time for mere 'deliberate speed' has run out" (Hochschild, 1984, p. 27).

While most of the early desegregation decisions focused on *de jure* situations in the South, some cases addressed *de facto* segregation in the North. In *Offerman v. Nitkowski*, when white parents in Buffalo, New York protested the adjustment of attendance boundaries to place white students in black schools and black students in white schools, the court noted: "That there may be no constitutional duty to act to undo *de facto* segregation, however, does not mean that such action is unconstitutional. Since *Brown* is the law, some attention to color count is necessary to see that it is not violated, for it affirmatively requires admission to public schools on a racially non-discriminatory basis. What is prohibited is the use of race as a basis for unequal treatment" (378 F.2nd 22, 2nd Cir. 1967).

On March 29, 1967, the Fifth Circuit Court of Appeals, in the case of *U.S. v. Jefferson County Board of Education* (380 F.2d 385, 1967) determined that the states within its jurisdiction (Alabama, Florida, Georgia, Louisiana, Mississippi, and Texas) must take whatever affirmative action was necessary to create a "unitary school system in which there are no Negro schools and no white schools--just schools." The Court, stating that "the only school desegregation plan that meets constitutional standards is one that works," in essence argued that where effectiveness and choice are in conflict, the former must prevail (Metcalf, pp. 10-11).

Following the same line of reasoning, the Court in *Green v. Board of Education of New Kent County* (391 U.S. 430, 1968) ruled that "passive 'freedom of choice' plans no longer sufficed. Schools had 'the affirmative duty to take whatever steps might be necessary to convert to a unitary system in which racial discrimination would be eliminated root and branch'" (Hochschild, p. 27).

Five years after the *Griffin* decision, the Court reiterated its refusal to tolerate further delay in the process of desegregation. In *Alexander v. Holmes County Board of Education*, the Court stated that "continued operation of racially segregated schools under the standard of 'all deliberate speed' is no longer constitutionally permissible. . . . The obligation of every school district is to terminate dual school systems at once and to operate now and hereafter only unitary systems . . . within which no person is to be effectively excluded from any school because of race or color" (396 U.S. 19, 1969).

The impact of this decision was further intensified by a shift in enforcement strategy. Instead of threatening to deprive districts of federal funds, which often disadvantaged blacks at least as much as whites, the Office of Civil Rights turned the cases over to the Justice Department for litigation. Districts were offered a simple choice: "comply or be sued." Although this at first appeared to be part of President Richard Nixon's southern strategy to retard the movement toward unitary schools, when the Justice Department brought suit against 81 Georgia districts in *United States v. Georgia* (Civil No. 12972, N.D. Ga., 1969), with the threat of eliminating state funding as well as federal aid, the recalcitrant districts were rapidly brought into compliance (Meier, Stewart, Jr., & England, p. 49).

Cisneros v. Corpus Christi Independent School District marked the political institutionalization of busing. When the defendant school board complained of the "dire effects" that would result from the transportation of white students, the judge responded that "the children who are being bussed now make no such claims, nor have I been shown any harmful effects on the individual children that will outweigh the harmful effects on the Negro or Mexican-American child who is in a segregated and dual system" (324 F. Supp. 599, S.D. Tex. 1970). President Richard Nixon's criticism of the Corpus Christi plan as "an example of the unconscionable busing of children for the sake of social engineering" heralded the beginning of an era where school desegregation and "forced busing appeared to be synonymous." (Gordon, 1989, p. 192).

Magnet schools have been one of the approaches tried to avoid compulsory busing. When in *United States v. Board of Education, Independent School District No. 1, Tulsa,* the Court found that the district was operating a dual school system and ordered it to desegregate, the final plan, after many failures, was a K-12 fine arts magnet program (429 F.2d 1253, 10th Cir. 1970). The building of an entirely new elementary school and the expenditure of three times the funds of any other school in the district enabled the magnet school, although located in a black neighborhood, to achieve the racial balance it sought and even to have a waiting list of white students (Gordon, 1989, pp. 198-99).

However, with the possible exception of Houston, Tulsa experienced the only successful implementation of desegregation through the use of a magnet program. Magnets were ordered in *Hart v. Community School Board of Education, New York School District No. 21* (512 F. 2d 37, 2nd Cir. 1975), where "a special curriculum and teacher interest [was] required" but an insufficient number of white students applied; in *Davis v. East Baton Rouge Parish School Board* (414 F. Supp. 869, M.D. La. 1981), where magnet schools were ordered but were never actually implemented despite 23 years of court litigation and the expenditure of several million dollars; and in *United States v. Chicago Board of Education,* where, with only four percent of the students participating, the majority of the magnet schools that were ordered did not achieve their goal of integration and, ultimately, it was accepted that all-black schools would be maintained and upgraded (554 F. Supp, 912, N.D. Ill. 1983); in *Liddell v. State of Missouri,* when the State of Missouri decided not to pay the full cost of transporting students who were to attend school outside of their district, a prohibition on further recruitment and acceptance of students was agreed upon and the magnet programs that had been developed were abandoned (717 F.2d 1180, 8th Cir. 1983).

There were far-reaching implications in the movement toward desegregation in *Swann v. Charlotte-Mecklenburg Board of Education.* The Court declared by unanimous vote that "All things being equal, . . . it might well be desirable to assign pupils to schools nearest their homes. But all things are not equal in a system that has been constructed and maintained to enforce racial segregation. The remedy for such segregation may be administratively awkward, inconvenient, and even bizarre in some situations and may impose burdens upon some; but all awkwardness and inconvenience cannot be avoided in the interim period when remedial adjustments are being made to eliminate the dual school systems. . . . Desegregation plans cannot be limited to the walk-in school" (402 U.S. 1, 1971).

A companion case, *North Carolina State Board of Education v. Swann* (402 U.S. 43, 1971), decided the same day, and again a unanimous decision authored by Chief Justice Warren Burger, "also endorsed the use of race-conscious remedial measures and placed the burden on school districts to justify the continuation of any one-race schools." The impact of judicial and administrative enforcement machinery between 1968 and 1972 was dramatic. "The number of Black children attending school with some Whites increased by 59%, while more than a million Blacks across the South entered majority White schools for the first time" (Vergon, 1990, p. 26).

When, in the autumn of 1971, the Department of Health, Education, and Welfare began to collect statistics on school desegregation, it discovered a "frightening disparity in racial isolation between North and South. Principally as a result of white migration to the suburbs, the public schools of New York, Chicago, Philadelphia, Baltimore, Washington, Cleveland, Detroit, and Los Angeles no longer had white majorities." While northern and western cities were increasing in school "blackness," comparable southern communites observed a falling rate. "Because of the North's failure to desegregate its schools, more--not less--racial segregation existed in America's public schools 17 years after *Brown*" (Metcalf, 1983, p. 130).

By stating only that *de jure* segregation was illegal, the Supreme Court allowed the North to escape the judgments handed down to the South. The North therefore enjoyed a "grace period of several years" before federal judges began to decide that what had been considered *de facto* segregation was in reality *de jure* (Metcalf, pp. 130-31).

Court and administrative actions were complemented by Congress when, in 1972, it passed the Emergency School Aid Act, which provided substantial funding (as much as $300.5 million in 1978) for schools that implemented desegregation plans. Schools created programs, purchased materials, and enlarged staffs to ease the transition to desegregated classes in what was intended to be improved educational settings. Attention then focused on the North, where *de facto* segregation has proven to be more difficult to eliminate than *de jure* segregation (Hochschild, 1984, p. 28).

In the first case involving a northern school district, *Spencer v. Kugler* (404 U.S. 1027, 1972), the Supreme Court affirmed the refusal of a district court to require integration in New Jersey because no intent to segregate could be shown. However, only a year later, in 1973, the Supreme Court, in a watershed decision, ruled in *Keyes v. School District No. 1 of Denver, Colorado* (413 U.S. 198,

1973) that even without a history of legislated dual school systems, Northern districts "could be found to have intentionally segregated their students and thus could be subject to the same mandates as the South" (Graglia in Stephan & Feagin, 1980, p. 83).

Not all Americans looked with favor upon the desegregation decisions of the Supreme Court, especially those that required busing. President Richard Nixon was among those who evinced little enthusiasm. Civil rights groups contended that the Nixon administration had relaxed its standards with regard to school desegregation and the implementation of Title VI of the Civil Rights Act of 1964 by the Department of Health, Education, and Welfare (HEW). They charged that there was no use of sanctions to cut off federal funds from noncomplying districts. Suit was filed against the Secretary of HEW and the United States Court of Appeals for the District of Columbia in *Adams v. Richardson* (356 F. Supp. 92, modified and aff'd, 480 F.2d 1159, D.C. Cir. 1973), ordered HEW to take "appropriate action to end segregation in public educational institutions receiving federal funds." The decision affected ten state-operated systems of higher education and more than 200 secondary and primary school districts (Kirp & Yudof, 1974, p. 394).

Attention was again brought South in 1973 when the Supreme Court took on the issue of providing protection of the rights of urban minorities and facilitating equal educational opportunities through equalizing the system of resource allocation in the case of *San Antonio Independent School District v. Rodriguez* (411 U.S. 1, 1973). The Court reversed the district court's decision by upholding the common system of financing public education. The ruling pronounced that education is not a fundamental interest and that a state need not provide equal education to all of its children (Showell in Levinsohn & Wright, 1976, p. 108).

However, in a landmark 1974 decision, in *Lau v. Nichols* (414 U.S. 563, 1974), the Supreme Court established the obligation of school districts, under the Civil Rights Act of 1964, to provide appropriate education for non-English speaking children (Orfield, 1978, p. xvi).

Also, in 1974, in *Milliken v. Bradley I* (418 U.S. 717, 1974), the Supreme Court "upheld an order of school desegregation for the City of Detroit, but the same court excluded the suburban school systems from the court order on the grounds that they had not been shown to be involved in the unconstitutional segregation in Detroit." The decision sealed off the city school district, 72 percent black, from the virtually all-white suburban districts that ringed it. Thus, despite a strenuous dissent from Justice Thurgood Marshall, who noted, "In the short run, it may seem an easier course to allow our great metropolitan areas to be divided up into two cities--one white, the other black--but it is a course I predict, our people will ultimately regret," a metropolitan approach to desegregation was not yet deemed appropriate by the nation's highest court (Feagin in Stephan & Feagin, 1980, pp. 31, 45; Vergon, 1990, p. 32).

Faced with the responsibility of providing the overwhelmingly minority Detroit students with an appropriate education and "without the expanded resources and political leverage that a metropolitan plan would have provided," school officials sought to create an effective remedial plan. When late in 1974, the district attempted to comply with the federal district judge's order to submit a Detroit-only plan for his consideration, it included thirteen educational elements as well as a limited pupil-reassignment plan. These components stressed reading and communications, multicultural and bilingual education, staff training, school-community relations, and a uniform code of student conduct (Vergon, 1990, pp. 32-33).

The district court and Sixth Circuit Court of Appeals affirmed the plan and told the State of Michigan to pay half the cost of putting into effect several of the components. The State objected and the case returned to the Supreme Court as *Milliken v. Bradley II* (433 U.S. 267, 1977). In a unanimous decision, "the authority of federal courts to order such broad programs of ancillary relief was affirmed."

The desegregation of the Boston schools also involved the incorporation of educational components in the plan approved by Judge Arthur Garrity. The Phase Two Plan, implemented in the 1975-76 school year, included the following provisions:

- Attendance options including community schools, magnet schools, and suburban schools;
- Programs that stress variety and innovation;
- Administrative reorganization that would ensure accountability to the community and the court;
- Pairing of schools with specific colleges, businesses, and labor organizations; and
- Closing of numerous buildings to upgrade the quality of services and enable the consolidation of students to further desegregation. (Case in Levine & Havighurst, 1977, pp. 162-63)

A 1976 case, *Washington v. Davis* (426 U.S. 229, 1976), in which a group of black applicants for positions as police officers in the District of Columbia challenged as racially discriminatory a written test of verbal ability used for selecting candidates for such positions, ultimately had much broader implications. The District of Columbia Court of Appeals found for the plaintiffs; however, the Supreme Court reversed the decision, "explicitly rejecting 'the proposition that a law or other official act, without regard to whether it reflects a racially discriminatory purpose, is unconstitutional solely because it has racial impact.'" Subsequently applied to school segregation cases, "*Washington v. Davis* makes clear that racial discrimination, and therefore segregation, cannot properly be found by simply finding racial separation resulting from the use of neighborhood schools." The Court carefully distinguished between "racial segregation, which is constitutionally prohibited, and racial separation, which is not" (Graglia in Stephan & Feagin, 1980, pp. 89, 93).

Also, in 1976, in a lower court decision, *Brown v. Weinberger* (417 F. Supp. 1215, D.D.C. 1976), "Federal District Judge John J. Sirica found the Department of Health, Education, and Welfare guilty of intentional nonenforcement of the Civil Rights Act of 1964 by continuing to subsidize unconstitutionally segregated schools in the North" (Orfield, 1978, p. xvi).

Another case, first heard in 1976, and decided by the Supreme Court in 1982, has particular relevance to Hartford. In *Crawford v. Board of Education of the City of Los Angeles* (458 U.S. 527, 1982), a *de facto* claim similar to *Sheff*'s, the California Supreme Court found a violation of the state constitution's equal protection clause and ordered busing. However, it turned out to be a Pyhrric victory for desegregation advocates: "voters in a referendum amended the constitution to conform to U.S. Supreme Court case law on liability for *de facto* segregation. Now the California constitution specifies, courts must find intent to segregate, as under the 14th Amendment to the U.S. Constitution. The U.S. Supreme Court later upheld the constitutionality of that referendum" (*The Connecticut Law Tribune*, November 30, 1992, p. 8).

Pasadena v. Spangler (96 S. Ct. 2697, 1976) was still another decision with implications for Hartford. In this case, the Supreme Court ruled that Pasadena, California need not redraw its school attendance zones each year when changes in housing patterns alter the racial makeup of the schools. *Hobson v. Hanson* (F. Supp. 844, D.D.C. 1971) involved similar circumstances with respect to the District of Columbia, as well as the issues of the implementation of a tracking system based on aptitude testing and the inequities of the distribution of resources within the schools in the District. *Bradley v. School Board* manifested an analagous situation in Richmond Virginia (412 U.S. 92, 1973). These decisions suggest that it is the Court's view that school officials are not required to redress circumstances that they did not cause.

The *Milliken I* decision was again reinforced and made more specific in *Dayton Board of Education v. Brinkman* (433 U.S. 406, 1977), another case requesting remedy for actions claimed to be in violation of the equal protection clause of the Fourteenth Amendment. The Court reiterated the theme that unless school racial separation was the result of overt acts by school authorities, it did not violate the Constitution.

The case of another city in Ohio was heard at the same time. In *Columbus Board of Education v. Pennick*, Justice White stated that "the district court had found "purposeful segregative practices with current statewide impact." White concluded that it is "the accepted rule that the remedy imposed by a court should be commensurate with the violation ascertained, and held that the remedy for the violations that had then been established in that case should be aimed at rectifying the 'incremental segregative effect' of the discriminatory acts identified" (443 U.S. 449, 1979).

The example of Wilmington, Delaware, demonstrated, however, that even when a school system ultimately attempted to desegregate in good faith, integration in public schooling might not be achieved. When *Evans v. Buchanan* (379 F. Supp. 1218, 1974) was first heard in 1957, the Court required that attendance zones in the City of Wilmington, which segregated African-American and white students, be abandoned and a unitary system be established. The Court noted that segregation in Delaware schools had been mandated by law until 1954, which made the facts of this case very different from those of Dayton, where *de jure* segregation was never at issue.

However, by 1970, the Wilmington school population was more than two-thirds African-American; effective school desegregation in such a context was virtually impossible. When the case was brought back to the Court in 1971, the plaintiffs argued that the only way to provide sufficient white students to enable the desegregation of Wilmington would be to implement a metropolitan solution that would include the surrounding suburbs, almost all of which were more than 90 percent white (Raffel, 1980, pp. 43-45).

Ultimately, the Supreme Court affirmed the order of the District Court prescribing a desegregation plan involving the City of Wilmington and 11 surrounding school districts (439 U.S. 1360, 1978).

In *Newburg Area Council v. Board of Education* (421 U.S. 931, 1975), where the Louisville City School System and the Jefferson County School System comprise the entire Kentucky county, a metropolitan solution was determined to be appropriate. Louisville, where the vast majority of blacks resided, supported combining the two districts for desegregation among other reasons, while the county, where two-thirds of the area's whites lived, opposed the consolidation. The court, guided by *Milliken*, ordered county-wide desegregation, observing that "school district lines in Kentucky have been ignored in the past for the purpose of aiding and implementing continued segregation." When the Louisville system lost in the district court, it voted itself out of existence. According to state law, this automatically transferred authority to the county, and the metropolitan remedy was realized.

While the courts refused to consider metropolitan remedies in Dallas, in *Tasby v. Estes* (517 F.2d 92, 5th Cir. 1975, cert. denied, 423 U.S. 939, 1975) and in Boston, Dayton, Columbus, and Birmingham, in the late 1970s, a successful interdistrict remedy was brought forth in *United States v. Indianapolis Board of School Commissioners* (573 F.2d 400, 7th Cir. 1978). The Court reasoned that since school system boundaries did not follow those of the city as it expanded into mostly white areas, the state was at least partially responsible for the school system's becoming predominantly black. The court's remedy was to transport black students from the city center to the white areas in the outer fringes of the city. This decision has been widely criticized by desegregation planners because no transportation was required in the opposite direction (Gordon, 1989, pp. 207-08).

It took several years of litigation before the courts finally determined in 1981 that the Commonwealth of Pennsylvania, in accord with the *Milliken* guidelines, had been the substantial cause of the segregated school systems in the case of *Hoots v. Commonwealth of Pennsylvania* (510 F. Supp. 615, W.D. Pa. 1981, cert. denied, 452 U.S. 963, 1981). The court ruled that there had been a "constitutional violation" because the state knew in creating the predominantly black General Braddock School District, which comprised the towns of Braddock, North Braddock, and Rankin, that "no other combination of school districts in the area would have yielded a school district with as large a percentage of black enrollment" (Gordon, 1989, pp. 208-9).

Although the surrounding districts to be included in the new Woodland Hills School District protested that they had not been guilty themselves, the verdict stood. Citing the decision in *Morrilton School District No. 32 v. United States* (606 F.2d 222, 8th Cir. 1979, cert. denied, 444 U.S. 1071, 1980), Judge Webber declared that "when the state has committed a constitutional violation in the use of its power, school district lines can be redrawn by the court to remedy those violations."

Ann LaGrelius Siqueland proudly recounted the voluntary desegregation of Seattle's schools in *Without A Court Order*, published in 1981, just one year before *Seattle School District v. State of Washington* (458 U.S. 457, 1982) was heard before the Supreme Court. Seattle, without judicial prodding, had adopted its mandatory citywide desegregation plan in December, 1977; its voluntary plan, implemented the year before, was superseded because the city found that partial voluntary desegregation was more than twice as expensive as total mandatory desegregation. Hochschild notes the irony that "the more successful the voluntary program, the greater the confusion and expense" (Siqueland, 1981, pp. 3-5; Hochschild, 1984, pp. 33, 75).

However, according to Ellen Roe, a Seattle school board member, by the fall of 1989, because of changing demography and general dissatisfaction with how the plan had evolved, the city had to abandon its ten-year-old mandatory desegregation plan. School enrollment had dropped from 58,000 to 44,000 during the ten-year period of mandatory desegregation, and minority enrollment had gone from 32 percent to 50 percent between 1978 and 1985. The new controlled-choice plan, which took two years to construct, realigned all schools to a K-5, 6-8 configuration and created attendance zones sensitive to the geography of the city. Eliminating the option of unrestricted choice greatly reduced transportation costs (*American School Board Journal*, February, 1990, pp. 26-27).

A 1987 New York case, heard in the Second Circuit Court, resulted in Judge Leonard Sand affirming the decision and remedies of the District Court. He agreed that segregated housing caused and perpetuated racial segregation in the public schools. Combined with city housing policies, the mayor's appointment of school board members, attendance zone policies, and race-based staff assignments, the policies of the City of Yonkers and its Board of Education sanctioned and maintained racial segregation in its schools. The Court ordered the construction of 200 units of low-income housing outside of primarily minority neighborhoods. And, specifically, to address school segregation, the Court required the city to fund a system-wide voluntary magnet school program to be implemented by the Board (*U.S. v. Yonkers Board of Education* , 837 F.2d 1181, 2nd. Cir. 1987).

The following year, in the Sixth Circuit, in apparent contradiction of its decision of a decade earlier, the Court of Appeals ruled that local school districts may not compel the state to fund court-ordered desegregation plans. In the case of *Kelley v. Metropolitan County Board of Education of Nashville and Davidson County*, the Court reversed a District Court ruling ordering the state to pay 60 percent of the future costs of a court-ordered desegregation plan, citing the sovereign immunity provision of the Eleventh Amendment, which does not allow states to be sued by their own citizens. The Court also noted that it was the responsibility of the legislatures and not the courts to regulate state spending (836 F.2d 986, 6th Cir. 1987).

In 1988, voicing a totally opposite opinion, the Superior Court of California ordered that that state must reimburse the Long Beach Unified School District for the 28 million dollars spent on its desegregation programs (No. 606020 slip op., Super. Court 1988).

A case heard before the Southern District Court of Ohio may have particular relevance to Connecticut in light of Governor Lowell Weicker's call to the legislature and the general population to voluntarily desegregate its schools by having the state divide into six regions and then having each district devise its own desegregation plan. In the case of *Mona Bronson et al. v. Board of Education of the City School District of Cincinnati et al.* (Case No. C-1-74-205; 604 F. Supp 68, 1984), Judge W.H. Rice found the Cincinnati School District in compliance with some provisions of a school desegregation consent degree from June 22, 1984 and not in compliance with others. The original decision was historic in allowing the school district charged with promoting or allowing unconstitutional segregation to choose for itself the means to arrive at desegregation goals. The Court was to determine compliance prior to June, 1991. At that time, the Court removed jurisdiction over those areas found in compliance and retained jurisdiction over those areas where compliance had not yet been achieved.

The issue of school desegregation has generated tremendous interest in the education community. During the last ten years alone, almost one thousand articles have been written on the subject. The entire spring, 1987 issue of *Metropolitan Education* was devoted to the St. Louis desegregation plan, while the February, 1988 issue of *Equity and Choice* featured a variety of articles on the topic of future designs for educational equity (ERIC 1/83-9/92).

Individual articles have appeared to describe positive aspects of reputedly poor schools, such as South Boston High School, and difficulties with programs deemed successes, such as that in St. Louis. Legal issues and court cases are the concern of many; others examine social attitudes and experiences. While the majority of the articles concentrate on high school and below, significant attention has also been given to the problem of segregation in higher education (ERIC 1/83-9/92).

Robert Crain was among the earliest, and has remained among the most important, researchers in the field of school desegregation. In his 1968 study, *Politics of School Desegregation*, he refers to the subject of school integration as "a new issue" where "rigid decision-making techniques have not yet been developed." His study of eight northern cities faced with the need to eliminate *de facto* segregation left him optimistic that "conflict is not unavoidable" (Crain, 1968, pp. 2-3).

In "Minority Achievement: Policy Implications of Research," written with Rita E. Mahard, he cites two findings that have appeared consistently in his studies. First, that "minority students in primarily Anglo schools score higher on achievement tests" and, second, that "this does not seem to be because of the 'whiteness" of the school but because predominantly white schools have student bodies with higher socioeconomic status" (Hawley, 1981, p. 56).

In 1985, he undertook a study of Hartford's Project Concern in which his findings supported those of Robert K. Gable and Edward F. Iwanicki, who have been evaluating the program since 1975. While Gable and Iwanicki found that "there were no major systematic differences in reading and mathematics achievement patterns between students who were bused to suburban schools as part of the Project Concern Program and their comparable counterparts who remained in the Hartford Public Schools," the authors continue that "[t]his finding should not be construed as evidence that Project Concern is not successful. . . . Other evidence, including participants' affective disposition and attitudes toward the program, Hartford and suburban parents' attitude toward the program, and suburban teachers' attitude toward the program are supportive of Project Concern." The authors, concurring with Crain, contend further that "Project Concern has had a positive effect on the career development and maturity of the high school graduates of the program who were bused to suburban schools" (*Metropolitan Education,* Spring, 1986, p. 76).

Among the most frequently discussed commentaries on the subject of desegregation have been the speeches and writings of James S. Coleman. Chief author of the widely circulated study, *Equality of Educational Opportunity,* published in 1966, Professor Coleman, a highly regarded sociologist, has continued to observe and report on school desegregation issues. Professor Coleman is credited, perhaps erroneously, for inspiring school busing to encourage integration. Subsequently, in his landmark article, "Racial Segregation in the Schools: New Research with New Policy Implications," which appeared in the October, 1975 issue of *Phi Delta Kappan*, he determined that urban school desegregation led to declining white enrollments, and this "white flight" in effect discouraged the very situation it attempted to promote.

However, according to Thomas F. Pettigrew and Robert L. Green in their *Harvard Educational Review* article, "School Desegregation in Large Cities: A Critique of the Coleman 'White Flight' Thesis," Coleman's research is "methodologically and conceptually faulty and . . . provides no basis for his highly publicized conclusion that urban school desegregation leads to massive 'white flight.'" Rather, they argue, his and other research tends to support metropolitan solutions to school segregation. Pettigrew and Green contend that "Coleman fails to distinguish between his scientific findings and his personal beliefs" (Pettigrew & Green, 1976, pp. 2, 4, 5).

Responding to James Coleman's "white flight" theory, Christine H. Rossell, in a 1975 article in *Political Science Quarterly*, contended that her study "demonstrated that school desegregation causes little or no significant white flight, even when it is court ordered and implemented in large cities." She noted that school desegregation had a minimal effect on white flight when compared with other, "more important, forces such as increasing crime and public fears of violence, rapid movement of jobs to suburban facilities, much greater housing construction in the suburbs than in the cities, decline in the actual level of some central cities services, major urban riots, and deteriorating city schools and declining achievement scores" (p. 688).

However, 15 years later, she reversed her views in *The Carrot or the Stick,* claiming that "the research presented in this book is really the first evidence that voluntary plans with incentives do indeed produce more desegregation than mandatory plans." Arguing that "the majority of white Americans do not see the difference in socioeconomic status between blacks and whites as a problem, because they believe it is caused, not by discrimination, but by a lack of motivation and skills among blacks. . . . Blacks have to earn this right by changing their behavior and values" (1990, pp. 183-84).

Rossell quotes Morris Abram, the former vice-chairman of the United States Commission on Civil Rights, as summarizing "the sentiments of many Americans when he writes that favoritism, affirmative action, and other forms of 'reverse discrimination' produce unintended negative consequences" as well as being unconstitutional. "There is a general acceptance of the notion that it is legitimate to force whites to stop discriminating but that compliance with affirmative action policies whose goal is social equality should be voluntary" (1990, p. 184).

When desegregation takes place in response to segregated living patterns, and the primarily one-race schools are the result of *de facto* as opposed to *de jure* segregation, as is the case most frequently outside of the South, some form of busing is almost always employed. Despite the fact that most non-urban schoolchildren travel to their classroom on a bus, the use of busing as a means of integration is rarely greeted with enthusiasm or even acceptance. In the introduction to his 1973 edited work, *The Great School Bus Controversy*, Nicolaus Mills notes that, although in the 1960s the black-liberal-labor coalition that made the 1964 Civil Rights Act possible supported busing, by the 1970s that coalition no longer existed. By the 1972 election, busing had become "the 'red-scare' issue, the code word for a series of widespread racial fears." A Harris Survey released in April, 1972, declared that "73 percent of the public opposed busing for racial balance, 7 percent were unsure, and only 20 percent favored it" (1973, p. ix).

However, these findings are mitigated by another Harris finding, which supported the contention of Kenneth Clark that at the time "more pupils [were] being transported at public expense to racially segregated schools--including public schools, private schools, parochial schools, and recently organized Protestant church related 'academies'--than for purposes of school desegregation." According to Harris, "of parents whose children are bused to school, the overwhelming majority, 89 percent,--were not unhappy with busing, that they found their children's [then existing] arrangements 'convenient'" (1973, p. ix).

In his background essay, Mills puts the busing controversy in historical perspective. He notes that its origins trace back to the nineteenth century and the first pupil transportation laws, which were an outgrowth of the school consolidation movement. Its purpose was to improve and equalize educational opportunity for rural children. By the 1970s, while nearly 20 million children were being bused to school (43.4 percent of the total enrollment), only three percent of those student rides were for racial reasons (pp. 3-11).

Christopher Jencks, in 1972, anticipating the Supreme Court's decision in *Keyes v. School District No. 1 (Denver)* and the implications it would have for other northern cities, contended that intense probusing efforts entail greater political risks than benefits and that energies would be wiser spent in improving employment opportunities for blacks (Mills, 1973, pp. 14, 25). Alexander Bickel was concerned that the busing issue would divide the national government with the more liberal Supreme Court on one side ordering integration and the more conservative executive and legislative branches on the other (Mills, 1973, pp. 30-32).

Following the issue six years later in another edited volume, *Busing, U.S.A.*, Mills noted that during that interval the number of children bused as a result of court order had increased from three to seven percent, while those being transported for other reasons had grown from 42 to 50 percent. At the same time, supporters of busing had also become more outspoken. Senator Walter Mondale, serving as Chairman of the Select Committee on Equal Educational Opportunity, forthrightly declared that "busing is one means--and at times the only means--by which segregation in public education can be reduced" (1979, p.1).

In a similar vein, sociologist Thomas Pettigrew, who was the principal author of the 1967 Civil Rights Commission Report, *Racial Isolation in the Public Schools*, contended, "To our knowledge there is actually no evidence whatsoever that 'busing' for desegregation harms children." But, according to Mills, the reality of the *Milliken* decision in Detroit and initial white resistance to busing in Boston pressured Congress to pay attention to the country's antibusing sentiment in the mid-1970s (1979, pp. 1-3).

However, as the decade of the 1970s moved to its end, as noted by Howard Husock in Mills and Charles W. Case in Levine and Havighurst's *The Future of Big-City Schools*, resistance to busing had so diminished that "two busloads of white students volunteered to go from South Boston to an innovative new high school in black Roxbury" (Mills, 1979, p. 6).

J. Dennis Lord approached the subject of busing from a geographer's perspective in his investigation of *Spatial Perspectives on School Desegregation and Busing*. While conceding that the charge that busing has not significantly improved the academic performance of black children, advanced by the National Association for Neighborhood Schools, has some validity, he asks, "What are the realistic alternatives that will provide equal protection of the laws for all students regardless of race?" (1977, p. 34).

Lord also suggests that busing may promote other desirable effects. He proposes that the "mental maps or images of the city held by both black and white students" must undergo substantial broadening when they become acquainted with the suburbs and central city ghetto, respectively (1977, p. 34).

Hawley, et al., examining *Strategies for Effective Desegregation*, concluded that the public has an inaccurately negative view of the social and educational consequences of desegregation. They attribute this false impression to six factors, which include assumptions that previously segregated schools were better than they really were, unrealistic expectations for the newly desegregated schools, a belief that minority schools are unlikely to be good schools, a tendency to believe negative evidence rather than positive evidence when both are presented, the media's emphasis on problems in preference to successes, and attributing all problems at school to the desegregation process (1983, pp. 161-62).

Conceding that the achievements of desegregation "have fallen far short of the hopes of its advocates," the authors contend that desegregation nevertheless has been more successful than is popularly believed. "Not surprisingly, those who opposed government efforts to foster social change. and especially those who have consistently opposed desegregation, have seized upon frustrations derived from unrealized high hopes to launch a new and powerful attack on desegregation. This attack focuses its attention on forced busing rather than interracial schooling. Despite abundant evidence to the contrary, the antibusing forces boldly assert that desegregation can be achieved voluntarily" (1983, p. 163).

In his fall, 1987 *History of Education Quarterly* review of four books dealing with busing, Ronald D. Cohen notes that the authors of all four books support busing because "they cling to a belief in equity, the unfairness of segregated schooling, and the hope that integration, voluntary or forced, will benefit all involved." Richard A. Pride and J. David Woodward, evaluating *The Burden of Busing: The Politics of Desegregation in Nashville, Tennessee* (1985) argue that whites benefited from the interracial contact and have not been educationally handicapped by busing, while blacks maintain their dream, although they are little better off educationally (Cohen, 1987, pp. 385-86).

In *Public Opinion and Collective Action: The Boston School Desegregation Conflict* (1986), D. Garth Taylor analyzes white's opposition to forced school busing while accepting interracial contact. He attributes the strong preference for voluntary compliance to the forceful leadership of antibusing community leaders who stressed the injustice of court-ordered busing. Bernard Schwartz, in *Swann's Way: The Second Busing Case and the Supreme Court* (1986), describes initial white community hostility to busing but concludes that a well-integrated, academically viable school system soon followed when the school board, supported by the Charlotte power structure, capitulated in 1973 (Cohen, 1987, pp. 381, 383).

In *Common Ground: A Turbulent Decade in the Lives of Three American Families*, J. Anthony Lukas follows three families: Yankee, Irish, and Black, through the tumultuous attempts to desegregate the Boston schools. Beginning his volume by describing the varying responses to the death of the Reverend Martin Luther King in 1968,

Lukas illustrates that all of the people involved, whatever their race or class, suffered in the chaos of the radical and sometimes violent social change that took place in the city (1985).

Kirby, Harris, Crain, and Rossell, discussing *Political Strategies in Northern School Desegregation*, distinguish between "busing" and "integration," contending that, when surveys were made, attempting to achieve the latter has been found to be far more acceptable. Further, it was found that busing, which brings black children into white neighborhoods, was much preferred to transporting white students to ghetto schools. The authors argued "that this fear is not simply prejudice. Ghetto schools, after all, are often bad schools with severe discipline problems. If blacks complain about these schools, one should expect whites to complain, too" (1973, pp. 130-31).

Kirby, Harris, Crain, and Rossell also reported that whites were far more likely to be accepting of integration once it was established in their school. "Objection was greater to the idea of government action than to the actual effect of the action. . . . [A] large segment of the population . . . express the feeling that they have nothing against integration, but resent any governmental decision which favors blacks as a special group" (1973, p. 131).

Thomas J. Cottle's qualitative study of *Busing* in Boston suggests that "inevitably, it comes down to the question, are you for or against busing? That's the basis of the division, and the proper answer to the question is your passport into the communities that have the most to gain and the most to lose from school desegregation." According to an involved woman in her fifties who discussed the issue with Cottle, "You [are] with them or with us. Just say yes or no. It's a black-white issue, you know what I mean? There's no place for nobody to be in between" (1976, p. 10).

Gary Orfield answered the question *Must We Bus?* by declaring that "desegregating big city schools through busing is not an ideal or even a natural solution to segregation, but it is quite simply the only solution available if there is to be substantial integration in this generation." Orfield noted that housing policies that encouraged a mixing of the races, if implemented, would be of assistance, as well. He continued that "there is no neat package of policies and programs that would solve all local problems, but there are many constructive policies that could ease the transition in the schools. Each year it will be harder to reverse the momentum of segregation in the big cities. The real choice now is not between busing and doing nothing, but between busing in an intelligent way that will begin to consolidate integration and busing in an ill-planned way that will reinforce the existing separation and deepen racial polarization" (1978, p. 7).

Among Orfield's conclusions were that metropolitan plans are more successful than those restricted to the central city, that resistance to desegregation and busing diminishes significantly after the first year among whites, and that blacks in general support desegregation plans despite having to do more of the traveling and usually experiencing a greater loss of political influence in school management (1978, p. 415).

Orfield noted that once the concept of desegregation has been accepted, there are "various policy changes that would ease the tension of the transition and increase the chances of a positive income. Many are relatively uncontroversial." Among these alternatives are aid for initial costs, multiyear educational aid, Title I funds, and federal and state bi-lingual and bi-cultural programs (pp. 424-35).

While supporting the concept that integrated neighborhoods provide the best means of integrating schools, Orfield contended that since "Congress outlawed housing segregation without providing any credible enforcement machinery," it was unlikely that this more desirable solution would occur in a suitably timely fashion. Whites are unlikely to move back into central cities in the near future, and suburbs tend to be too expensive for minorities who generally are poorer. Orfield suggested that "two modest congressional initiatives could help stabilize existing integration. The first would be to reward integrated neighborhoods by exempting them from citywide busing plans. The second would be to stabilize existing integrated schools by guaranteeing that their integration will be preserved if the neighborhood begins to resegregate residentially" (pp. 435-39).

Orfield's views have not changed significantly in the intervening years. Testifying as the final witness at the *Sheff v. O'Neill* trial on January 28, 1993, Orfield reiterated his views that "the only effective solutions to solve racial and economic desegregation have been court-ordered plans. 'The plans that are most stable are mandatory, metropolitan plans.'" Orfield continued that "a desegregation order should include a broad metropolitan area and that the court's chief role is to establish goals, set deadlines, and monitor progress" (*The Hartford Courant*, January 29, 1993, pp. 1, 9).

Orfield warned that "there should be a relatively short time for devising a plan," since "the transition period is a dangerous time when opponents can exploit racial fears and stir up resistance." In several cities, metropolitan plans promoted "'tremendous upheavals' in early stages"; however, "once a plan is put into effect, 'the uproar goes down extremely rapidly. Within two or three months, it goes off the front pages of the newspaper'" (1978, p. 9).

In a report prepared for the Joint Center for Political Studies in July, 1987, Orfield noted that the segregation of blacks in American public schools had changed little since 1972 and that, additionally, there was a consistent growth in the segregation of Hispanics in the schools. He reported that no branch of the federal government had taken any policy initiatives since 1971. He also could have mentioned the paucity of attention that has been paid to the subject of the segregation of Hispanics despite the rapid increase in this population.

Orfield's report, entitled "School Segregation in the 1980s: Trends in the United States and Metropolitan Areas. A Report by the National School Desegregation Project," offered five major findings. These are:

1. States with the greatest integration of blacks typically have extensive court orders requiring busing;
2. States in which blacks are most segregated have fragmented school districts within large metropolitan areas and no city-suburban desegregation plan;
3. A few states experienced a modest reduction in segregation due to state government monitoring of desegregation;
4. The northeastern United States is the most segregated region; and
5. In locations where Hispanic populations are concentrated there are no widely implemented desegregation plans.

For those who believe that voluntary measures are more effective in dealing with racially segregated schools, magnet schools have obvious appeal. President Gerald Ford, in the spring of 1976, was reported to be looking at magnet schools as a more acceptable substitute for busing as a means of achieving school desegregation. Describing "Voluntary Racial Integration in a Magnet School," James E. Rosenbaum and Stefan Presser in a February, 1978 article in *School Review,* explain that magnet schools are so called "because they attract--rather than force--students to attend" (1978, p. 156).

Rosenbaum and Presser, writing at a time when magnet schools were still a relatively new concept, warned that the idea of integration could get lost in the enthusiasm of the programmatic aspects of the individual magnet. However, they saw distinct advantages, including the ability to "desegregate a former black school in a largely black neighborhood . . . without violence." Also positive was that "many of the claims had the effect of becoming self-fulfilling prophesies" and that "a talent system can permit integration in music, art, and drama talent classes . . . and seem to have a carry-over in terms of informal integration in the lunchroom" (1978, pp. 180-81).

Writing in *Urban Education* in October, 1979, Christine H. Rossell examines "Magnet Schools as a Desegregation Tool: The Importance of Contextual Factors in Explaining Their Success." Rossell emphasizes the important difference between magnets used as part of a mandatory desegregation plan and those that are the sole means of school desegregation (1979, pp. 303-4).

Rossell contends that, in the short-run, magnet-only plans are more efficient in that "they are able to obtain greater increase in interracial contact for a given reduction in racial balance." However, this result becomes diametrically opposite when school districts exceed 30 percent minority (1979, p. 316).

Reporting on her research on magnet schools six years later in the same journal, Rossell asks "What is Attractive About Magnet Schools?" The primary answer to her question is location. However, if the school is situated in a racially isolated area, whites seek "a critical mass of white students, preferably a majority, plus an environment that is perceived to be more academically stimulating or selective" (*Urban Education*, April, 1985, pp. 18-19). Rossell is curiously silent regarding what black families would be looking for to encourage the attendance of their children.

In her testimony at the *Sheff v. O'Neill* trial in early February, 1993, Rossell, disputing the findings of Gary Orfield and Charles V. Willie, continued to warn against a forced plan. She contended that such a plan would prompt many white parents to abandon public schools. "When the middle class leaves a school system, that school system has a poorer reputation, despite the fact teachers may be just as good . . . [and] resources may be just as good." Rossell pointed out the "huge expense to implement any kind of desegregation plan" and argued that "the measured benefits are quite small" (*The Hartford Courant*, February 10, 1993, p. D1).

Writing in the December, 1984 issue of *Phi Delta Kappan*, Denis P. Doyle and Marsha Levine seek to free magnet schools from the charge that they are elitist, in their article, "Magnet Schools: Choice and Quality in Public Education." They contend that if more schools of this type were built (1018 were operating in the 1981-82 school year), preferably with significant aid from the federal government, all who wish to attend may do so (1984, pp. 267-68). Then many more children can enjoy the benefits of magnet schools: higher academic standards, greater integration, improved learning, high morale among students and teachers, and a sense of community. The authors suggested that in rural areas, boarding schools, modeled on the North Carolina School of Science and Mathematics, would solve the logistical and transportation problems that day schools would present (p. 269).

Appearing in the same journal, Rolf K. Blank evaluates "The Effects of Magnet Schools on the Quality of Education in Urban School Districts." Using a comparative case study approach, which included 15 school districts and 45 magnet schools representative of the population of 138 urban districts operating magnet programs, Blank determined that "magnet schools can and do provide high-quality education in urban school districts"; that "high-quality education in magnet schools does not stem from highly selective methods of admitting students"; and that "district and school leadership, community involvement, and small additional expenditures are important factors that produce high-quality education in magnet schools" (1984, pp. 270-72).

In the preface to her book, *Different by Design: The Context and Character of Three Magnet Schools*, Mary Haywood Metz describes the difficulty of creating schools that are designed to be diverse, attractive, and different enough to justify longer bus trips, but yet not so much better that they would offend those students who attended other schools within the same district (1986, pp. viii-ix). Metz also emphasizes the character and atmosphere evident in each school and the significant role the district's political life played in shaping the schools (1986, p. 3).

Between 1985 and 1990, the San Diego City Schools created 20 magnet themes. Elizabeth A. Tomblin and George T. Frey describe "A Process for Developing and Evaluating Magnet Schools" in their Winter, 1990 article in *ERS Spectrum*. In creating a magnet school outline, the authors advise preparing a mission statement, a special magnet curriculum emphasis, a program of staff development, and a strategy for parent and community participation (1990, p. 25).

The authors concluded that magnet schools have been a successful part of San Diego's voluntary intergration program since their inception in 1977. Evaluation had at first been on the basis of their drawing power--"the ability to attract and hold students, particularly those who improve the racial balance of the school." More recently, the quality of the instructional program was considered as well (p. 28).

Magnet schools offer options for some; "schools of choice" are designed to allow everyone within a system to exercise the right to decide. Minnesota became the first state in the union to allow parents to choose a public school for their child anywhere in that state by 1990 when then Governor Rudy Perpich signed the first open enrollment law in the nation in 1988. Choice has been enthusiastically supported by former President George Bush and, according to Stanford University Professor Michael Kirst, it has proven to be politically irresistible as a low cost educational reform (*Education USA*, September 4, 1989, p. 1).

Although the program had been in effect for less than a year, State Education Commissioner Ruth Randall declared the effort a success, and Administrator of the State Board of Education Ted Suss saw choice expanding opportunities for low-income students (pp. 1, 6).

Cambridge, Massachusetts has had a plan for parental choice since 1979. *The Cambridge Controlled Choice Program: Improving Educational Equity and Integration*, prepared by Norma Tan (October, 1990) explains and evaluates the program through its then 11-year history. Responding to increasingly segregated schools as minorities moved in and whites moved out, and the difficulties observed in Boston in response to court-ordered desegregation, Cambridge determined to take matters into its own hands (1990, pp. 1-3).

The Cambridge Plan allows parents to select three or more schools for their child, and assignments are made taking into account the racial balance of the schools (1990, p. 4). Evaluations have determined that the plan succeeds in achieving voluntary school desegregation while improving overall achievement levels in both lower and upper grades. Additionally, emphasis is placed on strengthening "the formal and informal networks linking government and community agencies, administrators, instructional staff, and parents" (1990, pp. 23-24).

In 1990, the Association for Supervision and Curriculum Development devoted an entire report in its *Issues Analysis* series to the subject of choice. In "Public Schools of Choice," the authors, chaired by Paul E. Heckman, Assistant Dean of the College of Education at the University of Arizona, Tucson, propose that choice has at least three agendas supporting it. These are those dissatisfied with education as it currently exists, those who see choice as a means for desegregating schools, and those who view choice as a catalyst for change (1990, pp. vi-vii).

While acknowledging that "the existing programs and structures of public schools have become suspect in light of poor student achievement, a lack of responsiveness to the concerns of parents and students, the shortcomings of overt desegregation strategies, and the difficulty of revitalizing public schools" (p. 5), the authors note that "choice is one largely unproven strategy being offered to meet the challenge." They warn that "educators and policymakers are charged with maintaining a balance between . . . the common goals of a democratic society and . . . the needs of individual students" (1990, p. 32).

Whether they are supporters or critics of the concept of school choice, most of the authors for the December, 1990/January, 1991 issue of *Educational Leadership* "agree that choice itself is not the panacea some advocates claim." Charles V. Willie advocates "Controlled Choice Avoids the Pitfalls of Choice Plans." This "equity planning tool" recognizes the "complementary relationship of freedom and conformity." While students rank order their preferences, each school's racial and socioeconomic diversity is guaranteed, and all schools are equivalent in range and quality of service (1990/1991, pp. 63-64).

Education and Urban Society also felt that the subject of choice was important enough to justify an entire issue, "School Choice Plans," and did so in February, 1991. Editor Frank Brown, reviewing the articles in the journal, contends that choice is proposed primarily by "neoconservatives as a cure for our educational problems, deregulation via parental choice of a school for the child and increased privatization of schooling by making it possible for more children to enroll in private schools." Brown argues that this action will not solve the problem of improving education for poor and inner-city children (1991, p. 117).

Despite many educators' continued skepticism regarding choice, President Bush maintained his support for the concept. *The Executive Educator* announced in its May, 1991 issue that the President's budget proposal included "$200 million in incentive funds for schools that have choice programs, $30 million for schools interested in developing choice programs of 'national significance,' and $100 million for magnet schools unrelated to those set up for desegregation purposes" (1991, p. 28).

Continuing the debate, Abigail Thernstrom, quoted in *The Executive Educator*, July, 1991, contended that a nationwide study "finds no evidence linking school choice and quality." According to Thernstrom, "Sound educational ideas and effective leadership, not consumer taste, are probably the key to good results. . . . [N]o evidence exists that parents who are passive and indifferent will become involved in a school of choice" (1991, p. 4).

Roy C. Rist, in his publications of 1978 and 1979, analyzed not only school desegregation but how this desired activity affected multiculturalism and assimilation.   In *Desegregated Schools: Appraisals of an American Experiment*, he began the discussion Christine Rossell continued 11 years later in *The Carrot or the Stick for School Desegregation Policy: Magnet Schools or Forced Busing*. Rist wanted to know "what the day to day realities are for teachers, students, parents, and administrators." What are "the subtleties of interrelationships between students and teachers, between whites and blacks, or between administrators and parents?" (1979, p. xii).

Rist concluded that "the results are mixed, even discouraging to those who have labored long and hard for school desegregation." He blamed "the decentralization of educational decision making, the mixed messages from Washington, the unwillingness of the white majority to support viable means of achieving school desegregation, the political web of schools, banks, real estate, and the city politicians plus the tenacity of racism within American education [which] have all mediated against any 'quick fix' of a difficult and complex problem" (1979, p. xiii).

David S. Tatel, Maree F. Snead, Kevin J. Lanigan, and Steven J. Routh described "The Responsibility of State Officials to Desegregate Urban Public Schools Under the United States Constitution" in 1988. They determined that state governments are losing an increasing number of desegregation cases. The basis of liability has changed from local agencies to the states during the 1970s and 1980s. The consequences are that some states continue to deny responsibility. Others, more wisely, are acknowledging their appropriate role and developing programs to desegregate as a matter of state policy (*Equity and Choice*, 4, 1988, pp. 56-59).

Tatel, et al. summarized trends in recent judicial decisions and described the situations that existed in Detroit, Indianapolis, Dallas, and Chicago. They also noted that in some instances, courts have restructured local governmental entities to consolidate previously independent school districts, thus enabling compulsory student reassignments among the schools.

With regard to financial responsibility, they cited Ohio, where Dayton, Columbus, and Cleveland have been awarded state funds to implement remedial and compensatory education programs. In Missouri, the courts not only ordered the 23 St. Louis County suburban school districts to consolidate with the city into a unified metropolitan school district, but they also required the State to pay totally for the cost of voluntary interdistrict transfers, including host district incentive payments, the cost of transportation, and the operating and capital costs of the interdistrict magnet schools designed to attract white county students into the city schools.

State funding for improvement of educational quality is another mechanism for correcting racial isolationism that Tatel et al. have found to be favored by the courts. States are frequently asked to develop programs to help local school systems deal with educational deficiencies resulting from past segregation.

Few of those who study the issue of school desegregation would disagree that its implementation is highly desirable. Funding from federal and state coffers eases the burden for the local district; however, everyone is aware that money is in short supply at all levels. The issue of how desegregation should be accomplished still provokes the greatest disagreement. While Gary Orfield is convinced that mandatory desegregation is the only effective method (1978), Robert Crain is equally supportive of the goals and benefits of desegregation, such as in Project Concern, but less certain as to the best means to accomplish that end (Crain, Mahard, Narot, 1982).

Charles V. Willie advocates controlled choice (1991), while Christine H. Rossell, who began her career as a supporter of mandatory desegregation, now argues that only voluntary measures will achieve true integration and interracial exposure (1990). Meanwhile, David J. Armor, who agrees with Christine Rossell on the desirability of voluntary as opposed to mandatory desegregation (Stephan & Feagin, 1980, p. 225) further contends that desegregated schools have demonstrated no significant effect on the achievement of black children (*The Hartford Courant*, December 16, 1992).

While there has been great interest in and discussion of magnet programs and more recently of choice as cities continue to increase in minority residents and to an even greater extent minority students, the case for metropolitan remedies appears to be all the more compelling. Desegregated schools are the law and should be supported. Resistance to desegregation, when it occurs, ultimately fades, especially when the metropolitan region is large enough to discourage white flight (Gordon, 1989, pp. 210-14).

Bibliography

PRIMARY SOURCES

U.S. Bureau of the Census Reports: 1970, 1980, 1990

Court cases as cited in the text

Newspapers

Arlington, Virginia:	*Education, U.S.A.*
Boston, Massachusetts:	*The Christian Science Monitor*
Dayton, Ohio:	*Dayton Daily News*
Hartford, Connecticut:	*The Connecticut Law Tribune*
	The Hartford Courant
	Journal Inquirer
	UConn Advance
	the Chronicle
Rochester, New York:	*A Visitor's Guide to Rochester, 1991*
	CQIE Newsletter
	Democrat and Chronicle
	Times-Union
Trenton, New Jersey:	*The Times*
	The Trentonian
Wilmington, Delaware:	*Wilmington News-Journal*

Reports

Dayton, Ohio:
> *Dayton Cares for Kids: From Court Order to Implementation,*
> 1977, Dayton Board of Education
> *Just the Facts*, 1988, Dayton Public Schools

Magnet Schools Assistance Program Application, 1989, Dayton
    Public Schools
Magnet Programs Evaluation, 1990, Dayton Public Schools
A School System of Choices, 1990, Dayton Public Schools

Rochester, New York:
Desegregation of the Elementary Schools, 1967, Rochester City
    School District
*Grade Reorganization and Desegregation of the Rochester Public
    Schools,* 1969, Rochester City School District
Needs Assessment, 1981, Rochester City School District
Magnet Schools, 1989, Rochester City School District
Neighborhood Diplomatic Corps Home Visiting Registry, 1989,
    Rochester City School District
Magnet Schools, 1990, Rochester City School District
Selections, 1990, Rochester City School District
Magnet Schools: Elementary Programs, 1991, Rochester City
    School District

Trenton, New Jersey:
*Questions and Answers on Commissioner Marburger's Trenton
    Decision on Desegregation,* 1970
Plan for Educational Excellence, 1984, Trenton Public Schools
Demographic and Geographic Considerations, 1986, Trenton Board
    of Education
Desegregation Plan for Educational Excellence, Revised, 1986, New
    Jersey State Department of Education
Observations and Recommendations, 1988
Reorganization Task Force Meeting Minutes, 1988
Desegregation Expansion and Continuation Plan, 1989-90, Trenton
    Public Schools
Desegregation Student Survey Results, 1990
Desegregation Teacher and Principal Survey Results, 1990
Outline for Desegregation, 1990, Trenton Board of Education
Seventh and Eighth Grade Magnet Program, 1990, Trenton Board
    of Education
Survey of Students, Staff and Administration, 1990, Trenton Board
    of Education
Districtwide Enrollment, 1990-91, Trenton Board of Education
Districtwide Enrollment, 1991-92, Trenton Board of Education
Art Museum Project Guide, 1992

Wilmington, Delaware:
Fact Book, 1978, New Castle County School System
*The U.S. District Court Opinion and Order on Remedy to
    Desegregate Wilmington Public Schools,* 1978, SANE of Delaware,
    Inc.
*Regulations for the Reorganization of the New Castle County School
    District,* 1980, Delaware State Board of Education.
Report of Suspensions and Expulsions, July 19, 1990

Hartford, Connecticut:

Design for Excellence, 1986, State of Connecticut Board of
Education

Minority Students and Staff Report, 1986, State Board of
Education

*A Report on Racial/Ethnic Equity and Desegregation in
Connecticut's Public Schools*, 1988, State of Connecticut Board of
Education

*Background and Discussion Paper on School Racial/Ethnic
Balance*, 1988, Hartford Public Schools

Indicators of Success, 1988, State of Connecticut Board of
Education

Quality and Integrated Education: Options for Connecticut, 1989,
State of Connecticut Board of Education

*Almost Twenty-five Years of Project Concern: An Overview of the
Program and its Accomplishments*, 1989, E. F. Iwanicki and R.K.
Gable, The University of Connecticut

*Creative Approaches for Reducing Racial/Economic Isolation in
Connecticut Schools*, 1989, Connecticut Associations of Boards of
Education

*Background and Discussion Paper on School Racial/Ethnic
Balance: Update*, 1990, Hartford Public Schools

Crossing the Bridge to Equality and Excellence, 1990, Governor's
Commission on Quality and Integrated Education

PAQIE Inventory of Progress to Reduce Racial Imbalance, 1990,
Capitol Region Education Council

Where We Stand, Part 2, 1992, Capitol Region Council of
Governments

Vision of Excellence, 1992-1993, Hartford Public Schools

General:

Orfield, G. (July, 1987). *School segregation in the 1980's: Trends in the
United States and metropolitan areas. A Report by the National
School Desegregation Project.* Washington, D.C.: Joint Center for
Political Studies.

Tan, N. (October, 1990). *The Cambridge controlled choice program:
Improved educational equity and integration.* New York: Manhattan
Institute.

BOOKS

Bastian, A., Fruchter, N., Gittell, M., Greer, C., & Haskins, K. (1986).
Choosing equality: The case for democratic schooling. Philadelphia:
Temple University Press.

Bell, D. (Ed.). (1980). *Shades of Brown: New perspectives on school
desegregation.* New York: Teachers College Press.

Bogdan, R. C. & Biklen, S. K. (1982). *Qualitative research for education:
An introduction to theory and methods.* Boston: Allyn and Bacon,
Inc.

Borg, W. R. & Gall, M. D. (1989). *Educational research: An introduction.* New York: Longman, Inc.

Brownell, B. A. & Stickle, W. E. (1973). *Bosses and reformers.* Boston: Houghton Mifflin Company.

Cataldo, E. F., Giles, M. W., & Gatlin, D. S. (1978). *School desegregation policy: Compliance, avoidance and the metropolitan remedy.* Lexington, Massachusetts: Lexington Books.

Coleman, J. S., Campbell, E., Hobson, C., McPartland, J., Mood, A., Weinfeld, F., & York, R. (1966). *Equality of educational opportunity.* Washington, D.C.: U.S. Government Printing Office.

Cottle, T. J. (1976). *Busing.* Boston: Beacon Press.

Crain, R. L. (1968). *The politics of school desegregation: Comparative case studies of community structure and policy-making.* Chicago: Aldine Publishing Company.

Crain, R. L., Mahard, R. E., & Narot, R. E. (1982). *Making desegregation work: How schools create social climates.* Cambridge, Massachusetts: Ballinger Publishing Company.

Cremin, L. A. (1964). *The Transformation of the school: Progressivism in American education, 1876-1957.* New York: Vintage Books.

Cumbler, J. T. (1989). *A Social history of economic decline: Business, politics, and work in Trenton.* New Brunswick, New Jersey: Rutgers University Press.

Dror, Y. (1971). *Ventures in policy science: Concepts and applications.* New York: American Elsevier Publishing Company, Inc.

Fine, D. R. (1986). *When leadership fails: Desegregation and demoralization in the San Francisco schools.* New Brunswick, New Jersey: Transaction Books.

Gaillard, F. (1988). *The Dream long deferred.* Chapel Hill: The University of North Carolina Press.

Glasser, R. (July, 1992). *Aqui me quedo: Puerto Ricans in Connecticut.* Middletown, Connecticut: Connecticut Humanities Council.

Grant, E. S. & Grant M. H. (1969). *Passbook to a proud past and a promising future.* Hartford: Connecticut Printers, Inc.

Grant, E. S. & Grant, M. H. (1986). *The city of Hartford 1784-1984.* Hartford: Connecticut Historical Society.

Green, R. L. (Ed.). (1985). *Metropolitan desegregation.* New York: Plenum Press.

Hawley, W. D. (Ed.). (1981). *Effective school desegregation: Equity, quality, and feasibility.* Beverly Hills: Sage Publications.

Hawley, W. D., Crain, R. L., Rossell, C. H., Smylie, M. A., Fernandez, R. R., Schofield, J. W., Tompkins, R., Trent, W. T., & Zlotnik, M. S. (1983). *Strategies for effective desegregation: Lessons from research.* Lexington, Massachusetts: Lexington Books.

Hillson, J. (1977). *The Battle of Boston.* New York: Pathfinder Press.

Hochschild, J. L. (1984). *The New American dilemma: Liberal democracy and school desegregation.* New Haven: Yale University Press.

Hoffecker, C. E. (1983). *Corporate capital: Wilmington in the twentieth century.* Philadelphia: Temple University Press.

Iwanicki, E. F. (1976). *An evaluation of the 1975-76 Hartford Project Concern program.* Bloomfield, Connecticut: Capitol Region Education Council.

Jeffries, J. W. (1979). *Testing the Roosevelt coalition: Connecticut society and politics in the era of World War II.* Knoxville: The University of Tennessee Press.

Katz, M. B. (1987). *Reconstructing American education.* Cambridge, Massachusetts: Harvard University Press.

Kerr, D. H. (1976). *Educational policy; Analysis, structure and justification.* New York: David McKay Company, Inc.

Kirby, D. J., Harris, T. R., Crain, R. L., & Rossell, C. H. (1973). *Political strategies in northern school desegregation.* Lexington, Massachusetts: Lexington Books

Kirp, D. L. & Yudof, M. G. (1974). *Educational policy and the law: Cases and materials.* Berkeley, California: McCutchan Publishing Corporation.

La Gente, *La Casa.* (undated). Hartford, Connecticut: La Casa de Puerto Rico.

Lasswell, H. D. (1971). *A Pre-view of policy sciences.* New York: American Elsevier Publishing Company, Inc.

Levine, D. M. & Bane, M. J. (1975). *The inequality controversy: Schooling and distributive justice.* New York: Basic Books, Inc.

Levine, D. U. & Havighurst, R. J. (Eds.). (1977). *The future of big-city schools.* Berkeley, California: McCutchan Publishing Corporation.

Levinsohn, F. H. & Wright, B. D. (1976). *School desegregation: Shadow and substance.* Chicago: The University of Chicago Press.

Lincoln, Y. S. & Guba, E. G. (1985). *Naturalistic inquiry.* Beverly Hills, California: Sage Publications.

Lord, J. D. (1977). *Spacial perspectives on school desegregation and busing.* Washington, D.C.: Association of American Geographers.

Lukas, J. A. (1985). *Common ground: A turbulent decade in the lives of three American families.* New York: Alfred A. Knopf.

McKelvey, B. (1961). *Rochester: An emerging metropolis (1925-61).* Rochester, New York: Christopher Press, Inc.

McKelvey, B. (1973). *Rochester on the Genesee: The growth of a city.* Syracuse, New York: Syracuse University Press.

Meier, K. J., Stewart, J., Jr., & England, R. E. (1989). *Race, class and education: The politics of second-generation discrimination.* Madison, Wisconsin: The University of Wisconsin Press.

Metcalf, G. R. (1983). *From Little Rock to Boston: The history of school desegregation.* Westport, Connecticut: Greenwood Press.

Metropolitan Community Studies, Inc. (1959). *Metropolitan challenge.* Dayton, Ohio: Author.

Metz, M. H. (1978). *Classrooms and corridors: The crisis of authority in desegregated secondary schools.* Berkeley, California: University of California Press.

Metz, M. H. (1986). *Different by design: The context and character of three magnet schools.* New York: Routledge & Kegan Paul.

Mills, N. (Ed.). (1973). *The Great school bus controversy.* New York: Teachers College Press.

Mills, N. (Ed.). (1979). *Busing U.S.A.* New York: Teachers College Press.

Myrdal, G. (1944). *An American dilemma: The Negro problem and modern democracy.* New York: Random House.

Neustadt, R. E. & May, E. R. (1986). *Thinking in time: The uses of history for decision-makers.* New York: The Free Press.

Orfield, G. (1978) *Must we bus? Segregated schools and national policy.* Washington, D. C.: The Brookings Institution.

Patchen, M. (1982). *Black-white contact in schools: Its social and academic effects.* West Lafayette, Indiana: Purdue University Press.

Persell, C. H. (1977). *Education and inequity: A Theoretical and empirical synthesis.* New York: The Free Press.

Prager, J., Longshore, D., & Seeman, M. (Eds.). (1986). *School desegregation research: New directions in situational analysis.* New York: Plenum Press.

Pride, R. A. & Woodward, J. D. (1985). *The burden of busing: The politics of desegregation in Nashville, Tennessee.* Knoxville, Tennessee: University of Tennessee Press.

Pula, J. S. (1985). *Ethnic Rochester.* Lanham, Maryland: University Press of America.

Raffel, J. A. (1980). *The Politics of school desegregation; The metropolitan remedy in Delaware.* Philadelphia: Temple University Press.

Rist, R. C. (1978). *The invisible children: School integration in American society.* Cambridge, Massachusetts: Harvard University Press.

Rist, R. C. (Ed.). (1979). *Desegregated schools: Appraisals of an American Experiment.* New York: Academic Press.

Ronald, B. W. & Ronald, V. (1981). Dayton: *The gem city.* Tulsa, Oklahoma: Continental Heritage Press.

Rosenberg, S. E. (1954). *The Jewish community in Rochester (1843-1925).* New York: Columbia University Press.

Rossell, C. H. (1990). *The Carrot or the stick for school desegregation policy: Magnet schools or forced busing.* Philadelphia: Temple University Press.

Schofield, J. W. (1982). *Black and white in school: Trust, tension, or tolerance.* New York: Praeger Publishers.

Schwartz, B. (1986). *Swann's way: The second busing case and the Supreme Court.* New York: Oxford University Press.

Sealander, J. (1988). *Grand plans: Business progressivism and social change in Ohio's Miami Valley, 1890-1929.* Lexington, Kentucky: The University Press of Kentucky.

Sedlacek, W. E. & Brooks, G. C., Jr. (1976). *Racism in American education: A model for change.* Chicago: Nelson-Hall.

Sheehan, J. B. (1984). *The Boston school integration dispute: Social change and legal maneuvers.* New York: Columbia University Press.

Siqueland, A. L. (1981). *Without a court order: The desegregation of Seattle's schools.* Seattle: Madrona Publishers.

Spring, J. (1976). *The Sorting machine: National educational policy since 1945.* New York: David McKay Company, Inc.

Stave, B. M. & Palmer, M. (1991). *Mills and meadows: A pictorial history of Northeast Connecticut.* Virginia Beach, Virginia: The Donning Company.

Stephan, W. G. & Feagin, J. R. (Eds.). (1980). *School desegregation: Past, present, and future.* New York: Plenum Press.

Stuart, I. W. (1853). *Hartford in the olden time: Its first thirty years.* Hartford: F.A. Brown.

Taylor, D. G. (1986). *Public opinion and collective action: The Boston school desegregation conflict.* Chicago: The University of Chicago Press.

Tilly, C., Jackson, W. D., & Kay, B. (1965). *Race and residence in Wilmington, Delaware.* New York: Bureau of Publications, Teachers College, Columbia University.

Verma, G. K. & Bagley, C. (Eds.). (1979). *Race, education, and identity.* New York: St. Martin's Press.

Violas, P. C. (1978). *The Training of the American working class: A history of twentieth century American education.* Chicago: Rand McNally College Publishing Company.

Washington, J. (1990). *In search of a community's past: The Black community in Trenton, New Jersey, 1860-1900.* Trenton, New Jersey: Africa World Press, Inc.

Weaver, G. (1982). *Hartford: An illustrated history of Connecticut's capital.* Woodland Hills, California: Windsor Publications, Inc.

Weinberg, M. (1983). *The search for quality integrated education: Policy and research on minority students in school and college.* Westport, Connecticut: Greenwood Press.

Wilson, W. J. (1980). *The declining significance of race.* Chicago: The University of Chicago Press.

Wilson, W. J. (1987). *The truly disadvantaged: The inner city, the underclass, and public policy.* Chicago: The University of Chicago Press.

Wolf, E. P. (1981). *Trial and error: The Detroit school segregation case.* Detroit: Wayne State University Press.

Wolfendale, S. (1983). *Parental participation in children's development and education.* New York: Gordon and Breach Science Publishers.

Wolters, R. (1984). *The burden of Brown: Thirty years of school desegregation.* Knoxville: The University of Tennessee Press.

Yarmolinsky, A., Liebman, L., & Schelling, C. S. (Eds.). (1981). *Race and schooling in the city.* Cambridge, Massachusetts: Harvard University Press.

JOURNALS AND PERIODICALS

Blank, R. K. (December, 1984). The effects of magnet schools on the quality of education in urban schools. *Phi Delta Kappan*, pp. 270-72.

Brown, F. (Ed.). (1991). School choice plans. *Education and Urban Society*, 23(2), pp. 115-230.

Case, C., & Shibles, M. (1990). Restructuring schools: A review. *Connecticut Leadership Academy.*

Challenging the myths: The schools, the blacks, and the poor. *Harvard Educational Review.* Reprint Series No. 5.

Cohen, R. D. (Fall, 1987). To bus or not to bus? That is the question. *History of Education Quarterly*, 27 (3), pp. 379-86.

Coleman, J. S. (October, 1975). Racial segregation in the schools: New research with new policy implications. *Phi Delta Kappan*, pp. 75-78.

Doyle, D. P. & Levine, M. (December, 1984). Magnet schools: Choice and quality in public education. *Phi Delta Kappan*, pp. 265-69.

Front Lines. (July, 1991). *The Executive Educator*, 13(7), p.4.

Gable, R. K. & Iwanicki, E. F. (Spring, 1986). The longitudinal effects of a voluntary school desegregation program on the basic skill progress of participants. *Metropolitan Education*, (1), pp. 65-77.

Gable, R. K., Thompson, D. L., & Iwanicki, E. F. (June, 1983). The effects of voluntary school desegregation on occupational outcomes. *The Vocational Guidance Quarterly*, pp. 230-39.

Giles, M. W., Cataldo, E. F., & Gatlin, D. S. (1975). White flight and percent black: The tipping point re-examined. *Social Science Quarterly*, 56(1), pp. 85-92.

Gordon, W. M. (1989). School desegregation: A look at the 70's and 80's. *Journal of Law and Education*, 18 (2), pp. 189-214.

Heckman, P. E. (1990). Public schools of choice. *ASCD Issues Analysis*, 53 pages.

Hidalgo, N. M., McDowell, C. L., & Siddle, E. V. (1990). Facing racism in education. *Harvard Educational Review*, Reprint Series No. 21.

Menacker, J. (1990). Equal educational opportunity. *Urban Education*, 25(3), pp. 317-25.

Perspectives on inequality. (1973). *Harvard Educational Review*, Reprint Series No. 8.

Pettigrew, T. F., & Green, R. L. (1976). School desegregation in large cities: A critique of the Coleman "white flight" thesis. *Harvard Educational Review*, 46(1), pp. 1-53.

Roe, E. (February, 1990). Striving in Seattle. *The American School Board Journal*, 177(2), pp. 26-27.

Rosenbaum, J. E. & Presser, S. (February, 1978). Voluntary racial integration in a magnet school. *School Review*, pp. 156-86.

Rossell, C. H. (1976). School desegregation and white flight. *Political Science Quarterly*, 90(4), pp. 675-95.

Rossell, C. H. (1979). Magnet schools as a desegregation tool: The importance of contextual factors in explaining their success. *Urban Education*, 14(3), pp. 303-20.

Rossell, C. H. (1985). Estimating the net benefit of school desegregation reassignments. *Educational Evaluation and Policy Analysis*, 7(3), pp. 217-27.

Rossell, C. H. (1985). What is attractive about magnet schools? *Urban Education*, 20(1), pp. 7-22.

School desegregation: The continuing challenge. (1976). *Harvard Educational Review*, Reprint Series No. 11.

Tatel, D. S., Snead, M. F., Lanigan, K. J., & Routh, S. J. (February, 1988). The responsibility of state officials to desegregate urban public schools under the United States Constitution. *Equity and Choice*, 4, pp. 56-59.

Tomblin, E. A. & Frey, G. T. (1990). A process of developing and evaluating magnet schools. *ERS Spectrum*, 8(1), pp. 24-32.

Vergon, C. B. (1990). School desegregation policy: Federal role in the 1990s. *Education and Urban Society*, 23(1).

Washington Windmill. (May, 1991). *The Executive Educator*, 13(5), p. 28.

Western, R. D. (Spring, 1986). Metropolitan school desegregation. *Metropolitan Education*, (1).

Willie, C. V. (1990/1991). Controlled choice avoids the pitfalls of choice plans. *Educational Leadership*, 48(4), pp. 62-64.

UNPUBLISHED MANUSCRIPTS

Daniel, R. (1959). *A case study of desegregation in the public schools of Trenton: 1944-54.* Unpublished doctoral dissertation. Rutgers University.

Klaff, V. Z. (March, 1981). *Metropolitan school desegregation: Impact on racial integration of neighborhoods.* Paper presented at the meeting of the Population Association of America, Washington, D.C.

Reid, L. (1984). *Progress of the Rochester city school district's desegregation efforts from 1975 to 1984.* Unpublished manuscript, S.U.N.Y. Brockport.

Index

About the Author

SONDRA ASTOR STAVE is Director of Adult Education and Coordinator of Community Services for the Mansfield, Connecticut Board of Education. She is the editor of *Hartford, the City and the Region* (1980).

ISBN 0-313-29523-9

EAN

9 780313 295232

HARDCOVER BAR CODE